IRISH POLITICS NOW

'THIS WEEK' GUIDE TO THE 25th DÁIL

BY

Shane Kenny
& Fergal Keane

WITH

Shane McElhatton
& Linda Sherlock

AND INCLUDING
CONTRIBUTIONS BY

Senator Michael Yeats
and Brendan Walsh

BRANDON

in association with

First published 1987
Brandon Book Publishers Ltd
Dingle, Co Kerry, Ireland
and 27 South Main Street, Wolfeboro,
New Hampshire 03894-2069, U.S.A.

© Radio Telefís Éireann 1987

ISBN 0 86322 095 9

Cover design: Paula Nolan
Cover photographs: The Irish Times

Typeset by Printset & Design, Dublin
Printed by Mount Salus Press, Dublin

Acknowledgements

This book could not have been undertaken without the help of
Jim Lynch and Dave Madden, of RTE, who spent endless hours
assembling and checking count figures and statistical analysis,
and Deirdre Horlacher, of "Today Tonight", whose
contribution was invaluable. We would also like to thank the
following: Vincent Finn, Director General of RTE, for giving
the work his sanction and support; Dave Holden for his
encouragement and advice; Wesley Boyd and Kevin Healy for
their support; Michael Curran for his technical assistance; Eddie
Liston and Donal Kelly for editorial advice; the journalists of
RTE News and Features/Current Affairs who supplied the
invaluable material for constituency sketches; the staff of the
Oireachtas party press offices for supplying biographical
material; Tim Sexton of the Department of the Environment
for assistance with count information; the staff of the RTE
library; Anne Courtney for inputting assistance; Michael
Gallagher for computer assistance; Colman Doyle of the *Irish
Press* and Peter Thursfield of *The Irish Times* for photographic
assistance; the RTE graphics department; Dr Garret FitzGerald
for assistance on transfer analysis; Anne Flaherty, Paula Murphy
and Simon Kenny for their forebearance.

Contents

PART ONE

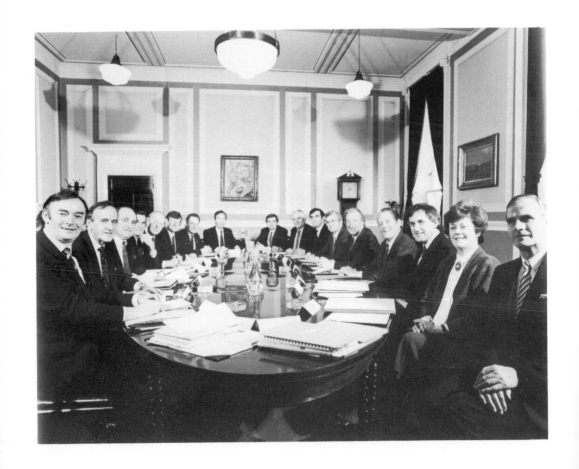

The Cabinet

Taoiseach and Minister for the Gaeltacht: Charles J. Haughey.
Tánaiste and Minister for Foreign Affairs: Brian Lenihan.
Minister for Finance and the Public Service: Ray McSharry.
Minister for Justice: Gerry Collins.
Minister for Agriculture: Michael O'Kennedy.
Minister for Social Welfare: Michael Woods.
Minister for Industry and Commerce: Albert Reynolds.
Minister for Energy (with responsibility for areas of Communications): Ray Burke.
Minister for Tourism, Fisheries and Forestry and the Marine: Brendan Daly.
Minister for the Environment: Padraig Flynn.
Minister for Labour: Bertie Ahern.
Minister for Health: Rory O'Hanlon.
Minister for Defence: Michael J. Noonan.
Minister for Education: Mary O'Rourke.
Minister for Communications: John Wilson.
Attorney General: Mr John Murray SC.

Ministers of State with Departmental Offices:

Minister of State for Forestry (attached to Department of Energy): Michael Smith.
Minister of State for Food Industry: Joe Walsh.
Minister of State for Trade and Marketing (attached to the Department of Industry and Commerce): Seamus Brennan.
Minister of State for Science and Technology (attached to the Department of Industry and Commerce): Sean McCarthy.
Minister of State for Horticulture (attached to the Department of Agriculture): Seamus Kirk.
Government Chief Whip and Minister of State at the Departments of the Taoiseach and Defence: Vincent Brady.

Other Ministers of State:

Department of the Gaeltacht: Denis Gallagher.
Department of the Taoiseach (coordination of Government policy on EEC matters): Maire Geoghegan-Quinn.
Department of Environment (urban renewal): Ger Connolly.
Department of Foreign Affairs (overseas aid): Sean Calleary.
Department of Health: Terry Leyden.
Department of Tourism, Fisheries and Forestry (marine): Pat the Cope Gallagher.
Department of Education (youth and sport): Frank Fahey.
Department of Finance (office of public works): Noel Treacy.

Chronology of Events

1986

17 Jan.   PDs make dramatic showing in opinion polls: 19 per cent of first-preference vote.

13 Feb.   Biggest cabinet re-shuffle since 1939. Barry Desmond, resisting a transfer to Justice, retains Health portfolio but loses Social Welfare to Gemma Hussey. FF table motion of no confidence in Taoiseach, on grounds of his failure to impose his authority on government ministers.

21 Feb.   FF motion of no confidence in Taoiseach and government is defeated by 82 votes to 77.

9 Apr.   Michael Keating TD leaves FG for PDs. Government working majority in Dáil cut to one.

11 May   FF pass 50 per cent mark, in *Sunday Press*/RSI poll. PDs drop to 11 per cent, FG 25 per cent, Lab 7 per cent.

10 June   Lab TD Joe Bermingham leaves the Party. Government now in a minority.

18 June   First challenge to the government's minority Dáil position: coalition survives FF motion condemning its economic performance by 74 votes to 68.

27 June   Divorce referendum results in heavy defeat for government. Divorce proposal rejected by 63 per cent of turnout.

7 Sept.   Lab Party leader Dick Spring says he will recommend against participation in coalition. Says that key party demands are non-negotiable. But he reaffirms Lab's commitment to staying in power.

18 Sept.   Liam Skelly threatens to withdraw support from the government if his plans for a transport complex in Dublin are dropped.

23 Sept.   Junior Minister Eddie Collins sacked by Taoiseach in row over his family business affairs.

1 Oct.   Exchequer returns published. Returns indicate possible overrun of £180m in government spending and a deficit of 8.5 per cent of GNP by year's end.

8 Oct.   FG discussion document proposes a tax band of 35 per cent for 75 per cent of taxpayers if personal allowances, including mortgage interest relief, were dropped. Cost of this change estimated at £130m.

12 Oct.   Wolfe Tone commemoration, Co. Kildare. FF leader Charles Haughey announces the party will seek to renegotiate the Anglo-Irish Agreement when it takes office again.

15 Oct.   PD policy document released. Aims to cut standard rate of tax to 25 per cent in five years. Aims at spending cuts of £375m to finance the 1987 package.

16 Oct.   Government publishes general targets for 1987 budget and estimates. Current budget deficit to be held to 7.4 per cent of GNP; Exchequer borrowing requirement to 11.8 per cent of GNP. Spending cuts of £250m planned. Lab members dissent from cabinet decision.

17-19 Oct.   FG Árd Fheis. Taoiseach accuses Charles Haughey of putting lives of nationalists at risk with his Bodenstown speech.

22 Oct.   New Dáil session opens.

23 Oct.   Government survives Dáil no confidence motion by 83 votes to 81.

4 Nov.   FF leader Charles Haughey outlines broad economic policy: freeze on government spending for four years and sectoral development aimed at annual growth rate of 2-3 per cent.

12 Nov.   NESC report "A Strategy for Development 1986-90" published. Calls for £500m in public spending cuts and action on unemployment.

26 Nov.   FF table motion calling on government to restore Christmas Social Welfare bonus

to £21m, instead of government's planned £18m. Government survives on casting vote of Ceann Comhairle, and last-minute change of heart by FG TD Michael O'Leary.

10 Dec. Alice Glenn formally resigns from the FG parliamentary party over controversy caused by her "Enemies of the People" remarks.

14 Dec. *Sunday Independent* poll shows FG at four-year low: 24 per cent. FF at 51 per cent, PDs 13 per cent, Lab 6 per cent.

19 Dec. Dáil adjournment debate: government defeats FF amendment calling for dissolution of the Dáil. Taoiseach says Dáil will resume on 28 January.

1987

2 Jan. Highest ever recorded current deficit published: £1.39b. Budget overrun on targets £145m, rather than predicted £180m. £300m worth of spending cuts to be agreed between ministers.

9 Jan. Record unemployment figures published: 250,178.

11 Jan. Des O'Malley says PDs would consider coalition with FF without Charles Haughey as leader.

20 Jan. Finance minister John Bruton issues document, "Framework for the Budget". Says public sector pay will cost £200m more in 1987 than in 1986, Social Welfare £80m more, and the servicing of the national debt £160m more.

20 Jan. Lab ministers withdraw from coalition leaving minority FG government. Taoiseach calls election for 17 February. FG budget manifesto unveiled.

21 Jan. President Hillery dissolves the 24th Dáil.

23 Jan. Des O'Malley says PDs will decide on the question of coalition with FG after election result is known.

27 Jan. FF leader Charles Haughey says FF will not be bound by the government's borrowing and deficit targets. Former Health Minister Barry Desmond says FG Health budget will overrun by £40m.

28 Jan. First poll of the campaign: *Irish Times*/MRBI poll shows FF with 52 per cent of first preferences, FG with 23 per cent, Lab 5 per cent, PDs 15 per cent.

29 Jan. FF manifesto launched. Aims for annual 2.5 per cent growth over five years. Aims at keeping 1987 government spending at 1986 levels.

30 Jan. Lab manifesto launched. Sets target of 4 per cent annual growth rate. Tax net to be widened, wealth tax to be reintroduced, to bring in £120m a year. Corporation taxes to be raised by 25 per cent.

2 Feb. PD manifesto launched. Aims for 25 per cent standard rate of tax by 1991. Funding to be secured through £100m worth of cuts in capital spending, £100m to be raised through privatisation of state assets.

5 Feb. *Irish Times*/MRBI poll gives FF 50 per cent of first preferences, FG 24 per cent, PDs 14 per cent, Lab 5 per cent.

12 Feb. "Today Tonight" debate between Garret FitzGerald and Charles Haughey.

14 Feb. *Irish Times*/MRBI poll shows FF lead slipping to 48 per cent. FG have 25 per cent, PDs have 16 per cent, Lab have 6 per cent. Taoiseach says no party will win an overall majority. Urges supporters to transfer to PDs. But PD leader Des O'Malley says the party is not entering any pre-election alliance.

15 Feb. *Sunday Independent*/IMS poll, the first to be taken after the debate. FG support up to 30 per cent, highest level for over a year. FF support falls to 45 per cent. PD support is 13 per cent, Lab 5 per cent.

19 Feb. General election results: FF 81; FG 51; LAB 12; PDs 14; WP 4; Inds. 4.

10 Mar. Charles Haughey elected Taoiseach by casting vote of Ceann Comhairle after tied Dáil vote 82-82. New cabinet announced.

11 Mar. Dr Garret FitzGerald resigns as leader of FG after ten years in office.

21 Mar. Alan Dukes elected as leader of FG.

31 Mar. Government's first budget aims to reduce current budget deficit to 6.9% GNP and borrowing to 10.7% GNP; public pay freeze after 2% payment 1987; mortgage interest relief clawback; home improvement and other grants abolished; new £10 hospital bed charge introduced, £10 outpatient charge retained; land tax abolished; social welfare cuts moderated.

The Phoney War

Tom Madigan's farm near Firhouse in County Kilkenny is in the middle of Fine Gael heartland. His family have tilled and tended eighty acres here for over a hundred years and they've been solid supporters of Fine Gael since the party's foundation in 1933. "From as far back as I can remember," says Tom, who is the kind of young farmer the party points to with pride as the model Fine Gael man of the land. It was here in the first week of October 1986 that Garret FitzGerald's black Saab and a retinue of camp followers and journalists came; the former in search of votes, the latter in search of an election. It was a beautiful sunny day, the kind of dry late autumn day that is any cameraman's dream. There was just the right amount of light and the stubble in the fields almost glowed as the Taoiseach and his entourage crunched across it.

After dutifully inspecting some freshly turned furrows and making polite enquiries about the harvest the Taoiseach was directed towards a circle of hay bales in the middle of the field. There the most powerful man in the state sat down on a bale and talked to local farmers about milk surpluses and fodder shortages and grants and all the other things which occupy the minds of farmers these days. It was a dream photographic opportunity and the sound of shutters clicking and whirring filled the air like the sound of crickets. Fine Gael's press officer, Peter White, hummed with pleasure as he directed a camera crew around the fringes of the crowd. And then it occurred to the journalists present that this crew was not part of the pack. They weren't from RTE and it was reasoned that no other network would be interested in what was apparently a routine visit by the Taoiseach to a Kilkenny farm.

It was all of course very simple: they were working for Fine Gael, filming the party leader among the plain people in the kind of situation beloved of image builders. But why, asked the journalists, was a party political broadcast being filmed if the Taoiseach had said there wouldn't be an election before June? "Nothing like being prepared you know — just routine preparation," quipped Peter White in his own earnestly credible way. The suspicious might have been forgiven for thinking that they were in the run up to or even in the middle of an election campaign. Earlier in the day there had been a vintage election pep talk for party workers in Carlow with the Taoiseach exhorting them to work hard to re-elect the government. "The alternative," he told them, "would be to bring in a Fianna Fáil administration and that would be a national disaster." Later that morning in Carlow regional technical college the Taoiseach launched a blistering attack on lazy Irish workers who, he claimed, were "voting with their feet to close factories because they are too lazy to turn up for work." It was the kind of attack that was certain to drive the trade-union support of the Labour Party up the wall, but it wouldn't, as one astute Fine Gaeler observed, lose the major government party any votes. And in October the battle was definitely on within Fine Gael to convince the party's supporters that what John Kelly had christened the "Labour monkey" would soon be cast off.

After the speech to the students the whirlwind sped off to Castlecomer where there was a stop for tea and handshakes with the local nuns before the journey up the dusty lanes to Tom Madigan's farm. As he sipped tea in the kitchen the Taoiseach seemed a man brim full of confidence, almost oblivious it seemed to the storm clouds gathering over his government in the first week of October. Perhaps it was the sunny day and the warm reception or perhaps a genuine belief that the wolves could be kept from the door for a decent interval that would allow the government to agree a budget and go to the polls with some vestige of credibility.

The confidence and the laughter in the Madigans' kitchen were at variance with what one would expect of a man who the previous week had been accused of running the country from a bunker by the Fine Gael deputy Liam Skelly. The outspoken TD from Dublin West made his attack at a parliamentary party meeting and repeated the criticisms in interviews with the newspapers and RTE. "Some of the cabinet members," he observed, were "not fit to run a sweetshop." To add bite to those criticisms Skelly threatened to withdraw support from the government if they did not agree to implement a £200m transport development plan for Dublin. It involved a Canadian consortium, Caneire, in a scheme that would involve, among other proposals, the building of new bus terminals on the north and south sides of the Liffey linked by an underground tunnel, in addition to an underground rail link between the city's two main railway stations. A study by economic consultants, Davey, Kelleher and McCarthy, commissioned by the government, concluded that the Caneire scheme was not "commercially attractive from the state's standpoint...and should not be proceeded with." The Skelly/Caneire plan was initially received sceptically by the party hierarchy who had long been wary of the controversial backbencher. Nonetheless they took his threat seriously. The margin for survival was too tight for the cabinet to merely brush him aside as an eccentric. Skelly was to pay for his outspokeness when the party in Dublin West failed to select him as a candidate for the general election, but that autumn he was a man of some considerable power.

And then there was Frank Cluskey, deputy for Dublin South Central, who was threatening to withdraw support on the Dublin Gas issue. Cluskey had a reputation as being a man of his word on such matters and the shock of his resignation from cabinet on the very question of Dublin Gas was still vivid enough for any threat of his to be taken seriously. His request was on the surface simple: that on behalf of the 440 permanent staff made redundant by the company he be given detailed information about its financial situation, the interest rate arrangements made for repaying loans and specifically the pension and lump sum, if any, arrangements made with senior company executives. He described the £124m which he said it cost to wind-up the company as a national scandal and said the man who had been the government's representative dealing with the Gas Company, Finance Minister John Bruton, should resign. Cluskey wisely figured that the information would have to be given — and given in full — if the impression of a cover-up was to be avoided. From Garret FitzGerald's point of view, however, the publication of the pension figure alone (the eventual cost was in the region of £600,000) could leave the government open to the charge that it had looked after top management but left the workers in the lurch. Although he had already been given some information Cluskey sensed that to get to the real meat of the question would require all his considerable political skill and more than a little brinksmanship. Hence the threat: reveal all or I bring down the government.

There were threats in the air too from Independent Kildare deputy Joe Bermingham who was demanding a £60-a-week flat rate of benefit for Social Welfare recipients as the price of his continued support. Bermingham, a former junior minister who had already announced his intention to leave politics, had resigned from the Labour Party because of the imposition of Councillor Emmet Stagg as his replacement in Kildare. Bermingham, who was still a little upset over the issue, had wanted Senator Timmy Conway, who subsequently defected to the Progressive Democrats, to be his heir apparent. Not to be outdone was the Louth Fine Gael deputy, Brendan McGahon, who hinted he too might join the swelling ranks of the refuseniks if he did not get a package of aid for the border counties. That threat was not taken seriously by the cabinet.

In addition to the threats of withdrawal of support there had been the embarrassment only the week before of the sacking of Junior Energy Minister, Eddie Collins, and his declaration that while he would remain loyal to Fine Gael he would not pledge a similar oath to Garret FitzGerald. The Collins affair centred around allegations, published in *New Hibernia* and *Magill* magazines, that while a minister Collins continued to be involved in his family's business affairs and more importantly that he had misled the Taoiseach the previous February about the exact nature of that involvement. While there was no question of Collins withdrawing his support from the government his pointed and bitter criticisms of the Taoiseach were not the stuff to inspire confidence on the part of the general public. Speaking about the affair later the Taoiseach would say it was a decision which he found painful but necessary. He refused to state whether or not he believed he had been misled by his junior minister, although it was evident to many that he had been embarrassed by the magazine allegations. Eddie Collins maintains to this day that he did nothing that was improper and he especially refutes the suggestion that he misled Garret FitzGerald. There was for Collins a certain irony to the whole affair. He had been one of the prime movers in the election of Garret FitzGerald as leader of Fine Gael after the departure of Liam Cosgrave in 1977. But bad as the embarrassment of the Collins affair was, the most politically unpleasant news for the government came in the first week of October with the publication of the exchequer returns which underlined the crisis state of the economy.

The returns showed that the projected overrun in borrowing would be £180m leading to a projected current budget deficit of £1,450m or 8.5 per cent of the nation's Gross National Product. The level was the highest in the history of the state and well wide of the target deficit of £1,250m which had been set by the government. That target had itself been an abandonment of the figure identified in the national plan, ''Building on Reality''. The hope in the plan was to get the deficit down to 5 per cent of GNP — a figure many cabinet members now admit was highly optimistic. The government explained the overrun by pointing to what it called once-off, non-recurring expenses like the teachers pay deal, the Dublin Gas deal and the money paid to farmers because of bad weather. They also admitted that the consumer boom they had predicted simply did not happen, leading to a fall-off in receipts from Value Added Tax. The scale of the overrun and the crisis which erupted almost simultaneously on the Dublin money market in October put the state's finances on a crisis footing and, certainly from John Bruton's viewpoint, left little option but to bring in a budget with widescale cuts in public spending programmes. The money market crisis saw interest rates jumping 2 per cent and government sources of funding literally drying up. One Fine Gael minister describes it as follows:

It was caused by a number of factors. In fact it was about sterling, the EMS and the fact that we hadn't done our borrowing. You see, what we tried to do in 1986 was to stay off the domestic market for borrowing for the first half of the year to keep interest rates down and assist what we thought was incipient economic recovery. In the event it didn't work because interest rates didn't come down as much as we had hoped, the consumer boom didn't happen and then we found ourselves, having taken this risk, being forced to raise a substantial amount of money domestically in the latter half of the year. This meant that those selling us money were in a position where they knew we had to buy and they had to sell and this forced the price up. It was that combined with the amount of money going out of the country because people were buying sterling [the £ sterling was being devalued] which caused it. That created the crisis. It had nothing to do with the DIRT tax driving the money out of the country. It was our mistake to leave over borrowing.

In other words the government, with the best will in the world, backed itself into the October crisis, thus ensuring a tough budget. Almost immediately the government issued a statement to calm the market and bring interest rates into line. They promised to keep the deficit at 7.4 per cent of GNP, thus committing themselves irrevocably to big spending cuts. The Labour ministers in cabinet opposed this parameter but were voted down. They faced the choice of resigning or agreeing to be bound by collective cabinet responsibility. They chose the latter course of action. On the Fine Gael side there was a feeling that the cuts should have been on the agenda anyway, irrespective of the money market crisis. A Fine Gael minister says of the time:

> We couldn't have brought in a budget with a deficit larger than 7.4 per cent anyway and maintained any sort of respectability, internationally and domestically. The financial crisis propelled us into doing something we should have done at an earlier stage, and if we'd done it earlier we wouldn't be in the state we're in today at all. If we'd faced the public expenditure decisions earlier, we'd have ten more seats than we have now.

On the weekend of 5 October John Bruton was quick to acknowledge the seriousness of the situation and he blamed it on the massive interest repayments on our foreign borrowings. Since 1984 the government had borrowed £4.5b and the interest repayments since then had been £6b. As Bruton ruefully pointed out: "We would have a current budget surplus of £1.5b for the past four years were it not for the interest repayments." In a "This Week" interview on 5 October he said it would take fifteen years for the country to get out of the financial mess. He was noticeably reticent, though, when asked what cuts he thought would be needed to put the finances of the state in order.

> I'm not going to get into specifics because I know what you're trying to do is get me to say something that will provide a headline for the papers tomorrow and I'll be dealing with that for the rest of the week. I think it's pretty clear there are going to have to be cuts in public spending and the proposals as to how this may be done are at an advanced stage.

They were, as we report later in this chapter, at a very advanced stage. In the preamble to the main portion of the interview he said the government's main mistake had been its failure to get a mandate for specific action to tackle the deficit problem. "So the result was that while we had a mandate for the figure we wanted to achieve we didn't have a mandate for the measures necessary to achieve it." It was a theme which was to form the basis of Fine Gael's challenge to Fianna Fáil in the general election campaign and which Bruton was to emphasise forcefully at the party's Árd Fheis in November. The message was simple: if you are contemplating unpopular decisions spell it out loudly and clearly on the hustings. Speaking on the same weekend the Taoiseach expressed himself confident that the government would see off the challenge posed by the forthcoming Fianna Fáil no confidence motion.

> I believe we will get through because whatever speculation there may be there is no general disposition amongst politicians to precipitate an election in which they themselves possibly might not always benefit from the outcome. It's going to be difficult. It's quite clear from the exchequer returns to everybody now, and I've been saying this for some time now but I'm not sure everybody's heard me or been listening to me, that there is no room for an election budget or an easy budget. It's quite clear the budget will have to involve very tight controls on expenditure.

Thus were the warning signs signalled to those who might have thought the hairshirt could be returned to the wardrobe. Despite the succession of body blows the government was publicly continuing to maintain that it would get a budget together although the exact flavour of such a budget differed acccording to the political colours of the minister speaking. For instance, on the same day that the Taoiseach was talking about the country walking a financial tightrope the Minister for Health, Barry Desmond, was telling political correspondents he believed there could be a "neutral budget" in the spring which would avoid major cuts. It was a public symptom of the kind of division which was coming to a head at the cabinet table. For the Labour members of the cabinet there was the difficulty of a growing feeling amongst rank and file members that it was time to get out of coalition at any cost. There was the worry, expressed openly at a later stage by Senator Flor O'Mahony, that the Labour cabinet ministers would be forced into going along with stringent cuts in areas like Social Welfare on the basis that they had a national duty to do so.

The report of the Party's Commission on Electoral Strategy, which had been leaked to the media in the early part of August, added to the pressure on the Labour ministers. The report took a strong anti-coalition line, recommending that the Party stay out of government for a period of ten years unless there were reasons of major national interest necessitating its participation. The clear thrust of the report was that coalition was not good for Labour and that they should go it alone. Dick Spring, himself a member of the Commission, sensed the mood within the party and said publicly that he wished to lead an independent Labour Party in the years ahead. However, the Party's Annual Conference coming up in Cork that November could possibly have seen a move from the floor to have Labour pull out of coalition straight away. But with ironic good timing a trade-union dispute in Cork forced the cancellation of the Conference and eased the pressure. Yet while cabinet members like Dick Spring and Barry Desmond may still have hoped privately that they would somehow or other get that "neutral budget" those on the left wing of the parliamentary party, like chief whip Mervyn Taylor and Senator Michael D. Higgins, the party chairman, thought otherwise. Earlier in the year, in response to a particularly poor poll showing by Labour, Taylor said it was time to "pull out of coalition" while Higgins, with the voice of a man who sensed severe difficulties, had predicted as far back as 31 August that the government would come to grief over the issue of cuts in the budget. He said at the time: "I think it is likely that there will be immense fighting within cabinet about all of those. I expect that there are difficulties at the present time." It is interesting to note the response of Dick Spring when he was asked on "This Week" on 7 September if he thought a budget could be put together in spite of the arguments over cuts.

> We have been dealing with a difficult financial situation since the day we went into government. I recall being advised on the day the government was being formed by senior civil servants that there was a serious financial crisis. There is not going to be an easy budget but we are determined to ensure that the programmes we have are continued. I believe that in the course of this budget we can continue with the protection of those we represent in the main — the less well-off members of society. If I said that there wasn't a difficulty in putting a budget together we'd all be living in Cloud-cuckoo-land. It's going to be difficult but I believe there is the resolve in the political parties to bring a budget in.

Those reading the political tea-leaves would have seen the fast-approaching election simply by looking at the pace of the government's legislative programme in the closing months of its administration. Literally galloping through the Dáil and Seanad went the Building Societies Bill, the Metropolitan Streets Commission Bill, the Electoral Reform Bill, not to mention the sanctioning of new hospitals in Sligo and Wexford — both strategically important constituencies for the government parties.

Inside Government Buildings and away from the charged atmosphere of the Dáil chamber the cabinet continued to meet, ostensibly trying to hammer out some form of agreement on a book of estimates. Throughout the autumn months and into January government ministers were saying publicly that they felt they could agree on a budget although they admitted the bargaining was hard. From discussions with cabinet ministers the authors can reveal that a full budget was actually presented to cabinet on 23 October: completely reversing the position whereby ministers made submissions through government memoranda on behalf of their own departments. It is believed that John Bruton's officials in the

Department of Finance, when asked to have the entire set of estimates ready for the new Dáil session, felt it couldn't be done. In the event the Department literally burned the midnight oil through September in order to have the budget estimates ready for presentation to cabinet. It was all on the face of it perfectly consistent with John Bruton's oft-stated desire to present estimates early and have them discussed and debated thoroughly. As a Fine Gael minister explained:

> The difference this year was that the whole budget was brought forward as one — the tax and the expenditure proposals, and the full book of estimates was presented. The whole lot was on the table from October. Everything. All the figures, how we got to 7.4 per cent, a complete budget on the table. We showed the full magnitude of what was needed to achieve 7.4. No surprises were sprung. That was deliberate because bitter experience has shown in the past that people lost sight of where they were going and ended up with a budget with a far greater borrowing requirement than was acceptable simply because it was done incrementally, and you gradually push it up and up and up. Each decision on its own would seem reasonable but you ended up with a totally unacceptable picture. That was why we decided to go for a complete presentation of the entire picture on day one; down to the last penny in the book of estimates.

The estimates were first agreed between the Taoiseach, Dr Fitzgerald, and the Minister for Finance, John Bruton, shown to Dick Spring, and then presented to the full cabinet on 23 October. We have been reliably informed that the estimates contained all of the cuts which appeared in the Fine Gael budget and in some cases the proposed chopping went even further. The October budget provided for the abolition of pay related benefit (PRSI) rather than the proposal to halve it which appeared in the later Fine Gael budget. It also proposed a charge for occupying a hospital bed, an old chestnut from the Department of Finance. The Taoiseach and the Minister for Finance had already engaged in a weeding-out exercise — but the cabinet asked for the full list they had considered so that the range of possibilities for substitution would be greater. While the Health proposals were teased out — with the hospital bed charges meeting resistance from Fine Gael ministers as well as Labour — the Social Welfare cuts which Gemma Hussey saw as possible were not discussed at all. Dr Garret FitzGerald told the authors:

> The health list was worked through, excluding the hospital bed charges, and while Barry Desmond was objecting, and the others were not accepting them, the proposals were not being ruled out "a priori" so one could say there was a possible basis for further discussion towards agreement. However, on Social Welfare, Labour made it quite clear that they had great difficulties, so they were not teased out like the Health cuts. We couldn't see how we could get a budget together within the agreed parameters unless it included these things. Labour were hoping maybe something would turn up, more revenue perhaps, since you don't really know the out-turn until the end of the year.

According to a Fine Gael minister there was no rush to agree the estimates between the two parties once they had been presented. "We gave them the whole budget in October. We never said hurry up and decide. We let them sit on it and stew on it for as long as they liked. We gave them four months." From Labour's point of view the presentation of the estimates put them irrevocably on the road to an election in the early spring or perhaps even January. As one Labour minister recalls:

> Gemma Hussey came in with a list of cuts in the Social Welfare area that were effectively the budget cuts. Normally we would object and she would back down or some bargaining would take place. But this time she stuck to her guns. She persisted

with them and was hell bent on it. I could tell then it was going to be a very different story with Fine Gael.

Fine Gael sources say they were surprised at the willingness of Labour to try and reach some consensus. However, there is agreement among cabinet ministers from both sides that that a breakup over the budget was clear to all from October onwards. As one senior Fine Gael source put it:

> We thought the breakup was on the cards from the very beginning of the budgetary considerations when it became clear we were going to have to go for a budget with fairly substantial cuts. It was fairly likely that the government was going to break up on this issue. What surprised us was the willingness or the apparent willingness of the Labour ministers to hang in there, and apparently face up to some of these things which they had failed to face up to or had indeed vetoed for the previous three years. And there were a lot of reassuring sounds from the Labour Party about their anxiety to settle, to reach a conclusion.

The background to Bruton's decision to present the full budget to cabinet in October lies in his apparent disillusionment at what had happened to the state's finances, not only during the government's term of office, but through ''overspending for 15 years'' as he put it at the Iveagh House news conference to publish the Fine Gael budget proposals in January this year.

A Fine Gael source spelt out the problem, particularly in relation to Labour ministers of cabinet, in this way:

> They went on thinking there were new taxes to be invented, new wheezes like the DIRT tax and the life insurance tax which were going to come riding over the horizon and solve the problem. The sort of ''there's money out there if you could only find it'' mentality…and indeed there was up to a point. But you reach the end of the line and we did reach the end of the line as far as taxation was concerned.

The change in attitude of the coalition partners towards handling the state's financial crisis was intertwined at this stage with John Bruton's return to the Finance portfolio. That Bruton, who was to be recalled to the job in the cabinet reshuffle on 13 February 1986, was unhappy with the specific drift of government economic policy is beyond doubt. His general views on the level of state borrowing and the lack of action to counter it by successive governments are well known. A Fine Gael economist told us: ''He felt he was fighting every year against the tomorrow never comes consensus, the long term never arrives, the our job is to survive this year, let's be politically realistic school of thought. People had been running away from the financial crisis for years, and they couldn't run away from it anymore.'' Certainly Bruton's re-selection as Minister for Finance in the reshuffle made, in retrospect, the likelihood of budget agreement between Labour and Fine Gael a slim chance indeed. Labour's Barry Desmond found Alan Dukes an easier man to reach agreement with:

> I put together four budgets with Alan Dukes and while he is definitely to the right, let's say centre right, of Irish politics he is a pragmatist. I think we might have agreed a budget if Alan Dukes had been Minister for Finance.

His view of Bruton is one of personal admiration for his capacity for work, which he describes as ''hardworking to the point of exhaustion'', but disdain for his political position. ''He is an ideologue of the New Right in Irish politics. He is also a very stubborn man and he has thought out his position very well. But he has a set of right-wing economic principles and all debate oscillates around these." John Bruton rejects the description of himself as representing the New Right: "It's another label which is used to put around ideas which some don't want to have to answer, or to listen to. It's essentially intellectual laziness." To the charge of being stubborn and disorganised, he replied: "Stubborn, yes, I can't really argue with that. Disorganised...well, I tend to rely on officials to do official's work and politicians to do politician's work."

Whatever about the widening chasm between them neither Fine Gael nor Labour had any stomach for going to the polls just yet. There was an unwritten agreement that both parties would stick with it, perhaps with the outside chance of reaching some form of agreement. To get to Christmas they had first to deal with the Fianna Fáil motion of no confidence looming on the agenda. On the face of it their chances of survival were, in betting terms, about 50/50 thanks to the threats of Frank Cluskey, Liam Skelly and Joe Bermingham. To add to the uncertainty Labour chief whip Mervyn Taylor said he would be voting against the government in support of Frank Cluskey's demand for more information on Dublin Gas. With the polls showing dismally for Fine Gael and Labour there was no way either could afford to be voted out of office by one of their own backbenchers. The government moved first to placate Cluskey and Taylor. In the space of a day the information Cluskey had been seeking on the pension funds and interest rates was handed over to him. The details were given by Dick Spring and showed that a pension fund of £600,000 had been established for a company executive. There is still a degree of mystery as to why it took a threat to bring down the government to get Frank Cluskey — and the public — the information he was looking for. Fine Gael cabinet sources say the Department of Energy was at all times responsible for seeking out and handing over the information.

Garret FitzGerald himself was dissatisfied with the information given initially and he was determined to pursue the matter. Frank Cluskey visited him at Barrettstown Castle when the government was meeting there and FitzGerald told him he would insist on full disclosure. Labour on the other hand say the delays were due to simple logistical problems. As one Labour minister explained:

> There was no desire to hold back the information. Our major problem was that Dublin Gas was a private company with a receiver and we had to ask the receiver to dig out the information. The amount of paperwork was voluminous. We couldn't just go in there and dig out the material. There was an enormous amount of work for the receiver to do.

With Frank Cluskey back "on side" and the disappearance with that of Mervyn Taylor's threat, the cabinet turned its attention to the problem of Liam Skelly and the Caneire plan. They had less than a day to secure his support. Already a fairly substantial amount of government time had been taken up by the Skelly plan. There were at least twelve meetings between Skelly and senior Fine Gael cabinet figures like John Bruton, Paddy Cooney, Peter Barry, Jim Mitchell and the chairman of the Fine Gael parliamentary party, Kieran Crotty. There were several meetings between Skelly and the Taoiseach. According to a reliable source there were at least six government memoranda on the subject in addition to the inter-departmental task force and the Davey, Kelleher and McCarthy report. That estimated that the project could cost the state £259m — a figure hotly disputed by Liam Skelly. We have learned that the cost to the state of researching the proposals was around £60,000. At least two senior Fine Gael cabinet members believe the problem with Skelly might have been avoided had his plan been seriously examined when it was first proposed in 1985. As one of them explained:

> I think what happened was that Skelly got the feeling from an early stage he was being fobbed off by the Department of Communications and that he wasn't being taken

seriously. The whole thing was so complicated that people only began to understand it at the end. We should have had it appraised thoroughly from the very first moment and given a definite answer without allowing ourselves get into the position where our backs were to the wall. It was our fault that we allowed it to develop to the extent that we were in the position of having to make a last minute decision.

Fine Gael sources defend the time devoted to the Skelly plan saying that at first their disposition was to knock the whole thing and tell him "nothing doing" regardless of the consequences, but when he met various ministers he convinced them the proposal was not necessarily absurd. Skelly provided reasonable answers to objections, so they formed the view that they must examine his plan in further detail. One said that if even part of the proposal could have been desirable, satisfying the Department of Finance criteria for a worthwhile investment, then it would be "irresponsible" not to examine it further. However, a Labour cabinet minister described the Skelly/Caneire affair as "horrific".

The amount of time taken up with it was enormous. It was an exercise in psychological warfare trying to keep him on board the ship without any major commitment of public money. As far as we were concerned the project was wholly unfeasible and we were not going to commit public money to it.

That wasn't, however, what the dissident deputy was told in the final hours before the vote of no confidence. At a meeting with Peter Barry, Kieran Crotty, John Bruton, Jim Mitchell and chief whip, Fergus O'Brien, a formula was hammered out that would allow both sides to save face. The government agreed to consider the plan and deliver a decision by 20 November. Afterwards the party floated the word to journalists that Skelly might be re-selected to run for the party in the general election if, as *The Irish Times* reported, he "kept his nose clean".

The final obstacle facing the government was Joe Bermingham. In the end he was the easiest to placate. He said his fears over the position of single people living alone on unemployment assistance had been given what he called "sympathetic consideration" after a meeting with the Taoiseach. In reality there were sympathetic noises but no promise of a £60-a-week flat rate. Thus Joe Bermingham along with Frank Cluskey and Liam Skelly walked into the Government lobbies when the vote on the Fianna Fáil motion of no confidence finally came on the evening of 23 October. The government won the vote by 83 votes to 81. The day had been saved, for the day at least. Although disappointed at the defeat of their motion, Fianna Fáil made it clear that they would pile on the pressure and force the government into as many perilous divisions as possible. To this end the party's chief whip, Vincent Brady, tabled a private member's motion that was to bring the government careering close to the edge once again with the help of Cluskey, Taylor and the former leader of the Labour Party, Michael O'Leary.

The issue was an EEC directive on equality in Social Welfare legislation for men and women. In essence the directive removed the dependent status of women under the Social Welfare code. Although the thrust of the directive was progressive and aimed at removing discrimination, it had radical implications in terms of the Irish Social Welfare code. It meant, for instance, that the working wives of men who were on the dole lost their automatic dependent status and the £20-a-week that went with that. In short, about 20,000 families on Social Welfare would lose money. As the harsh reality of this dawned along the backbenches there was a hue and cry against it. For government backbenchers from working-class constituencies there was an acute potential for electoral disaster. In addition to this the government had decided to reduce the amount of money for the Christmas Social Welfare bonus from £21m to £18m. Fianna Fáil seized on this and immediately tabled a motion calling on the government to restore the Christmas bonus to its previous level. Taken together the two issues placed the government right back in the hot seat.

This time there was no equivocation on the part of Joe Bermingham. He announced he would not be voting with the government on the Fianna Fáil motion, a move that did not surprise the cabinet, given Bermingham's stated convictions on the whole Social Welfare issue. The figures then, as the Fianna Fáil motion approached, were 80 votes on the government side and 80 on the opposition benches. With Independents Sean Treacy, Neil Blaney and Tony Gregory voting against the government along with the Workers Party, the government could not afford any defections. With Bermingham committed to at least abstaining they would have to rely on the casting vote of the Ceann Comhairle, Tom Fitzpatrick to survive. It was not, however, going to be that simple. The two Labour rebels, Cluskey and Taylor, announced that they would vote against the government on the Fianna Fáil motion in protest at the equality directive. To make matters worse, former Labour leader, Michael O'Leary, now a Fine Gael backbencher, announced he was withdrawing support on the issue of the Christmas bonuses. Then, on the weekend prior to the vote, the cabinet took a decision to appease Cluskey and Taylor. Just one day before the Dáil division Gemma Hussey told the two Labour TDs she would be making compensatory payments to 17,000 families affected by the equality legislation. The money, according to the government, would come from savings identified in their weekend discussions on the estimates. The two said they would consider the position but it was clear that they would now support the government. That left Michael O'Leary standing alone on the edge of the precipice with the government backed up behind him.

It is fair to say that nobody, not even O'Leary himself, knew how he would vote eventually. On the morning of the crucial vote, 27 November, O'Leary appeared on RTE's ''Morning Ireland'' programme to explain why he wouldn't be supporting the government.

> For the people concerned it's the difference between having a Christmas and having no Christmas. I've always represented constituencies with large pockets of low-income families and I know their problems and they are bargaining on that amount being in their pockets. I don't see myself being able to support these cuts. A woman I met in Tallaght told me she wouldn't be able to give a present to her grandchild because of it. I'm not supporting the cuts at any rate.

That was at five minutes to nine on the day of the vote. On the news at 1.30pm O'Leary repeated his determination not to support the government. In cabinet there was an air of panic. As one Fine Gael minister recalled: ''We weren't sure at all what way it would go. Although it was a private member's motion and we wouldn't have to go to the country because of it we saw the word ELECTION in capital letters staring us in the face.'' At six o'clock O'Leary was telling Charlie Bird of RTE television news that he wasn't supporting the government. There was talk all over Leinster House of secret meetings between O'Leary and senior cabinet members. The pressure was mounting. In the chamber the final speeches were being made for both sides, with Fianna Fáil launching an all-out assault on the government frontbench. Their Social Welfare spokesman, Dr Sean McCarthy, glowered across at Gemma Hussey and declared: ''The government blackmailers are now being bribed purely to save this government's political skin. Credibility and political honesty have been thrown out. You are a collection of political frauds.'' It was Padraig Flynn who produced the finest lines for Fianna Fáil. He fixed a questioning stare on Mrs Hussey.

> What is £5 to you, Minister? It is the price of two gin-and-tonics in the room next door to here. Five pounds to an unemployed person is all he has to provide food, shelter, clothes and transport and the necessities of life for one day of his existence.

As the division bells tolled the government still didn't know where it stood. Eventually it was Paddy Cooney who saved the day. Michael O'Leary strolled into the chamber at the last minute. With him was the Minister for the Environment, John Boland, dressed rather incongruously in full evening dress. As O'Leary leaned against a pillar, Paddy Cooney and Peter Barry engaged the wavering TD in furious debate. From the distance of the press benches Barry could be seen to smile. Cooney was completely straightfaced and continued talking intently to O'Leary. When the tension seemed ready to go beyond breaking point, O'Leary at last made his decision. He smiled grimly and followed Cooney and Barry into the government lobby. The chief whips of Fianna Fáil and Fine Gael walked towards the Ceann Comhairle with the result. It was a tie: 80 votes to 80. The casting vote of Ceann Comhairle Tom Fitzpatrick saved the government from the embarrassment of defeat.

There were howls and jeers from the Fianna Fáil benches and gasps of relief on the government side. On the press bench there was a scramble for the phones. A Labour cabinet minister gave us this version of what happened:

> It was Paddy Cooney who saved the day. He told O'Leary in no uncertain terms that he was dead, gone as far as Fine Gael was concerned if he didn't support the government. He made it very clear to him that he wouldn't get a nomination for the party if he abstained or voted for the Fianna Fáil motion.

After the vote Fine Gael organised a news conference at which Michael O'Leary explained his position. He told journalists that it had been made clear to him that by abstaining or voting against his position would have been misinterpreted as a vote of no confidence in the government. It would, he said, have set in motion a chain of events that would have led to a general election. He admitted: "You are looking at somebody tonight who was defeated from what he set out to get. Yes you are." Asked what he thought it had done to his credibility as a politician, he replied: "I said what I was going to attempt to do with the government and I failed to manage to get that done. I failed. It's not an uncommon experience for somebody to fail in achieving something. I failed and I'm disappointed. I on that matter was defeated."

On the morning following the vote O'Leary contacted the RTE newsroom and told a journalist he wished to come on the "Morning Ireland" programme to explain his position. He was told that the station already had an interview with him which it was going to broadcast. O'Leary then told the journalist he wanted to come on and announce that he was quitting politics. He would come on the programme live he said. The arrangement was made and the programme makers sat back and waited for him to arrive. About half an hour later he rang again to say his car wouldn't start and he would not be coming on the programme. That was the end of his quitting politics, for the time being at least.

The morning after the vote there was depressing news for the government and Fianna Fáil in the shape of opinion polls. One in the Cork Examiner showed the PDs making strong gains in Cork and the other, carried out for "Today Tonight" in Galway, showed that Bobby Molloy of the PDs would be the poll-topper in the Galway West constituency. It also tipped Michael D. Higgins to take the last seat in the constituency. The polls make interesting reading in the light of events in Galway West and the eventual victory of Mairin Quill of the PDs in Cork North Central. While the government agonised over the budget and Fianna Fáil waited for the off the Progressive Democrats were flexing their fiscal muscles with the publication on 16 October of an economic policy document which left Fine Gael scrambling to keep up when it came to cost-cutting proposals. The party had been dipping sharply in the polls since the 25 per cent high of their formation. In October they hit an all-time low of nine per cent. This produced claims from their detractors that the gloss of the new party had at long last worn off. The party's ideological principles had been clear from the start but there was a clear demand for specifics from the rank and file. The party's "think tank", which included people like Professor Martin O'Donoghue, architect of Fianna Fáil's 1977 manifesto, got to work and came up with the policy document. It was to be steel behind O'Malley's rhetoric. The cuts promised went into every area of public spending. They would, the PDs promised, cut £50 million in the first year and £100m in each succeeding year. Among the cuts promised were:

— to cut £45m from the budget of the Department of the Environment.

— to cut £2,370,450 on Education spending.

— to cut £47,424,750 from the Department of Labour budget.

— to cut £29,210,000 on Social Welfare spending.

— to cut £23,534,080 from the budget of the Department of Health.

The cuts on Health and Social Welfare provoked a strong attack from Health Minister Barry Desmond who accused the PDs of playing games with figures. There was criticism too from Fine Gael although Finance Minister John Bruton made the PDs' promise of a 25 per cent standard rate of tax the main point of his attack. But among many on the Fine Gael backbenches there was a clear appetite for the kind of moves suggested by the Progressive Democrats. In addition to the swingeing cuts the party set out proposals for privatising state owned bodies or, as they preferred to describe it: "shifting power from the state back into the hands of the people". Among the possible targets of such measures would be big semi-state companies like Aer Lingus, the profitable parts of the B and I line and the hotel chain, Ostlanna Iompar Éireann. The whole notion of privatisation was to become one of the contentious issues in the general election campaign and was to prove a source of major aggravation to Labour when Fine Gael spokesmen like Michael Noonan began to float the idea publicly in the middle of the budget negotiations.

The PDs' document had more than a tinge of populism. As any taximan will tell you, one of the greatest sources of annoyance to the plain people is the payment of ministerial pensions to former ministers who are still members of the Dáil. With one stroke of a word processor the PDs announced they would, if in power, abolish the system along with the subsidy for the Oireachtas restaurants. Although calls for a change in the system were not new the PDs, with all the skill of professional marketers, gave the old bogey new life.

There is immense and justifiable public cynicism with politics in Ireland. Exhortations by politicians to the public to make sacrifices are rightly dismissed when the public perceive politicians to have featherbedded themselves. The Progressive Democrats believe that if politicians lead by example, the people will respond to tough and equitable policies to sort out the country's problems.

Fine Gael and Labour have been quick to point out that to date neither Desmond O'Malley nor Bobby Molloy, the party's deputy for Galway West, have signalled their intention to take the lead and forego the pensions which the party criticises so strongly. For the Progressive Democrats the October document was to be the manifesto on which they would go to the country. Its critics described the policies as "Thatcherite" and the politics of the rich. The PDs reject this totally saying they are a party for all the people.

Meanwhile, in Fianna Fáil, party leader Charles Haughey was predicting an election by Christmas on the basis that the government would not get through his party's no confidence motion or that it would not survive the debate on the adjournment of the Dáil. He said on 5 October that he regarded himself as being "virtually on the campaign trail," and with so many threats to the government's survival from within its own ranks he was one of many in those perilous months who could not see them coming through. While Garret was visiting Carlow-Kilkenny on his constituency tours Charles Haughey was heading for Dingle to launch a new trawler and shake a few hands in South Kerry where

Fianna Fáil had designs on a second Dáil seat in addition to existing TD, John O'Leary. On board the plane as it soared over the Bog of Allen and down over the plains of Munster Charles Haughey buzzed with confidence. He said then as he was to say so often since that Fianna Fáil would secure an overall majority. Down in Dingle there was the familiar skip across the road to say hello to old friends and potential voters and a trip around the harbour in the new boat Mr Haughey was launching. The boat was named "Boru", after Mr Haughey's hero, Brian Boru, and onto its slender bows were crammed more county councillors, party officials and journalists than ever took to sea together before. It was clearly more than a routine launching. As the boat ploughed out into the choppy waters of Dingle Bay it was chased by a dolphin which had stayed on in the bay long after the rest of its school had departed for the warmer waters of the south. Charles Haughey took the helm and played chase with the mammal out into the bay. As he did the cameras clicked and he was asked when he expected to be at the "real helm" again. He grinned at the pun and then composed himself to deliver a call on the government to declare an immediate general election. He talked for a few moments about the country being in a shambles and then, as the spray splattered into the wheelhouse, he turned the boat towards the pier where there were hands to be grasped and photographs to be taken.

As he flew back to Dublin that night Charles Haughey allowed himself a rare drink of brandy and Irish spring water. He normally doesn't drink while "on business" but somehow he felt he'd earned it. And anyway, as those around him say: "the humour was good". Just out of Farranfore airport he was asked if he thought he was on the election trail. "I wouldn't exactly say we are on the election trail, or an election campaign, but from now on everything the political parties say, everything the people in the political parties do, will be looked at in the light of a general election." A senior member of Mr Haughey's shadow cabinet has told us that the party was straining at the leash for an election from October onwards.

> Once the word started filtering out that they were having trouble with the book of estimates there was a feeling on our part that they might just decide to call the bluff of Skelly and the rest of them and cut and run. We were really hyped up and ready to go. It was what you might call gung ho. From our point of view there never was going to be a budget but we didn't estimate that they would get as far as they did.

On the face of it Fianna Fáil had every reason to be confident. Looking at the situation as it was in October they could have been forgiven for thinking that nothing short of a miracle would see the government through to the budget stage. The signs from the Fine Gael Árd Fheis on 19 October did nothing to dispel the view that an election might be imminent. From the first speeches it was apparent that the message of the Árd Fheis was "go it alone". In the weeks leading up to the gathering at the RDS the party's general secretary, Finbar Fitzpatrick, and press officer Peter White were feeding the message to political correspondents that the Labour "monkey's" hour was fast approaching. Any temptation to cut and run was quickly curbed though by the news which reached the ministers and the delegates on Saturday night. As the delegates cheered Garret FitzGerald's speech euphorically the newspaper vendor stood outside in the bucketing rain with early editions of the *Sunday Independent*. The news on the front page was the last thing the delegates wished to see as they streamed out of the hall. An opinion poll carried out by Irish Marketing Surveys for the newspaper gave Fianna Fáil 53 per cent of the vote compared to a drastic 27 per cent for Fine Gael. Dr Fitzgerald trailed 12 percentage points behind Charles Haughey as the people's choice for Taoiseach.

The Árd Fheis, although low-key and lacking the razmatazz normally present, was significant in that it laid out the specific issues on which Fine Gael would ultimately campaign in the general election. Throughout the weekend speakers concentrated on the credibility of Charles Haughey, particularly in relation to Northern Ireland. It was clear that whatever about subsequent intentions Northern Ireland and the Anglo-Irish Agreement were very much part of the pre-election warm-up. There was Dr Fitzgerald's allegation that Mr Haughey was putting the lives of northern nationalists at risk through his speech at Bodenstown promising to renegotiate the Agreement. Peter Barry compared the Fianna Fáil leader's opposition to that of the Provisional IRA and the extreme Unionists. In the light of those comments it was perhaps naive to hope that the Agreement and Northern Ireland would not become an issue in the campaign that followed. The newspaper reports the Monday after the Árd Fheis headlined the ''go it alone'' message from Dr Fitzgerald to the delight of Fine Gael's party managers. The word coalition was disappearing from the political vernacular with remarkable speed. The government did have two final hurdles to cross before the Christmas recess — the debate on the Extradition Bill and the vote on the adjournment. Once again their defeat on either of these bills would almost certainly ensure an immediate general election. And again they were threatened, but this time by a dual combination of illness and dissident trouble.

The dissident was Alice Glenn whose continual criticisms of the leadership — in August she described the government as a juggernaut out of control — had thrown a doubt over her voting intentions since the beginning of the new term. She had stayed out of the fray, voting with the government on the no confidence and Social Welfare votes, until November when she returned to the headlines with a vengeance thanks to the famous ''Alice Glenn'' report. The ''report'', which was Alice Glenn's private newsletter, accused the leaders of the minority churches, among others, of being ''enemies of the people'' because of their support for the pro-divorce case in the constitutional referendum on divorce. The remarks passed off without notice initially but were brought to the attention of the media and the Fine Gael party generally by two of Mrs Glenn's most implacable enemies, fellow backbenchers Alan Shatter and Monica Barnes. Once given media attention the remarks provoked outrage on the part of minority church leaders. Fine Gael disowned the remarks and Mrs Glenn found herself out in the cold. None of her fellow conservatives on the Fine Gael backbenches, like Tom O'Donnell or Liam Cosgrave junior, were heard to breathe a word of support. The Dublin Central TD found herself completely alienated not only from the parliamentary party but, as events were to prove, her own constituency party as well. The crunch came on Friday 28 November in a stuffy, crowded room in Wynne's Hotel when the Dublin Central constituency of Fine Gael met to select candidates for the forthcoming general election. Alice Glenn was roundly rejected by the convention and on 3 December she announced that she would be resigning from the party, thus placing the government in a minority position. It also left Fine Gael without a sitting TD in Dublin Central where they had taken two seats in the February 1982 election (Alice Glenn and Michael Keating, who defected to the Progressive Democrats). The departure of Mrs Glenn meant that even if the Labour and Fine Gael ministers did agree a budget it would stand little chance of getting through were she to follow the logic of going independent and vote against the government.

The voting position in the Dáil was further thrown into doubt by the illness of the father of the house, Oliver J. Flanagan, who was being treated in a Dublin hospital for a serious illness. Throughout the month of December the rumours abounded about Oliver J.'s exact state of health. There were reports that he would not under any circumstances be able to come to the House for the vote, leaving the government almost certainly facing defeat. Even if Oliver J. Flanagan was fit enough to attend the Dáil, the government would still be dependent on the vote of Independent Joe Bermingham, with the casting vote of the Ceann Comhairle just seeing them through if Alice Glenn voted against. Shortly after becoming an Independent Mrs Glenn said she would not support the government on the Extradition Bill. She cited the cases of the Birmingham Six, the Maguires and the Guildford Four as reasons why the extradition of Irish citizens to Britain should not be made easier. The government was faced with further difficulty when the Progressive Democrats announced their intention to challenge key sections of the Act. In the event the Extradition

Bill was passed on 17 December but only with the help of the Ceann Comhairle's casting vote, producing a result of 81 — 80 in favour of the coalition. Neither Oliver J. nor David Andrews of Fianna Fáil, who was recovering from a back operation, attended the debate. Everything now hinged on the adjournment debate scheduled for the following day, 18 December.

The Fianna Fáil motion called for the Taoiseach to dissolve the Dáil at a convenient date in January 1987. A victory would, in the government's terms, have meant that Fianna Fáil would set the date for the election, thus allowing them to say they had brought the government down. The coalition received a boost the day before the vote with the announcement by Joe Bermingham that he would support them. On the day itself Alice Glenn intimated she would abstain on the vote. It was now down to Oliver J. and David Andrews. The word came from Fianna Fáil a short time before the vote that Andrews would be coming. Fine Gael deputies waited anxiously for news of Oliver J. Then there was news that Peter Barry had visited the Laois-Offaly TD and had been assured he would be in the Dáil for the vote. And he kept his promise in one of the most emotional and dramatic moments seen for many years in Leinster House. As the debate was being wound up with the last-minute speeches of both sides the word went around Leinster House that Oliver J. had arrived by ambulance. He entered the chamber with the aid of a walking frame, looking frail and tired. As he moved towards the government lobbies he was assisted by another of the Fine Gael old guard, Tom O'Donnell, and the deputy for Tipperary South, Brendan Griffin. As he did David Andrews was wheeled to the Fianna Fáil side by colleague Dr Donie Ormonde. Oliver J, who had refused a pair that would have allowed both himself and David Andrews to stay away, shook hands with his colleagues and was congratulated by the Taoiseach, the Ceann Comhairle and by Charles Haughey who crossed the floor to shake his hand. It was to be the last characteristic gesture of a man who had always spoken his own mind and done his own thing for over fifty years in Dáil Éireann. His gesture saved the government and saw them defeat the Fianna Fáil motion by 82 votes to 81. The two sick TDs returned to hospital and the deputies from all sides streamed out of the chamber, some for Christmas drinks in the Dáil bar, others to their constituencies for the hard slog of an election most believed to be imminent.

What was going on in cabinet in these critical weeks and why was there such a determination to stay in power until after the Christmas recess? The answer lies in a mixture of some slight hope on the part of both coalition parties that the other would back down on the question of spending cuts, and more importantly, the basic political reason of not wanting to be brought down from the outside. To be dragged down by Fianna Fáil and the Independents, perhaps even by one of their own backbenchers, would have placed the government at an enormous disadvantage in the eyes of the electorate. The degree of sincerity with which both sides sought agreement is hard to guage. Since senior members of both parties have admitted they knew the "game was up" on the budget from late October onwards, it begs the question: Just what were they doing in cabinet. During the Christmas recess a senior Labour figure, outside the cabinet, told one of the authors jokingly: "I'm convinced they're playing cards in cabinet". It appears there was a good deal of what one Fine Gael minister described to us as "political reflection". Another gave us this perspective:

There was no confrontation at any stage. The thing was like a slow bicycle race. There were an awful lot of people who sort of hoped something might turn up, but one of the merits of putting things down on the table at the beginning was that the something might turn up brigade had it put up to them. It was saying: "This is the budget. Everything is there, and if you have any other ideas what are they?" To try and get a government to agree to cuts in spending was a radical step if you compared it to the previous three years.

The Fine Gael cabinet source quoted was unsure as to why Labour were prepared to "stick with" the discussions for so long.

One possibility is that that they wanted to stay in until the end of the year, that they wanted another three months at it and were prepared to jolly us along for that purpose. The other is that they genuinely wanted to contribute to solving the country's financial problems.

From mid-December it was apparent to Barry Desmond, for one, that there was no possibility of agreement on budget cuts. However, he gave this reason for Labour "hanging on":

But the Labour ministers had taken a decision to go all the way with them, right up to the book of estimates. We wanted it on paper, out in the open so people would see the estimates and know why we were quitting. We were determined that the differences between the parties on the estimates would be written into the public record. We were very bitter about those who said we should come out in mid-'86. We had to come out on specifics and not on generalities or some piece of individual opportunism.

There had been some speculation that Fine Gael might opt for an election immediately after their Árd Fheis, before the no-confidence motion, but the Taoiseach had a major concern which made that unattractive. He was convinced that the coalition must put through the Extradition Bill so that the Republic would be seen to have delivered on the Anglo-Irish Agreement. He believed that Charles Haughey and Fianna Fáil would not have been able, or willing, to put that Bill through, and thus Britain would have been given an excuse not to deliver on its side. He expressed that view to the authors at the outset of the election campaign. But the political considerations, getting the economic battleground right and staving off destruction by dissidents, Independents and Fianna Fáil were more at the core of things. A senior Fine Gael cabinet source put it this way:

In the latter stages, we had to produce a budget no matter how bad it was, and fight the election on that, rather than just break up in disorder and disappear. Failure to produce a budget would have rightly led people to have little faith in us as a government. If we had broken up, Labour and ourselves, and we had nothing to offer, we weren't able to say "this is what should be done," then we would have been decimated, and rightly.

It is believed that Desmond and the party leader Dick Spring were those pressing the hardest line against the Fine Gael cuts at the cabinet table. The pressure from the parliamentary party eased up substantially in the final weeks of the Dáil despite Flor O'Mahony's stated fears that the Labour ministers were being led into a trap. As one Labour minister commented:

Towards the end there was no real pressure from the parliamentary party. Most people knew we weren't coming back. We knew there was no way we would be able to carry out the kind of cuts Fine Gael were talking about. But we had no intention of letting ourselves be hijacked by Frank Cluskey and company. We knew that if those cuts were published with our names on it there would be a motion of no confidence in the government before the Labour parliamentary party as quick as you'd look around you.

On 2 January the highest ever deficit figure of £1.39b was published. As a result the budget overrun would be £145m. Although short of the predicted £180m the overrun would necessitate cuts of £265m in spending programmes. It ruled out any hope of agreement.

Yet throughout the Christmas period and into January there were continuous soothing noises to the media from government spokesmen who insisted that there would be a budget. In early January when the cabinet were reported to be in deep discussion over the cuts Peter Barry told RTE he believed there would be a budget agreed on by both Labour and Fine Gael. At the time Fine Gael's election strategists were making their final preparations. It is interesting that on the same day Peter Barry talked about an agreed budget, Fine Gael Senator Sean O'Leary predicted, in response to a question, that there would be an election on or about 19 February. To make matters worse for the government the unemployment figures published on 10 January were a record 250,178. Four days later *The Irish Times* was reporting that civil servants expected the government to split up within a week — the deadline for the publication of the book of estimates loomed on 21 January. It is now clear that in the final weeks both parties were simply waiting to name the day. Both used the time to prepare their election machinery. Fine Gael's election manifesto had in fact been drafted much earlier, alongside the budget, giving credence to the suspicion that it had been the strategy all along to go to the country on a budget that would be Fine Gael's alone. We have been told that John Bruton wrote substantial portions of the Fine Gael manifesto. A Labour minister admitted frankly that the party's participation in government had weakened the party's organisational base. Thus any time which could be bought before the actual election was called was very valuable. "In my own case it would have been politically disastrous to go before my constituency party was ready," he said.

Fine Gael's managers had been busy too, booking a room in the Burlington for their manifesto launch and organising a helicopter to take the party leader on a tour of the Sligo, Roscommon and Galway constituencies as soon as the election was declared. Both of these arrangements were made a week in advance of the actual day and the information passed on to key constituency organisers. In the final week, when there was still talk of possible agreement and "crisis meetings" of the cabinet, the ministers were busy preparing themselves to take to the road armed and equipped with their respective policy documents and manifestos. The final day, which had been agreed between Garret FitzGerald and Dick Spring, dawned on 20 January in a welter of media speculation. The newsrooms of the country buzzed with rumours. The first reports were that the Taoiseach was going to Áras an Uachtarán to dissolve the Dáil at midday. The story was that he was going to form a minority Fine Gael administration and seek to introduce a budget. Then word came that the Labour ministers had resigned amicably and would be giving a press conference at the Setanta Building opposite Leinster House around noon. Sometime around midday the copy desks were told that a story was to be filed shortly from Government Buildings on the Taoiseach's statement. It came within minutes, bearing the news the nation had been anticipating for months. The President was to be asked to dissolve the Dáil and an election would be held on Tuesday 17 February.

The Campaign

As he stood with his fellow Labour ministers on the steps outside Government Buildings in the rain Dick Spring smiled and seemed to be quite pleased with himself. The strategy had paid off and the millions in cuts had been left behind in the hands of the new Fine Gael government. Inside the same building the jobs the Labour men had left behind were being shared out among their former colleagues. It was not, however, a division of the spoils in the normal sense of the word. The ministers were aware that they would not have long to enjoy the honour of these new offices. It was simply a holding operation and an interesting moment for the party historians. This was the first Fine Gael government since the party's foundation over fifty years before. The newly rearranged government lost no time and immediately presented its proposed budget — effectively the first manifesto of the campaign with all the wide-ranging cuts that had been predicted for months beforehand. One look at those cuts reinforces the view that there was never any realistic prospect of the government parties agreeing to go ahead with them. They included a £10 charge for out-patient services at hospitals for all but medical card holders; a £1 prescription charge for all, with refunds for amounts over £5 spent in any one month; increases in the health contributions ceiling; rates of pay related benefits to be halved for new claimants from April and an increase in the conditionality of disability benefit. Later, on the day the government quit, the Labour leader and his fellow backbenchers, as they had now become, hosted a news conference in the Setanta Buildings just across the road from Leinster House. With posters of Dick Spring in an open-neck white shirt on the walls behind them the former ministers sat down to explain why they had resigned. Their leader looked sternly into the cameras as he spoke of the unjust nature of the cuts. Beside him Ruairi Quinn folded his hands like a man deep in prayer; Barry Desmond was armed with a detailed explanation of his reason for quitting and looked fit to take on all-comers while Liam Kavanagh was, as ever, quiet and composed. Spring summarised the Labour position by saying they simply could not accept what they claimed amounted to £140m in Social Welfare and Health cuts.

> They represent a fundamentally unacceptable imposition on insured workers and on the poorest sections of the community. They will affect the rights of women and of young people entering the workforce for the first time. They will make life difficult and costly for old people, for people living alone and for the mothers of children. Neither I nor my cabinet colleagues can defend these cuts since we regard them as fundamentally wrong.

Barry Desmond in the meantime circulated copies of his own detailed response to the cuts in Health and Welfare spending. It was all part of the strategy that had been agreed months before.

Later in the day Fine Gael launched the minority government budget proposals in the colonial splendour of Iveagh House, the headquarters of the Department of Foreign Affairs. The ministers walked in solemnly and went to a long table at the top of the room. Sitting strategically to the right of Garret FitzGerald was John Bruton. It was a pairing that the electorate would see a lot more of during the campaign, thanks to a decision by Fine Gael's managers to use the Taoiseach and the Finance Minister as the principal front-men. The two, with Alan Dukes, Michael Noonan and Peter Barry in supporting roles, travelled the country blasting home their message of rectitude and responsibility. In a sense the budget that was presented in Iveagh House overshadowed the Fine Gael manifesto which was launched the following day. Fine Gael now regret this. In the eyes of the public and media the two became indistinguishable. The budget provided for £210m in cuts with substantial reductions in the estimates for Health and Social Welfare. The manifesto which was published the following day contained policies on a wide range of issues including education, law and order, neutrality and a brief section on Northern Ireland. It was clear though that the agenda throughout the campaign would, until the appearance of the Anglo-Irish Agreement in the final week, be dominated completely by the key issues of unemployment, emigration and the economy. Fine Gael's main economic planks, then, as they faced the public were:

— to reduce public spending in 1987 by £210m and cut borrowing by 1.2 per cent of GNP per annum.
— to reform the tax system by getting two thirds of taxpayers onto the standard rate of tax and to introduce a system of self assessment for farm and corporation tax.
— to sell up to 49 per cent of shares in public companies like Aer Lingus, NET and Irish Steel. To sell off all of the Great Southern Hotels Group.
— to lower the starting salaries in some jobs so that a greater number of people could be employed (a particular priority of Garret FitzGerald's). To remove what the party described as the conservative, shackled and worn-out attitudes of the trade unions.

The latter definition of ''conservative'' was broadened to include the Labour Party and drew a fiery riposte from Labour's chairman, Senator Michael D. Higgins. It was, observers agree, all part of the process of distancing that had been taking place at a furious speed since the two parties went their separate ways. Labour were quick to go on the offensive themselves against Fine Gael. The man carrying the sword into battle was Barry Desmond, the party's most combative performer. He challenged the Fine Gael Health estimates saying in blunt language that they could not work. In private he is believed to have described the Health estimate as ''sharp practice'' and ''contrivance at an estimate''. This was rejected by Garret FitzGerald but it did provide Fianna Fáil with a useful stick with which to beat Fine Gael.

Fine Gael's proposals to sell shares in firms like Aer Lingus, NET and Irish Steel as well as £3m worth of trees from the state forests also provoked strong criticism from Fianna Fáil, Labour and the Workers Party. The Fianna Fáil leader dispatched a letter to the Irish Congress of Trade Unions without hesitation, assuring them that — whatever about Fine Gael or the Progressive Democrats — his party was solidly behind the public sector. In his letter he did, however, say that Fianna Fáil would support joint ventures between the public and private sectors. The issue bubbled for about two days and then slid down the agenda as the more pressing problems of the state's finances and unemployment came surging to the fore. Fianna Fáil had taken a deliberate decision not to publish their manifesto until ten days after the campaign had started. In the end it was a strategy that many in the party now admit backfired on them. From the outset they were aware that the Taoiseach's decision to go for a long campaign could only work to their disadvantage. The four-week campaign would allow the coalition parties time to put some of the past four years behind them. Barry Desmond certainly believes the four-week campaign was to Labour's advantage. ''Remember, in many cases we had to build a campaign from the ground up," he says. Fine Gael's strategists were keenly aware of the old maxim that a week is a long time in politics. A four-week campaign would, they felt, expose Fianna Fáil's reluctance to give specific details on how they would handle the problems of the budget deficit and the national debt. When he appeared on the "This Week" programme just three days before the official start of the campaign, Charles Haughey had this criticism of the four-week campaign:

> I think it would be outrageous, just prolonging the agony. I don't think anybody wants or needs a four-week campaign. We can put our case to the people in a much shorter period of time than that. And they are also probably hoping, and I think we intend to disappoint them on this, they're probably hoping the longer the campaign goes on the more likely it is for somebody to make a sort of political blunder that will be to their benefit.

On the same programme he affirmed his determination to abolish the DIRT tax despite, as he conceded himself, the budgetary cost of roughly £100m to £150m. "I have no doubt that the reduction in interest rates you would achieve by bringing the £1.4b to £1.5b which has gone out of the country because of DIRT back into the Irish system would more than compensate for the budgetary loss." Asked if he would be making any commitments to the electorate during the campaign he answered in a very definite tone: "We are making no commitments. Absolutely no specific commitments." Everything would be subject to budgetary considerations. And while he ruled out promises, Mr Haughey also ruled out going into specifics on just how Fianna Fáil would cut the deficit and the national debt.

However he did say that government spending would be contained in real terms at 1986 levels. In the Fianna Fáil manifesto it was made clear that spending would be kept at those levels as a proportion of GNP. In other words the growth factor in the economy would be all-important in determining the severity of cuts in public expenditure or, indeed, if there would be any possibility of loosening the state purse strings.

The decision not to go into specifics was reaffirmed two days after the election was called. The official line was that the party would not consider itself bound by the estimates published by Fine Gael and would instead publish overall spending figures for each department. Charles Haughey took the view that it would expose the party to the "worst of all worlds" to publish cuts while out of government. It was a view apparently shared by most of his shadow cabinet. The Fianna Fáil view was that until such time as the party had access to the nation's accounts it could not make any specific commitments. One of Mr Haughey's frontbenchers now believes this to have been a mistake.

> Let's face it, the fashion of the moment was to go out and say in as hard terms as you like what should be done. What did we do? We abandoned the stage to Bruton and Dessie who paraded around the place telling the people that we were afraid to tell the truth. People wanted to know exactly what we were going to do and a lot of the time we simply couldn't tell them.

However, another senior figure took the opposite view, the one shared by the party leader:

> There was a right-wing swing out there and we couldn't go after that. It's not what Fianna Fáil is about. We would have been completely marginalised if we got into the game of competing on cuts. We weren't in a position to be specific on cuts or commitments. Look where we'd be now if we'd gone around the place making promises. That sort of thing leaves you with no room to manoeuvre if you're in a tight corner.

At their meetings the shadow cabinet also decided that they would try to shorten the campaign by holding off on the release of their manifesto until at least a week after the official declaration. The result was that for the first week of the campaign Fianna Fáil spokesmen like Seamus Brennan and Ray McSharry found themselves facing opponents who were fully briefed on the specifics with programmes to put to the people. The Fianna Fáil representatives were restricted to criticising the government and talking in general terms about the need to "go for growth" and boost the economy. It was McSharry, according to a very senior member of Mr Haughey's cabinet, who suffered most.

> It wasn't Ray's fault at all. The night the election was called he appeared on "Today Tonight" only four-and-a-half hours after getting off a plane from Brussels and he had missed the whole buzz of the day. You couldn't expect him to be hyped up and raring to go the way Bruton was on the same night.

There was worse to come for McSharry when he seemed unable, again on "Today Tonight", to answer repeated questions about the party's policy on the confidentiality of savings accounts under a system of self assessment. The incident occurred when John Bruton stated that Fine Gael would consider allowing tax inspectors access to such accounts if they suspected a person was avoiding tax. What was Fianna Fáil's position Ray McSharry was asked. The Sligo TD and MEP was unable to answer the question despite repeated attempts by the interviewer to elicit the specific detail. The following day the party leader announced that Fianna Fáil would observe the confidentiality of accounts. Fine Gael's press officer, Peter White, said of the programme: "Ray had an impossible brief and that was to go on and say nothing".

Fianna Fáil officially launched their campaign on 29 January in the conference room of Jury's Hotel. In the hallway Fionnuala O'Kelly, Niamh O'Connor and Sinead Corby of the party's press office handed huge wads of documentation to the arriving journalists. As they filed in and camera crews fiddled and fidgeted with innumerable wires, the strains of Beethoven's Emperor Symphony drifted calmly over the crowd. Busily directing people to their seats and checking microphones was the ebullient P.J. Mara, press secretary to Fianna Fáil and confidant of Charles Haughey. With everybody settled in their seats, pens and microphones at the ready, the signal was given backstage and the party leader and his frontbench trooped onto the podium. For the next hour-and-a-half he gave a performance that bristled with confidence. The repeated questions about what he would cut if elected were grabbed in the palm of the hand and sent flying back down the hall. Sometimes they boomeranged back but gradually the journalists were worn down, the realisation that they were not going to get specifics finally coming home to rest. The target of the party's "Programme for National Recovery" was, they heard, to contain expenditure at 1986 levels in real terms as a proportion of GNP. In simpler terms that meant cuts but the size of the cuts would not be known until the growth level for the year was determined. Fianna Fáil's ambition was to reduce the level of public spending progressively and achieve an annual growth rate of 2.5 per cent over five years. The programme identified unemployment as the key problem and suggested a wide range of state programmes and plans to reverse the trend.

The best news line of the launch came following a series of questions from Vincent Browne, editor of the *Sunday Tribune*. Browne asked the Fianna Fáil leader if the targets had not been achieved after two years, would he consider his government a failure. Charles Haughey agreed that he would, in so far as that target was concerned. The redoubtable Browne pursued the issue and asked if the Fianna Fáil leader would resign if he felt his government had failed to do what it set out to do. To this question there was laughter and when it was pursued there were shouts from Fianna Fáil supporters at the back of the room, to "shut up Vincent". The conference did, however, see a major policy change, described as a U-turn by the media, on the issue of DIRT tax. Although he had said on 18 January that he would abolish the tax, Mr Haughey now said the party would review it. The reason for this change of heart: the large sums of revenue the tax was producing.

On campaign in Cork John Bruton attacked what he called the ''U-turn'' and accused Fianna Fáil of looking for a ''blank cheque'' from the electorate.

> What Fianna Fáil are proposing is more spending and more borrowing. This means increased interest rates and no prospect of lower taxes. This is just cowardice masquerading as cuteness. As far as the most immediate issue facing an Irish government in 1987 is concerned — the budget for the year — Fianna Fáil have nothing to say.

Also quick to respond were the Progressive Democrats. The party leader accused his old adversary of failing to be specific — the charge that was to be thrown again and again at Fianna Fáil throughout the campaign.

> In short, in its present form, the Fianna Fáil programme is asking the voters to buy a pig in a poke. It is a catch-all formula from a catch-all party that is not going to fool the people.

There was criticism also from Labour and the Workers Party but some soothing praise from the Construction Industry Federation which welcomed the measures aimed at boosting the industry. Ray Burke believes the party scored with the electorate on the construction issue.

The following Sunday the Fianna Fáil leader pulled out of a pre-arranged interview on the RTE ''This Week'' programme prompting allegations from Fine Gael's director of elections, David Moloney, that he was unwilling to discuss his manifesto. However he did, the day before, answer questions for RTE at a news conference while campaigning in Meath. The Taoiseach was to accuse the Fianna Fáil leader of being afraid to debate the issues because of his ''refusal to go on the programme'' and because he allegedly turned down an opportunity to go on the live television programme ''Questions and Answers'' in which the two party leaders would answer questions from the public. Fianna Fáil's P.J. Mara reacted with anger to the allegations and in turn accused Fine Gael of refusing to agree to two debates between the party leaders on ''Today Tonight''.

The day after Fianna Fáil's launch the Labour Party produced its manifesto. It aimed at growth of 4 per cent a year and focussed on a major role for the National Development Corporation which had been established at Labour's insistence during the lifetime of the previous government. Labour also proposed a widening of the tax net; the reintroduction of wealth tax which they claimed would net £200m in revenue; an increase of 25 per cent in corporation taxes; the extension of social insurance to farmers and the self-employed and a drive to bring the standard rate of tax to 35 per cent. It was a document with a strongly leftward drift designed to win back some of the support which had been eaten away by the Workers Party. As subsequent events were to prove, Labour, although entering the election in poor wear, managed to distance themselves from the coalition image, helped no doubt by the clear anti-coalition line which had been established by the party's Commission on Electoral Strategy.

Their opponents on the left, the Workers Party, set the question of tax reform at the centre of their campaign accusing the bigger parties of being ''afraid to hurt their friends'' in big business and the farming sector. The message was: ''Tax the greedy not the needy''. The Party also targeted agriculture as an area where they would introduce greater planning. On the question of the national debt the Party urged either a re-scheduling of the national debt or a freeze on repayments with the basic message of expansion rather than fiscal rectitude. Also competing for the left-wing vote, but with little realistic chance of taking a seat, were Sinn Féin, now committed to taking their seats in the Dáil. The party proposed, in addition to re-scheduling of debts, a major drive to develop natural resources and to reap tax revenue from big business and large farmers. The question of Northern Ireland was clearly not going to be an issue in the Republic and this, the party say, was reflected on the doorsteps. Throughout the campaign the party leader, Gerry Adams, who toured the targeted constituencies of Cavan Monaghan, Louth, Dublin Central and Dublin West, maintained that the party might have a chance of taking seats. The real target though was the next election, he said.

The Progressive Democrats had given a clear indication of their manifesto as far back as October but their actual election document was not launched until the second week of the campaign. It proposed, among other things: a standard rate of tax of 25 per cent by 1991 with a 2 per cent tax cut for PAYE workers to take effect immediately; proposals to cut £250m in public spending; a deferrment in public sector pay increases and privatisation of some state enterprises and the state forests. The tax reform proposals, aimed directly at the party's middle income, suburban constituency, would according to economists give PAYE workers the equivalent of a 4 per cent pay rise. And in terms of cuts in public spending the PDs surged ahead of Fine Gael with proposals to slice £100m more in capital spending than the government party. It was a document designed to challenge both of the major parties. It was a challenge to Fianna Fáil to spell out specifics, and it threatened Fine Gael for the majority share of the fiscal responsibility vote. Both Fianna Fáil and Fine Gael now admit they did not take the threat seriously enough. Apart from criticism by John Bruton and by Charles Haughey himself, the PDs never faced the kind of sustained attack to which Fianna Fáil and Fine Gael subjected each other.

The first major opinion poll of the campaign, which appeared on 28 January in *The Irish Times,* just one week into the campaign, bore up the view that where Fianna Fáil and Fine Gael were suffering the PDs were gaining. The poll gave Fianna Fáil a clear lead of 14 per cent over the combined support of the Progressive Democrats and Fine Gael; but Desmond O'Malley emerged as the most popular leader with 47 per cent of the vote compared with 46 per cent for Charles Haughey. The Fine Gael leader, Dr Fitzgerald, had 36 per cent as against 33 per cent for Dick Spring and 25 for Workers Party leader, Tomas MacGiolla. The state of the parties was: Fianna Fáil — 52 per cent; Fine Gael — 23 per cent; Labour — 5 per cent; Progressive Democrats — 15 per cent; Others (including Workers Party and Sinn Féin) — 5 per cent. The poll was taken after the launch of the Fine Gael budget and manifesto and before Fianna Fáil's publication of their ''Programme for National Recovery''. It showed them with a clear lead and set to win an overall majority. They would never have it so good again. For Fine Gael the figures were, to say the least, disappointing. They had dropped by 6 per cent from the post-Árd Fheis figure of 29 per cent. It was at this stage in the campaign that one of their senior managers told the authors: ''We'll be lucky not to be coming back to the Dáil in a minibus.''

The party's director of elections, David Moloney, took some consolation in the relatively high number of people who had answered ''I don't know'' when asked who they would be voting for. The figure, according to *The Irish Times*/MRBI poll was an exceptionally high 22 per cent. ''We are confident,'' said Moloney, ''that there will be a dramatic improvement between now and polling day.'' The Fine Gael leader had privately said to his election strategists at the beginning of the campaign that he expected the party would suffer in the first polls but gradually recover once the campaign got properly underway. Nevertheless, there were many in party headquarters on 28 January who felt a twinge of panic when they saw the front page of *The Irish Times* headlined: ''Poll shows Fianna Fáil in clear lead over all parties.''

But it was the Fianna Fáil electoral strategy and a faux pas over Northern Ireland which was to give relief to the other parties and deny an overall majority to Charles Haughey. A decision was taken by the inner cabinet and the party leader to go for a restrained approach to the campaign with no major attacks on the other parties, no ''going for the jugular''. The idea, from the leader's viewpoint, was to present the positive; not to try and outdo the other parties on cutbacks but concentrate on ''growth and good things''. It was a strategy which senior figures in the party now admit backfired. One of them commented:

A decision was taken to go for the laid-back approach. We completely changed gear from the mood before Christmas. I don't know who took that decision or why it was taken but it changed the pace completely. The new idea was to be statesmanlike and responsible when, at the time, many of us felt we should be putting the boot in. Let's face it, the hard-hitting approach got us to 52 per cent of the poll at one stage. Once we started to go laid-back we began to slip.

This source also said that Fianna Fáil spokesmen found themselves being savaged on radio and television debates because their instructions were to "go easy". At the same time, Fine Gael were conducting that party's most aggressive campaign ever, with little regret about personalising the debate. The so-called "Haughey factor" was resurrected within days of the campaign starting, on an official party political broadcast, putting in doubt the party leader's stated hope that the campaign would not be personalised. The first appearance of the "Haughey factor" in Fine Gael's election material was on 28 January. After dwelling for some moments on the achievement of "Fine Gael in government" the broadcast turned its attention to Fianna Fáil with the key word, "remember". "Remember the deals, dissension and scandals," a voice said, as the camera panned across newspaper clippings from 1982. "Remember the tapping of journalists' phones, remember the growing threat of political interference in the Garda Síochána." The screen then cut to shots of Ray McSharry, Gerry Collins and Sean Doherty and the voice asked the public to "remember the incompetence of Mr Haughey's cabinet". The shadows of other days were being brought back to haunt Fianna Fáil.

The Haughey factor was not laboured in the broadcast but it did, from a Fine Gael point of view, serve to remind people of things which had been largely forgotten in the years since the last Fianna Fáil government. The pre-election publicity surrounding the High Court awards to two journalists, Geraldine Kennedy and Bruce Arnold, for the tapping of their phones on the instructions of the then Justice Minister, Sean Doherty, cannot have helped Fianna Fáil. Fine Gael succeeded, to some degree, in their other aim which was to erase the bad memories of the previous four years. The policy of the party managers was to get Fine Gael far away from the image of a coalition government as fast as possible:

> We were selling people the gin without the bitter lemon. We produced ideas and policies we would never have gotten away with had we been tied to Labour. We were saying in straightforward terms that the country was banjaxed. It turned out to be much easier for us over the four weeks to put the bad stuff behind us. And we knew the longer it went on the harder it would be for Fianna Fáil to say nothing. If there had been a three-week campaign I believe Charlie Haughey would have an overall majority by now.

A Fine Gael strategist admitted that the party was "throwing muck at Charlie," but says they failed to take on the Progressive Democrats. "The PDs were let away with murder but it is hard to fight a war on two fronts," he commented. Fianna Fáil did go on the offensive sporadically to remind people that Fine Gael had been in government for the past four years and were the majority partners in an administration of record unpopularity. It was all to little avail. Fine Gael were succeeding, to quote L.P. Hartley, in convincing people that the past was a foreign country. Within Fine Gael there were those who believed the party should have been taking a tougher line with the PDs. Others counselled against alienating PD voters who might transfer to Fine Gael. Others still agreed with what the PDs were saying and saw no real reason to attack them. The only strong criticism of the PDs came from John Bruton who attacked the party's plan to cut capital spending by £100m.

It was like selling the furniture to pay for the groceries, Bruton declared. He debated the issue with Des O'Malley on radio the morning after the PDs launched their election manifesto. It was a particularly bitter and acrimonious debate with Bruton accusing the

PDs of indulging in once-off gimmicks. A badly stung O'Malley responded: "It is not a once-off gimmick and John Bruton's arguments are totally false." The debate continued with some anger.

"This is one of the authors of the 1977 manifesto talking," Bruton pointed out disparagingly.

"I would love to be able to explain what I have in mind," O'Malley persisted, "without being shouted down by John Bruton."

It was the first and last real battle between Fine Gael and the PDs and it is perhaps significant that Bruton was the man doing the attacking. In the course of that "Day By Day" interview, Bruton also challenged Des O'Malley to have his proposals costed by the Department of Finance. The PD leader recalled:

> Bruton spoke many times about our economic policies. But we kind of took the steam out of that by going to the Department of Finance to have the proposals costed.

O'Malley claims there was an element within Fine Gael which wanted to "get at" the PDs. That group prevailed for a couple of days, he says, with the publication of some newspaper advertisements proclaiming, "Dessie can't do it". He says they found the advertisements counterproductive as they soon stopped.

The possibility of an alliance between the PDs and Fine Gael, whether formal or informal, was discussed at a senior level in both parties during the election. There had been suggestions from Peter Barry and Paddy Cooney that a PD/Fine Gael coalition would not be a bad idea; and there was Des O'Malley's pointed refusal to engage in any coalition with Fianna Fáil as long as Charles Haughey was leader. There were those in both parties who believed that an alliance would prove the only valid alternative to a Fianna Fáil government. The authors can confirm that there were talks about a transfer arrangement between senior representatives of both Fine Gael and the Progressive Democrats from the earliest stages of the campaign. Among those engaged in discussions were Fine Gael's director of elections, David Moloney, and the PDs' general secretary, Pat Cox. According to Fine Gael the discussions reached the stage where both parties agreed to a transfer arrangement. Peter White, the Fine Gael press officer, has confirmed that the PDs were told in advance that the Taoiseach would be advising Fine Gael voters to transfer to O'Malley's party on Valentine's Day, 14 February. Fine Gael say that Pat Cox was given the exact text of the Taoiseach's offer and told that the speech would be delivered in time for the evening television news on RTE. In return Fine Gael were given a form of words that O'Malley would deliver the following day. Peter White describes these as, "neutral to mildly positive". According to Fine Gael the PDs were to advise their supporters to bear in mind "the importance of electing a government which will face up squarely to the economic crisis". While not giving an explicit directive the PDs urged their supporters to "consider how the country's true interests can best be served" when deciding their transfers.

The Taoiseach made his offer but, according to White, the response from O'Malley the following day was "totally at variance" with what had been agreed. The PD leader firmly rejected any deals or alliances in advance of the election. Fine Gael claim that the PDs "lost their nerve" and decided at the last minute not to go ahead with the arrangement. Des O'Malley denies that there was any such arrangement. He cites as evidence the statement by the Taoiseach on election night that he did not expect the PDs to enter any arrangement with Fine Gael. Des O'Malley claims that there has subsequently been a row within Fine Gael between those who wanted an all-out attack on the PDs and those who supported the "softly softly" approach. Mr O'Malley also believes that Garret FitzGerald's attempt to link the two parties cost his party votes from disaffected Fianna Fáil supporters who might have been tempted to vote PD. Pat Cox also said that there was "no deal". Asked if he had agreed a form of words with Fine Gael, he answered: "I'm not going to get involved in that at all''. He said the Fine Gael claims about a deal reflected a disagreement within that party about its attitude to the PDs during the election. ''At no stage during the campaign did we seek to indicate to anybody that we were ploughing anything other than an independent furrow. All that is doing is lining up points in what is essentially an unresolved row within Fine Gael.''

The Fianna Fáil leader, for his part, likened the Taoiseach's offer to a ''kiss of death'' and accused Dr FitzGerald of abandoning Labour to the wolves in ''one of the most cynical acts of our times''. Fianna Fáil's attitude to the PDs and vice versa was much less complex. The bitter personal differences between the two party leaders made an alliance of any sort impossible. Yet in spite of the anti-PD feeling within Fianna Fáil the attacks on Des O'Malley and his party were few and far between. The attitude was, as one Fianna Fáil minister has told us: ''Don't give them publicity by paying attention to them.''

For the Progressive Democrats there were obvious dangers in being seen to be aligned with Fine Gael, however tempting the prospect of gaining transfers might have been. A party whose *raison d'etre* was to break the mould in Irish politics would have to do so even-handedly if it were to avoid the charge of being nothing more than a Fianna Fáil rump. The evidence of the opinion polls also suggested that the independent course was the wisest. In the first *Irish Times*/MRBI poll the Progressive Democrats stood at 15 per cent; by the time of the second poll of the campaign in the *Sunday Independent* they had moved up to 17 per cent. That poll, on 4 February, confirmed for Fianna Fáil organisers that their lead was slipping substantially. They were down from 52 to 48 per cent and the initial certainty of winning an overall majority was beginning to disappear. For Fine Gael there was a new low of 22 per cent while Labour — to their own great relief — had moved up a percentage point to 6 per cent.

The alarm bells were starting to ring within the Fianna Fáil camp. Still, few were willing to believe that they would be denied an overall majority. As he toured the border counties in the second week of the campaign Charles Haughey acted every inch a winner. He said again and again that Fianna Fáil would win an overall majority and put the fall in his party's position down to the large number of ''don't knows'' among the electorate. The *Independent*/IMS poll put them at 11 per cent, a record figure suggesting to the parties that everything was there to play for. As the battle moved into the third week the debate on the economy lapsed into stalemate. In the second half of the campaign Fine Gael tried to rekindle the debate on the economy. They held a major press conference, hosted by John Bruton and Michael Noonan, to assert that Fianna Fáil's programme would in fact cost the state £900m. Since they had been arguing up to this time that the programme was too vague the media were decidedly suspicious of this belated costing. It disappeared as an issue within 48 hours. A senior Fine Gael minister admitted: ''It just didn't work''. Time and time again Fine Gael, the Progressive Democrats and most of the media demanded that Fianna Fáil spell out their plans to cut public spending. Fianna Fáil refused to be budged and continued to talk in calm, soothing tones about prudent financial management and ''getting the country going again''. Only occasionally was there a glimpse of specifics. On the second Sunday of the campaign the party's finance spokesman, Michael O'Kennedy, told the *Sunday Press* that a Fianna Fáil government would probably have to implement most of the provisions in the Fine Gael budget. It was, on the face of it, only logical. No incoming government would have time to put together an entirely new budget for presentation in March. Thus Fianna Fáil would have to, whether or not they agreed with them, implement most of the cuts in Health and Social Welfare. It was a message the party did not expand on, save for a confirmation of O'Kennedy's statement by the party leader.

There was a slight reprieve for Fianna Fáil in the next opinion poll, published on 5 February in *The Irish Times*(MRBI), which saw them with 52 per cent of the vote; the PDs had slipped back to 14 per cent; Fine Gael with 24 per cent were slightly improved and Labour were back to 5 per cent. It was the last poll before Charles Haughey became embedded in the mire of the Northern problem and his hopes of an overall majority evaporated.

Traditionally, Northern Ireland has had a low priority with voters in the South, the notable exception being 1981 when two H-Block candidates were elected on a wave of public sympathy during the Maze prison hunger strike. At the start of the campaign there were statements from Garret FitzGerald and Charles Haughey that neither wanted the North to be a campaign issue. Yet, since the founding of the state, the North has never failed to erupt as an issue during elections. More often than not it has been helped into the headlines by politicians. And no single party has had a monopoly on playing the green card. The November '82 election saw Fianna Fáil accusing the Taoiseach of consorting with the Duke of Norfolk who, they suggested, was a spy; they also suggested that the RUC would be allowed to cross the border into the South in hot pursuit of IRA suspects as a result of Anglo-Irish discussions at the time.

Both were allegations designed to hurt Fine Gael in constituencies where there were a substantial number of "sleeping" Republican voters. Fine Gael say the allegations hurt them in North Kerry, particularly when a Fianna Fáil official raised the spectre of RUC men stalking the streets of Kerry villages in pursuit of the IRA. For months before the campaign Mr Haughey's media advisors were telling him in blunt terms to "steer well clear of the North". There was, however, one major obstacle in his way — his promise at Bodenstown to renegotiate the Anglo-Irish Agreement if returned to power. The crux of this was Mr Haughey's stated objection to the "constitutional implications" contained in Article One of the Agreement. Two days before the election, Mr Haughey said on "This Week", for the first time, that in government he would accept the Anglo-Irish Agreement; he would not throw out any progress which had been made but, nonetheless, he could not accept the constitutional implications of Article One. "All our actions in regard to it will radiate from that non-acceptance," he said. A few days later Dr FitzGerald said he was glad that the Fianna Fáil leader had "gone back on talk of renegotiating the Agreement". He said he would not be making Northern Ireland an issue but reserved the right to set out his government's achievements there. Fine Gael were to do more than that. In reality the party strategy committee were pressing the Taoiseach to make the Agreement an issue from the start of the campaign. On Friday 6 February, Fine Gael indicated that Garret FitzGerald would be making a statement about Northern Ireland the following day. They said that Peter Barry would be available to the media to criticise Mr Haughey on the North in the wake of FitzGerald's speech. The word from Fine Gael was that Barry would say that the Anglo-Irish Agreement was "gone" if Charles Haughey was returned to power. The clear message from Fine Gael was that Barry was ready to "put the boot in" to Fianna Fáil on the Agreement. That was the beginning of the end of Northern Ireland as a non-election issue.

The following day the Taoiseach made his promised speech on Northern Ireland. It was a long address, reflective and seen by many commentators as valedictory. Nonetheless, it did not criticise Fianna Fáil. The main target of attack was Sinn Féin which was campaigning for the first time on a participationist ticket. The attack prompted Sinn Féin president Gerry Adams and a cluster of supporters to converge on the hotel and confront the Taoiseach. It was one of a series of such protests by Sinn Féin against Section 31 during the course of the campaign. Ironically, it was the Taoiseach's suggestion of an all-party economic forum which made the headlines rather than the comments on Northern Ireland. Some hours after the Taoiseach delivered his speech newsdesks were alerted to an imminent speech by Desmond O'Malley attacking Fianna Fáil's position on the Agreement. The speech was couched in strong terms and moved the North centre stage from a media point of view. The people had a right to know, said O'Malley, if the gains won on behalf of the nationalist minority in the North would be thrown away because of an insistence on renegotiating the Agreement. He accused Fianna Fáil of entering sly reservations on "so-called" constitutional grounds.

That party is now unwilling to declare itself unambiguously on this topic for fear of alienating any group of voters, however small, in the election run-up. For the sake of a pocketful of votes in some small marginal or border constituencies they are prepared to disturb the political consensus which otherwise backs the Anglo-Irish Agreement in this state.

Now that O'Malley and FitzGerald had brought the Agreement into play the stage was open for a full-scale debate. On Sunday 7 February Gerry Collins of Fianna Fáil faced Peter Barry, Des O'Malley and Frank Prendergast of Labour on "This Week". Before going on the programme Collins was briefed at length by Mr Haughey and the Fianna Fáil press office on the party's policy. It was agreed that he would repeat the strategy that had been enunciated from the start of the campaign: Fianna Fáil would try to build on any progress that had been made through the Agreement, though retaining its constitutional objections. However, on the programme, Collins said the party would honour the implications of the Agreement, "and improve it if we possibly can". This appeared to contradict the party leader's line, which sought to change the constitutional implications. The following day Charles Haughey denied that there were any contradictions. "If Gerry said anything else...he didn't mean to...there's no change at all in the party's policy," he told *The Irish Times*.

On that Sunday night the Labour leader, Dick Spring, moved to distance himself from Fianna Fáil after speculation about a possible coalition between the two parties. On the North he said that Fianna Fáil had a fundamentally different approach to the Labour Party, "which regards any ambivalence in relation to violence, or in relation to the issue of consent generally, as both dangerous and misguided." The battle was stepped up in Macroom on Tuesday. Again leading the charge for Fine Gael was Peter Barry. "The Irish people must take the most serious account of Fianna Fáil's record and of their totally untenable present position on this fundamental issue," he said. Using the strongest language possible he went on to accuse Mr Haughey of "behaving atrociously and working openly against the national interest in ways that have never been seen before in Ireland." It was the type of attack which had been given a test-run at the Fine Gael Árd Fheis and which produced extreme nervousness in Fianna Fáil. The Fianna Fáil leader was again asked by Peter Barry to test the constitutionality of the Agreement in the courts.

Mr Haughey now talks of renegotiation. Mr Collins of seeking improvements by agreement. What is it to be? The former is simply not on and it is dishonest to pretend that it is; the latter is a dangerous proposition at this stage.

Peter Barry's speech was delivered at one o'clock, an hour after Mr Haughey had appeared on a "Day by Day" phone-in. It was what Charles Haughey said on that programme which laid the trap for him in the television debate the following Thursday. Towards the end of the programme he was asked why the party had not contested the constitutionality of the Agreement in the courts. His answer was that he did not believe the courts were the place to conduct political business and that a constitutional action would impede the work of the Anglo-Irish Conference. The crucial phrase came in his summary: "Now, if we have to accept that Agreement as being in place, we will then strive through political action and diplomatic action to see if we can change those constitutional implications to which we take objection." The remarks were reported on RTE news and in the *Irish Press* and *Irish Independent*. On the following day the Taoiseach was asked about them. He seemed surprised at what had been said and warned that any attempt to renegotiate the Agreement would threaten its foundations. Dr FitzGerald's reaction to the comments was reported in the newspapers. More importantly, Fine Gael's press office set to work transcribing the Haughey interview. His exact words about "political and diplomatic action" were written up and stored for the television debate.

Towards the latter part of that debate the presenter, Brian Farrell, raised the subject of Northern Ireland. In his opening remarks on the subject Garret FitzGerald accused the Fianna Fáil leader of saying he would use all political and diplomatic efforts to try and remove the constitutional difficulties involved in the Agreement. It was a crucial moment for the Fianna Fáil leader. He moved immediately to try to limit the damage:

> That's a misunderstanding. That statement of mine about using every diplomatic and political initiative applied to the position of illegal…young Irish people who have illegal status in the the United States. I was talking about a major diplomatic and political initiative to try to get the American government to give a legal status to those people. The Taoiseach misunderstood me. It was out of context.

The Taoiseach, however, was sure that it was not:

> Mr Haughey's memory is in fact extraordinarily defective. May I read out what in fact was said? At the end of a long piece trying to explain what was meant by his constitutional difficulties about the Agreement, solely about Northern Ireland, the following words were added: ''We will then strive through political and diplomatic action to see if we can change those constitutional implications to which we take objection''. What's that got to do with emigration to America? Mr Haughey should not evade the issue.

Again the Fianna Fáil leader denied that he had been talking about the Agreement and repeated his explanation about emigration to the United States. The damage, however, had been done and an important psychological victory scored for Garret FitzGerald. Fine Gael and the PDs had managed to make the North an issue and had provoked Charles Haughey to deny his own words. One member of Mr Haughey's shadow cabinet said the debate *faux pas* harmed the party badly.

> The North can be a minefield for us. It revives all sorts of memories and creates a mood of suspicion and uncertainty in people. They end up saying to themselves, ''are Fianna Fáil to be trusted on the North?'' and once that doubt is there they start to mistrust us on the economy and everything else. It just revives memories that we can do without.

Charles Haughey was well aware that he had strayed into an area that holds many pitfalls for him. He is believed to have told friends that Fianna Fáil's position was impossible because most people in the South wanted the Agreement to work. The reaction of his shadow cabinet at being drawn into the ''Northern trap'' is understood to have been one of despair according to several we have spoken to. One political commentator said of the incident:

> Fianna Fáil was behaving like an Italian soccer team winning by a goal. They were playing to stop losing. So by the time the own-goal came during the last days of the campaign it was too late to change tack. The added element was that the team captain was the one who scored the own-goal.

The Handlers and the Handled

In far-off foreign places when an army gets tired of the government and stages a coup d'etat the first thing that is siezed is the television and radio service. After that it is the newspapers and magazines. Control the media and you control the masses, the logic goes. In an election the media are not taken over but they are besieged. Lined up on all sides are hostile, competing forces battling for limited air-time and column inches. Ever since the American presidential elections of the '60s the old style of electioneering, with its big rallies and countrywide tours, has been gradually taking second place to the war that is waged on the airwaves and in the newspaper columns. The concept of mass communication is still relatively young in Irish election campaigns, beginning in 1977 when Fianna Fáil blitzed the country with the message of their manifesto. The age of the professional communications manager had arrived. It was Fine Gael who perfected the art of image building for the 1981 election. The team headed by party general secretary, Peter Prendergast, and which included people like Enda Marren, Frank Flannery and Derry Hussey, created a whole new image for the party. It was outward looking with an eye to the commentators and opinion makers. It drew heavily on the marketing experience of men like Prendergast and Hussey to present the party as fresh, vibrant and united. Before long these men were dubbed "national handlers" by John Healy in The Irish Times. A new political phrase and a new approach was born. Over the past ten years Irish elections have increasingly become media events. Without exception the political parties now concentrate their efforts on maximising coverage and image-building. In the February 1987 election the media war reached a new peak. It was less of a battle for hearts and minds than one for eyes and ears. This was recognised by the editors of the national newspapers each of whom devoted a daily column to reviewing the debate on the airwaves. For the political parties it involved the expenditure of millions of pounds and endless hours of strategy meetings.

On the Fianna Fáil side the media team was led by the party leader, Charles Haughey, who took a particular interest in the nomination of spokespersons for interviews. The party's press team was led by P.J. Mara with a core of advisors providing research and advice on policy. The man with responsibility for policy was generally Martin Mansergh, an Oxford graduate who is Fianna Fáil's head of research. He is a close friend of the party leader and compiled the book *Spirit of the Nation,* which featured the speeches of Charles Haughey. The party also engaged the services of the Carr Communications School to prepare spokespersons for television appearances. The fine polishing for television interviews was done by Tom Savage, a broadcaster and communications expert from Carr's. He had long experience of current affairs work with RTE and had trained spokespersons from both Fianna Fáil and Fine Gael in the past. A representative from Carrs attended the Fianna Fáil strategy meeting in party headquarters every day during the election.

For Fine Gael the press team was led by Peter White and director of elections, David Moloney, a Thurles-based solicitor and former TD. White was a former press officer with the Federated Union of Employers and a long-time devotee of Garret FitzGerald. Fine Gael assigned Senator Sean O'Leary, the assistant director of elections, to take full responsibility for the "great debate" on television. He had for many years been the party's most prominent electoral strategist. In the background physically, but to the fore of the strategy committee, were: Frank Flannery, the head of the National Rehabilitation Institute and a member of the RTE authority; Derry Hussey, the husband of the Minister for Social Welfare, Gemma Hussey; Enda Marren, a Dublin solicitor, and Pat Heneghan, a leading figure in public relations.

The PDs' core team centred around general secretary, Pat Cox, and press officer Stephen O'Byrnes, both former journalists. In the past Cox had spent elections working as a presenter of "Today Tonight". Stephen O'Byrnes was News Analysis editor of the *Irish Independent* before joining the PDs. He also authored a book on Fine Gael under Garret FitzGerald entitled *Hiding Behind A Face*. Assisting them with the media battle were people like Gerry Callanan and Jim Hoblyn, both marketing experts, and Noirin Slattery, a former leading strategist for Fianna Fáil in the 1977 and 1981 elections. The Labour team centred around general secretary, Ray Kavanagh, press officer Kathleen O'Meara and former assistant head of the Government Information Service, Fergus Finlay, a close friend of the party leader, Dick Spring. The Workers Party media strategy was coordinated by press officer, Tony Heffernan. Throughout the campaign these core teams pored over every newspaper article, watched every televison debate and listened to every radio programme. They harried the opposition and they harried the journalists, they counted the time given to each side and shouted loud if they felt they were being edged out of the race for coverage.

Although the battle for votes was intense it was a campaign which, as one commentator said, "died of boredom". The party leaders took to the road but with none of the colour and gusto of 1977 or indeed '81 or '82. It was a reflection, perhaps, of the gloomy economic times, a realisation that a campaign which reeked money and glamour would not sit well alongside the message of fiscal responsibility. In addition to that it was a campaign largely without incident, and devoid of scandal. There were no interventions by the grand old Duke of Norfolk and others who have enlivened election campaigns in the past. The only major row of the campaign was about Northern Ireland, an issue about which most of the electorate seemed indifferent. And while Charles Haughey had his setback on the North the nearest Garret Fitzgerald came to a *faux pas* was his comment advising retailers to travel over the border if they found it cheaper to shop there. It was a comment that may have cost Fine Gael votes in the border counties but it did not last as an issue. There were other attempts to inject some life. Fine Gael's allegation that the Fianna Fáil programme would cost £900m was a case in point. The story lasted for a day but never took off into a fully fledged row because the media were suspicious of the Fine Gael claim. How, they asked, can you cost it if you are saying all along that it is not specific?

Until the actual day of the count the public are rarely participants in the election campaigns, which are, to all intents and purposes, shows put on to try to woo them. In many senses the parties, on the road, are like participants in a great amateur drama festival. The party leaders' tours are, if organised properly, elaborately staged set-pieces. Contrary to the impression given on television, there are rarely huge crowds waiting to greet the aspirant Taoisigh. On the contrary. In this campaign the crowds were small, mostly composed of local party workers with the inevitable gaggle of school children grasping for autographs and party hats. The walkabouts were stage-managed to perfection. Nothing was left to chance. Before the leader's arrival the crowds were scanned by local "handlers" for any troublemakers who might be likely to make a scene in front of the cameras. Occasionally one slipped through, as in Cork when a PD supporter rounded on Garret FitzGerald and Peter Barry in Patrick Street. With the cameras rolling the woman accused them of ruining the country. She was delighted and so were the media. Even Garret FitzGerald knew a good stroke when he saw one. He shouted after the woman: "Well done, fair dues to you".

Between them the party handlers, the politicians themselves and the media play their own agreed parts in the drama. Election tours are full of created "photo opportunities". A favourite is the construction helmet photograph. This normally crops up on front pages after a party leader has been to a building site or a new factory. For the media it is an entertaining photograph, because the politicians nearly always look embarrassed; for the handlers it is a "symbolic" image which shows their leader as a man of action, ready to get stuck in and start rebuilding. There were several instances of the "action man" photograph in the last campaign: Des O'Malley driving a JCB, Dick Spring walking through freshly dug drains, Charles Haughey posing amongst the woodcutters at Aughrim. During the February 1987 campaign some of the walkabouts went wrong because of a deliberate policy of disruption and harrassment by Sinn Féin. The Sinn Féin protests, against Section 31, saw Desmond O'Malley and Garret FitzGerald both being harrassed, and because the drama was played out in front of the television cameras it gave Sinn Féin publicity they would never have gained otherwise.

In addition to organising the photographs and delivering the scripts, the handlers also quite often provide travel facilities and meals for the journalists and camera crews. There are party cars, buses and helicopters, all travelling to an itinerary carefully planned months in advance. The media are "invited along" to cover an event which more often than not is staged for their benefit. The party will regularly provide facilities for journalists to get themselves and their material back to base. During the last campaign Fianna Fáil hired a huge Sikorsky helicopter to take journalists to Killybegs in Donegal for the launch of their fisheries document. The investment paid off; the following morning's front pages carried handsome photographs of Charles Haughey at the wheel of a modern, brand-new fishing boat. In Limerick the Fianna Fáil chopper ferried journalists from the *Limerick Leader* across the county to make their deadline. That evening the Leader carried a big front page picture spread of the Fianna Fáil leader campaigning in County Limerick.

Party press conferences and major statements are often timed to coincide with television news bulletins. An example of this was Garret FitzGerald's instruction to Fine Gael voters to transfer their second preferences to the Progressive Democrats. The statement was made in the late afternoon during a walkabout by the Taoiseach. It featured prominently that night on the six and nine o'clock news bulletins. Fine Gael acknowledge quite openly that the statement was timed for the television news. Similarly, the political parties target particular television programmes and publications with statements. They may decide to give an interview to *Hot Press* magazine in search of the young vote, to *The Irish Times* for the urban professional vote. In the same way, major interviews for radio and television are given to programmes with the maximum and most appropriate audience. Throughout the campaign itself journalists and editors are showered with a paper blizzard of press releases, policy documents and candidate profiles. Much of this ends up in the waste bin, to the frustration of the party press officers, who go to endless trouble churning it out. After the last campaign, Fianna Fáil's press office complained that many of their policy documents were ignored by a media intent on extracting specific commitments from the party. Fionnuala O'Kelly, a senior press officer with Fianna Fáil, complained that the media were too concerned with colour and ignored vast amounts of what was sent to them. "Agriculture wasn't debated once on television," she pointed out.

However, during the campaign journalists complained about the lack of colour. The lengths to which some of the handlers went to inject some excitement is well reflected in an incident which occurred on the campaign bus during the Taoiseach's tour of Munster. The bus was three-quarters empty. At the back three reporters were chatting among themselves, complaining about the lack of "lines" in the Taoiseach's script. They were bored. The campaign was four days old and, for the reporters, very boring. Not a sign of a decent row, nobody saying the wrong thing and being attacked and no discernable enthusiasm on the part of the voters. As the reporters moaned, one of the Fine Gael organisers on the bus came down to give them "a really good story". The organiser was younger than the other more experienced hands on the bus, what reporters might call a "trainee handler". The good story revolved around the fact that he had organised several former Kerry football captains to meet the Taoiseach in Tralee. It would look lovely on the front page of the nationals and the *Kerryman,* he suggested. On a bad news day this amounted to a good story, albeit of the "colour" variety.

One of the reporters, an industrial correspondent with a particularly black sense of humour, decided to play a joke on the trainee handler. He suggested that the handler organise for the Sam Maguire cup to be brought along to the Tralee meeting. A look which said: "Why the hell didn't I think of that one?" crossed the young man's face. When the bus stopped in a village for a few minutes he bolted to the nearest telephone. The reporters took care to be seen alighting as well. After about ten minutes of handshaking the Taoiseach and his entourage boarded the bus again. The trainee handler was glowing. "Lads: I've organised it," he enthused, "I've organised the Sam Maguire." As he went back to his seat the reporters got to work. The first paragraph of the story read:

> A major row erupted today between the Taoiseach and GAA chiefs over the use of the Sam Maguire cup in the Fine Gael election campaign. The secretary of the GAA, Liam Mulvihill, accused Dr FitzGerald of trying to "blatantly politicise" the organisation "for his own electoral purposes."

Now, it is unusual for reporters to work with such diligence at ten o'clock in the morning, a fact that did not go unnoticed by the Taoiseach who was sitting in the row opposite them. "What's that you're up to?" he asked; "I think I've got a right to know." One of the reporters, a religious affairs correspondent and novelist, replied: "There are some things even a Taoiseach shouldn't know." Hovering nearby was one of Fine Gael's senior handlers, Pat Heneghan, who enquired what was happening. He was shown the story. "Ah lads, you're not serious. You're not going to do that," he gasped. He was told it was a joke and that he was to pass the story on to the trainee handler without saying anything. He did. The trainee handler almost passed out. He rushed to the back of the bus. "How could you? How could you set me up?" The reporters told him they had a duty to the public. He was inconsolable: a promising future in handling was disappearing before his eyes. Eventually the reporters had pity on the youngster: it was all a joke; they were bored, they explained, and there were no stories. The colour returned to the young man's face. He would have liked to have been able to insult them and throw them off the bus but he couldn't. Such are the joys of handling. Yet for a campaign fought very much through the media it was, by and large, devoid of stunts.

There were, however, local rows between candidates from the same parties. Stories of internecine rivalry abounded; tales of punch-ups between rival sets of Fianna Fáil canvassers in Limerick East, of bitter infighting between Fine Gael candidates in Dublin Central and, most interesting of all, the extraordinary leafletting campaigns in Dublin West and Dublin North Central. In the Dublin West constituency there was an open row between Fianna Fáil deputy leader Brian Lenihan and his running mate, Liam Lawlor. The latter claimed, and *Magill* magazine produced evidence to support it, that a small group of Lenihan's election workers had spread misleading "midnight" leaflets in his name. In North Central there was a row between the junior Foreign Affairs Minister, George Birmingham, and the junior Industry Minister, Richard Bruton. It centred on a leaflet distributed by Birmingham's supporters telling voters that his seat was in danger and asking for their No 1 votes. Bruton was to get the No 2. Bruton's outraged supporters called in headquarters who issued a countermanding instruction.

In any election the political parties have one guiding principle when it comes to dealing with the media. That is to present their side and their spokespersons in the best possible light while at the same time trying to show their opponents in the worst light. As a result of this broadcasters and print journalists find themselves the target of competing and sometimes hostile forces, all believing that their message is the most important, most correct and in need of most amplification. Any slip by the other side will be quickly pointed out to the media while mistakes by their own side are played down, if they are minor enough for that to be done, or, if that isn't possible, presented as "unintentioned", "unfortunate" or "blown up out of all proportion". The latter phrase is most often used to describe something that is more than likely true, probably of interest to the public and embarrassing for the party. The parties also bargain hard with editors and programme makers to get the best possible deal for their side. It is parties that nominate their own spokespersons to appear on radio and television. This allows each party to plan its media campaign and control its image on air. Programme makers sometimes complain that this system restricts them and allows the parties to dictate the agenda. The party which runs the tightest ship in terms of nominating spokespersons is Fianna Fáil, whose party press office will complain bitterly if a spokesperson is called, during or outside election time, without the press office first being consulted. From Fianna Fáil's point of view the system minimises the risk of somebody coming on air and saying things which are not in accordance with party policy. It also eliminates the danger of dissenting voices being heard too often.

In RTE's case there is a statutory obligation to provide balanced and impartial coverage. This means in effect that RTE must balance the amount of time given to each party against the number of Dáil seats it holds. To coordinate coverage and ensure balance an election steering committee is established under the chairmanship of the Director General. The time given to each party in debates and constituency reports is strictly measured by the stopwatch and balanced against the party's electoral support. This means that Fianna Fáil and Fine Gael will naturally dominate the election coverage, while parties like Labour, the Progressive Democrats and the Workers Party receive progressively smaller slices of the air-time. Sinn Féin are prohibited from being interviewed under Section 31 of the Broadcasting Act and the party claimed in the wake of this election that the lack of coverage had badly hindered their campaign. In order to understand how the "stopwatch" system works it is worth looking at the arrangements made for television news coverage of the party leaders' tours. The air-time was divided up as follows: Garret FitzGerald: 3 x 3 minute reports; C.J. Haughey: 3 x 3 minute reports; Dick Spring: 1 x 1.5 and 1 x 2 minutes; Desmond O'Malley: 2 x 1.5 minutes; Tomas MacGiolla: 1 x 2 minutes.

In the case of radio it was agreed that the daily programmes like "Morning Ireland", "News at 1.30", "Today at Five" and "Day by Day" would concentrate on the political news stories of the day. They carried a series of constituency profiles and reports on the tours of the party leaders and, for the first time ever, the party leaders also participated in election phone-ins on "Day by Day". The major radio interviews with the party leaders were carried on "This Week" which, along with "Day by Day", featured debates between key spokespersons. The same system of time balance operates on radio.

There are conflicting views on the "stopwatch" system. Eugene Murray, editor of "Today Tonight", believes that it is a faulty system but that the balance of argument is on the side of it remaining.

> In an election we are hidebound by legal and public service obligations. We are also tied by precedent. However, it is possible, within the system, to counteract that by concentrating on issues and in that way you can dictate, to some extent, what the agenda of the programme should be.

As evidence of this he points to the series of election "specials" dealing with unemployment, taxation, the state of the economy and the special programme on Denmark — a country which had problems similar to Ireland but managed to find its way out of the economic wilderness. The special reports were followed by studio discussions with representatives of all the parties in the Dáil. The PDs' general secretary, Pat Cox, a former "Today Tonight" presenter, is critical of the present system.

I've seen the dilemma from both sides. In 1982 I remember chairing what I can only describe as political tennis matches and feeling bored and oppressed by the system I was working within. It is a system which is not easily susceptible to the changing political circumstances. For instance, the opinion polls right up to this election indicated far greater support for us than was reflected in our five seats yet we only got the air time of a party with five seats. In the print media we were getting a huge amount of coverage. What happens is that news value does not dominate and it ends up putting the programme makers in a ridiculous bind. The instinct is to go for the story of the day but you end up having to have people who might not be relevant to it in studio simply for the sake of giving them their allotted time.

Fine Gael say they were fairly treated, but during the campaign the party was critical of the "Today Tonight" debates which included spokespersons from all of the Dáil parties. They objected in particular to the Workers Party being allowed to have a representative on each debate, even though their time was restricted, on the basis that they had only two seats in the Dáil. At one stage Fine Gael threatened to pull Michael Noonan out of a debate because they felt that there were too many other panellists. After a lengthy wrangle Michael Noonan eventually appeared. The Fine Gael press officer, Peter White, also complained that with television news the news value was often sacrificed for the sake of time balance. He suggests that important speeches and scripts, like one on the North delivered by Peter Barry in Macroom, were overlooked and "lumped together" with scripts of little importance on news bulletins. Rory O'Connor, head of television news, rejects this: "News value is our main criterion. Apart from this we use balancing factors when covering set-pieces like leaders' tours and manifesto launchings." He also points out that speeches and scripts are handled by a special election desk in the newsroom.

From the point of view of the smaller parties the statutory obligations provide a guarantee of air-time. For independents there is no such guarantee. Tony Gregory, Alice Glenn, Sean Treacy and Neil Blaney, although each just one seat short of the total held in the 24th Dáil by the Workers Party, had no right to contribute to the television debates which always featured a member of the Workers Party. It is a point of some contention with Tony Gregory who complained during the campaign about the absence of statutory air-time for independents who are sitting members of the Dáil. The time allocated to party political broadcasts is governed under RTE's own house rules. Theoretically the station is not obliged to provide time for broadcasts. Under the rules any party or grouping with at least seven candidates who share a common policy platform are entitled to broadcast time. In past elections groups like the H-Block Committees have been given time under this ruling. This time out the only non-Dáil party to look for a broadcast on the basis of the seven candidate rule was the "Green Alliance". The figure of seven is picked on the basis of the Dáil rule which allows a party offices and other facilities if they have at least seven deputies. Independents are covered in what is known in RTE as the "great march past". In the case of the last election, where there were 80 independents, this involved reading out the biographical details of a selection of the candidates on the News at 6.30 each evening.

Labour also say they were fairly treated during the campaign. They feel the party's strategy of distancing from Fine Gael worked well and that the media did not "tar Labour with the Coalition brush". There is also a feeling among Labour members that the battle between the major parties for the "right wing" vote allowed them greater freedom to concentrate on presenting an alternative. It also meant that with Fianna Fáil, Fine Gael and the PDs concentrating on each other, the left-hand side of the pitch was confined to Labour, the Workers Party, the left-wing independents and, to a minimal extent, Sinn Féin. There was never any real debate through the media on a left-right basis. On "This Week", midway through the campaign, Des O'Malley and Dick Spring faced each other. The debate never ignited. They were competing for vastly different audiences and they knew it. Labour's media campaigns have tended, on occasions in the past, to give the appearance of disorganisation. This time, although it was a low-key campaign, it ran smoothly. The highpoint was the exquisitely stage-managed walk-out from government.

Tony Heffernan of the Workers Party, although critical of the newspaper coverage given to his party's policies, feels the campaign worked well from a media point of view. He says the party's only party political broadcast, the "Fastermind" test, was the best produced by any party although it cost only £1,500 to make. Heffernan is critical of the coverage afforded to the Workers Party by the national newspapers. He maintains the papers reflected the predominantly right-wing approach to solving economic questions. Conor Brady, editor of *The Irish Times,* agrees that the newspapers are "centrist" in their approach to the economy but he suggests that the left failed to provide specific policies to tackle the financial crisis. "There was," he says, "a lot of rhetoric but not a great deal else behind it."

Although the papers shared a common view of the need for, at the very least, firm financial management they had different ideas as to who should do it. The *Irish Press,* as might be expected, supported Fianna Fáil; the *Irish Independent* took a line described by one commentator as being "somewhere between Fine Gael and the PDs"; *The Irish Times* and the *Cork Examiner* talked about the need for stability and courage but did not tell their readers who to vote for; the *Sunday Tribune* called for a "grand coalition" of Fianna Fáil, Fine Gael and the PDs and suggested massive cuts in public spending to solve the economic crisis.

Party strategists at the heart of the campaign cite few examples of what they consider amounted to bias, although Fine Gael's Peter White is critical of a story carried in the *Irish Press* during the campaign which suggested Garret FitzGerald was simply waiting to step down as leader of the party. In the light of his subsequent resignation one could be forgiven for thinking that the *Press* were on the right trail. Tim Pat Coogan, editor of the *Irish Press,* feels that Fine Gael were "let off too easily" by the media.

> We certainly didn't reflect the kind of hatred they were meeting on the doorsteps. They ran a good media campaign but they were very barefaced about it when you consider their record in government. They kept the Haughey thing alive expertly and ruthlessly.

Coogan also believes the PDs ran an effective media campaign, "second only to Fine Gael". Fianna Fáil, however, "should have fought it much harder. They neglected the obvious and they failed to attack the PDs." As editor of the *Irish Press* he was never pressurised to take particular stands on issues by the Fianna Fáil leader. "There was no attempt at all at a heavy hand, none whatsoever." Charles Haughey is still suspicious of the media perhaps, he suggests, with good reason. "It's like the old saying: 'Just because you're paranoid, it doesn't mean they're not out to get you'."

Conor Brady considers that it was a good election from the newspapers' point of view and he points to the fact that his paper had its highest ever net paid sales for the duration of the election. "The issues on which this campaign was to be fought were decided on and defined with some precision by the parties well in advance. I think there was also a realisation that personality politics are something we just cannot afford. If the moulds weren't exactly broken then they were given a damn good rattling." Brady shares the view expressed by Fianna Fáil that the campaign was too long. "It was a very dry campaign and it just went on for too long. I think that the electorate knew that whoever was victorious the medicine was going to be tough." As an editor he feels the newspapers played it down the middle and did their best to highlight the important issues. "There was a lot of analysis of economic issues by ourselves and by the *Independent,*" he adds. No real pressure was applied by the political parties but that there was, on the Fine Gael side, a lack of tolerance of editorial criticism.

We described the Fine Gael view as rather dismal, not giving hope, and they came back at us outraged that we couldn't see their position. There was a certain intolerance to criticism on the Fine Gael side. As well as that there were the usual complaints from Fianna Fáil and Fine Gael that we weren't printing enough pictures of their respective leaders.

There is agreement between Conor Brady of *The Irish Times* and Tim Pat Coogan of the *Irish Press* that the PDs ran an extremely effective media campaign. "They had an enormous appeal. They were able to offer a simple analysis and a way out. They also presented themselves as a party of young, fresh candidates offering people material improvement," says Conor Brady. He is also of the view, though, that some of the PD economic policies were "shot full of holes before they got out of traps".

From a British media perspective the election had one major focal point — Charles J.Haughey. In the British tabloids his role as the "enemy of England" was kept to the fore throughout the campaign. At Fianna Fáil news conferences the men from the tabloids could always be depended on to enliven matters with questions about Mr Haughey's past. The normal response from the Fianna Fáil leader was a contemptuous scowl or a sharply delivered put-down. He reserves a particular loathing for the *Daily Mail* and the *Telegraph* group, both of whom dispatched reporters to produce profiles of the man "the tabloids love to hate". One British journalist felt the sharp edge of Charles Haughey's tongue when he asked him what kind of a relationship he hoped to have with Mrs Thatcher. "Mr Thatcher," replied Haughey, "I don't intend to have any kind of relationship with Mr Thatcher." The journalist tried again. "I said Mrs Thatcher." Charles Haughey gave a pitying glance and said in a voice that oozed sarcasm: "Ah, I see. It's your accent you see, so difficult to understand." It was a moment that reflected the complete lack of sympathy both Charles Haughey and the British media, with a few exceptions, have for each other. Both pay a price for their mutual dislike. For Charles Haughey the price is a very uncomplimentary press; for the offending British journalists it is the guarantee of no cooperation from the Fianna Fáil leader. Thus BBC and ITN crews tend to be kept waiting until the last minute to be told yes or, more often, no to their requests for interviews. For the representatives of most British newspapers the price is the near-certainty of never being granted an interview with the Fianna Fáil leader.

The "quality" newspapers like the *Financial Times,* the *Guardian* and the *Independent* concentrated on the economic crisis facing the country. The coverage given to the debt and deficit problems annoyed the Industrial Development Authority and the Fianna Fáil leadership. They were particularly incensed at an article in the *Economist* magazine which described the country in terms more familiar to a Latin American banana republic than a modernised western nation. In the wake of the election Fianna Fáil said they would be trying to find out what the various Irish embassies had done to counteract the bad foreign press which the country received. There were murmurs from the party about the role of the influential "Friends of the Union" group. A number of the leading British commentators writing on Ireland during the campaign were members of this strongly pro-unionist grouping. The chairman of the "Friends of the Union" is Sir Ian Gow who resigned from the Thatcher cabinet in protest at the Anglo-Irish Agreement. It has been suggested by Fianna Fáil that this group were, to say the least, unsympathetic towards the Republic.

Apart from some conflict with the British media it was by far the most relaxed election campaign, in media terms, ever undertaken by Charles Haughey. Fine Gael say the Fianna Fáil strategy was to go for pictures but no words, to "keep Charles Haughey in vision but out of sound". Peter White puts it that

P.J. Mara wanted the campaign to die of boredom. Our idea was to get the ball onto the pitch and kick it around for all it was worth. But Fianna Fáil wouldn't play and that annoyed us. They were frightened that if they put Charlie into a bear-pit of an argument he would get mad and say something unpleasant.

Long before the campaign started Fianna Fáil had decided to go for a non-aggressive campaign, a decision many in the party now believe was a mistake. Certainly Charles Haughey himself now believes the party should have been more aggressive. Just why the party decided as it did has a great deal to do with the media perception of the Fianna Fáil leader. As one of those involved in the Fianna Fáil media campaign explained: "There is no percentage for Charlie Haughey going out and acting aggressively on television or radio. It just doesn't make sense, there are no bonus points in it for him if he is seen to be arrogant." The "softening" of Charles Haughey's media image began shortly after the November 1982 election. Most observers agree that the man responsible for the success of that "softening process" was P.J. Mara, a former senator with an easy-going manner and a disarmingly irreverant sense of humour. He has acted as a buffer between the blunt edges of both the media and his leader. There is now a sense of regret among many of those close to the Fianna Fáil leader that there were so few sharp attacks on Fine Gael and the PDs.

However, Fianna Fáil's media advisors believe that the party's spokespersons performed well throughout the campaign, pointing to Ray Burke's creditable performance against Alan Dukes on "Today Tonight" and Haughey's own interviews with Una Claffey on the same programme. The Fianna Fáil leader was also judged by the media to have performed well on the "Day by Day" phone-in. There is general agreement, however, that the great debate and the McSharry "Today Tonight" appearances were disappointing. Ray McSharry is aware that senior Fianna Fáil figures have expressed disquiet over the "Today Tonight" debates with John Bruton and that media pundits felt he came off worst in the encounters. The first contribution by McSharry was on the night the election was called. He appeared to those watching to be tired and withdrawn, having just flown in from Brussels, whereas John Bruton exuded confidence and dominated the debate. The next discussion, on income-tax confidentiality, took place on the night before the party leaders debate. It was McSharry's apparent unwillingness to answer a specific question on the confidentiality of bank accounts for income tax purposes that earned him the criticism of some of his shadow cabinet colleagues. However, Ray McSharry believes that some of the criticism directed against him is the result of jealousy. He believes also that he did "quite well" in the debates, given that the priority in the Fianna Fáil campaign was not to make commitments. "The overriding factor was not to get caught on promises. We were being screwed to make promises and we didn't." In some of the television debates he feels it was a case of "four others against one for Fianna Fáil". He rejects the suggestion that he was "beaten" by John Bruton in the television debates. "If that is supposed to be the case I would like to point out that I was elected on the first count with a higher first preference total than Mr Bruton who had to wait until the tenth count to be elected," he adds. McSharry rejects the widely held view that it was an election fought through the media.

> It wasn't really. If it was fought through the media then Fianna Fáil wouldn't get a look in. Any election is fought and won by knocking on doors and talking to people about their problems. The GNP or the deficit doesn't matter a curse to the widow who is trying to survive on an old age pension.

Another senior person involved with the Fianna Fáil campaign reflected in retrospect:

> The main focus at the daily committee meetings was on the media and what they were saying and how we were doing compared to the other parties. The important things like the reports from the marginal constituencies and that were way down the agenda. We should have concentrated far more on getting efficiency on the ground, on sorting out the problems that were appearing in the local party organisations. We were more media conscious than we need have been.

The media war, whether conducted through the newspapers, television or advertising billboards, costs huge amounts of money. It is a time when the resources of political parties are stretched to the limit and generous donors are approached for further contributions. We asked the political parties what they spent in this election. The figures quoted to us are approximate and may, in cases, be less than what was actually spent. Those parties which receive private contributions — Fine Gael, Fianna Fáil and the PDs — are reluctant to name the donors. For the record the following details indicate what the parties say they spent in the February 1987 election campaign:

Fianna Fáil: £2m, of which £1m was spent from headquarters and the other £1m in the constituencies. The money was mainly spent on advertising, on major display ads in the newspapers and on billboards around the country. The party started their billboard campaign in October with the highly effective "passport" ads. The advertising was run by O'Kennedy Brindley, recently taken over by Saatchi and Saatchi who ran Margaret Thatcher's victorious election campaigns. According to Fianna Fáil the money was largely raised through the party's national lottery and constituency fundraising events. The party also received substantial donations from business people.

Fine Gael: £800,000 from head office and between £5,000 and £15,000 in each of the 41 constituencies. Again the vast proportion of the money was spent on advertising and printing. The party's advertising campaign was handled by Arks Ltd. and the party set up its own television studios in party headquarters. Substantial donations are received from private individuals.

Labour: £175,000 from headquarters and between £1,500 and £9,000 in each of the 33 constituencies in which they campaigned. The majority of the money was spent on newspaper advertising and posters, and advertising was handled by Quinn McDonnell and Patterson. Labour began raising funds for the campaign 18 months before the election was called and constituencies were asked to fund their own campaigns.

Progressive Democrats: £450,000 from headquarters and approximately £330,000 in the constituencies giving a total figure of £780,000 according to the party general secretary Pat Cox. Roughly half of that money was spent on advertising. As in the case of Fianna Fáil the PDs' billboard campaign began well before the election with the "Dessie Can Do It" posters. Press officer Stephen O'Byrnes said the party had an overdraft of £150,000 for the campaign; they raised £100,000 in a national collection and about £200,000 was spent on newspaper advertising, which was handled by Kennys Ltd.

Workers Party: £80,000 in total. The money was largely spent on postering in key constituencies and virtually nothing was spent on newspaper advertising. The funds were raised through a national lottery and from various internal functions, and the party borrowed £25,000 from the bank which is still outstanding; it also owes a similar amount in printing bills. The party says that it receives no donations from business.

The single greatest focus of the media battle came in the final days of the campaign with the great debate on television. It was to be the final duel, the battle between two men for the right to govern the country, brought to the sitting rooms of Ireland. It was to be a chance for Fianna Fáil to at least consolidate their position, for Fine Gael to fight back and deny Charles Haughey his majority. Here, television was judged to have replaced the after-Mass meetings and the monster rallies as the weapon with which to win votes.

Prior to the debate "Today Tonight" sent an agenda to the two parties. The debate would concentrate in the main on the economy with a very brief section, about four minutes, devoted to Northern Ireland. Both leaders were extensively briefed by their communications managers. The core advisors for Fianna Fáil were: Martin Mansergh, Tom Savage of Carr Communications and P.J. Mara. The man with overall responsibility for the debate on the Fine Gael side was Senator Sean O'Leary who, with Peter White and the Taoiseach's special advisor, Catherine Meenan, carried out the final briefing. On the day of the debate

Charles Haughey's advisors handed him a brief which advised him, amongst other things, not to invite the Taoiseach to agree with him on any issue and not to "dive in" when answering a question. He was told to relax, look confident and smile. Meanwhile Garret FitzGerald was preparing the opening statement he intended to make. He planned to use Charles Haughey's comments on the Anglo-Irish Agreement from the "Day by Day" phone-in as a weapon in the debate.

Later that evening the party leaders travelled to Montrose with a carefully planned fifteen minute interval between their respective arrival times. Garret FitzGerald, who arrived first, went straight to make-up. As he sat down and waited for the make-up to be applied he asked his press secretary, Peter White, for the transcript of Mr Haughey's comments. Peter White said he didn't have them and turned hopefully to Sean O'Leary. No, he was told, I don't have them. There was an immediate rush to the phone to call Headquarters. After some delay the vital words were produced and dictated to Peter White who scribbled them on a piece of paper. The note was given to the Taoiseach who put it in his pocket and headed down to the studio. About three-quarters way through the debate the critical moment arrived. In response to a suggestion by the Taoiseach, Charles Haughey denied using the words "political and diplomatic action" in relation to the Anglo-Irish Agreement. Fitzgerald reached for the scribbled note. Out of his pocket came what he thought was the piece of paper. Alas, there was nothing on it. Blank. Again he rummaged in his pocket. This time, to FitzGerald's great relief, it was the correct note. The Taoiseach rounded on the Fianna Fáil leader. It was the turning point in a debate which, up until then, had seen both men competing on fairly equal terms. Now the Fianna Fáil leader was twice forced to deny his words, asserting that he had really been talking about diplomatic and political action to help young Irish people emigrating to the United States. He appeared to have been genuinely taken by surprise and he never fully regained his composure. Afterwards he is believed to have told advisors that he had been "far too relaxed" and he now regrets not having taken the battle to Dr FitzGerald.

However, the trauma was not confined to Fianna Fáil on the night. Earlier Senator Sean O'Leary had threatened to withdraw the Taoiseach from the debate because, he claimed, the agenda was not being adhered to. The dramatic moment came just after Brian Farrell's opening question which asked the Taoiseach why he expected people to vote for him in the light of the country's economic situation. Sean O'Leary objected that this was in breach of the agreement whereby the Taoiseach was to be asked a general question and invited to make an opening statement. The editor of the programme, Eugene Murray, maintained that the agenda was being adhered to, that it was a general question, and that the Taoiseach was being allowed to make an opening statement. The row raged in the hospitality suite outside the studio. The Taoiseach was being withdrawn, the programme editor was told. Eventually, after some discussion, peace was restored and the spectre of Garret FitzGerald being withdrawn live on air disappeared. While these scenes had been going on outside the studio the apparent change had caused Garret FitzGerald some panic. He was so disconcerted for the first fifteen minutes of the debate that he was unable to follow his brief. However, he concentrated on the economy and succeeded in recovering his sense of direction and composure.

The following morning the newspapers agreed that while the economic section of the debate had produced a draw, the Fianna Fáil leader had suffered badly because of his apparent *faux pas* on Northern Ireland. Other commentators suggested that he had been too relaxed and had smiled too much. It must have seemed to Charles Haughey that whether he smiled or scowled his critics would damn him. One Fianna Fáil source commented: "It was not so much a question of us losing support because of the debate, it was more a question of failing to convince those who had deserted us to come back." Another commentator, with his tongue in his cheek, proposed that the real winner of the debate had been the PD leader, Desmond O'Malley. In fact, O'Malley and the Labour leader, Dick Spring, had given two of their finest performances on the previous evening when they joined Workers Party leader, Tomas MacGiolla, for separate interviews in advance of the great debate.

The two main party leaders gave their final interviews and news conferences of the campaign on the following Sunday. On "This Week" both gave what the critics would describe as "solid performances". On Charles Haughey's part there was considerably more aggression and fire as he answered questions on the economy and the North. Afterwards he said quite openly that he should have been more aggressive in the great debate. The opinion poll which appeared in that Sunday's *Independent* had been taken just after the debate and it bore depressing news for Fianna Fáil. The party had slipped from 43 per cent of first preferences in the first *Independent* poll to 38 per cent. On the other hand Fine Gael were up to 25 per cent of the first preference vote compared to 21 per cent in the first poll. For the PDs there was an encouraging 11 per cent, while Labour were down from 5 to 4 per cent. The number of "Don't knows" was a relatively high 15 per cent. It was to these people, the undecided ones, the floating voters, that the parties now looked for salvation. With so many of the electorate apparently undecided there was a feeling, as voters walked to the polls in the bright sunshine, of a battle that would be close and perhaps inconclusive.

Irish Politics Now

By nine o'clock on the evening of Wednesday 18 February the make-up of the 25th Dáil was still in the balance. Although Fianna Fáil would be by far the biggest party, a strong overall majority was out of the question; the most they could hope for was a slim majority of one or two seats. Yet there was optimism, albeit cautious, in the Fianna Fáil headquarters in Mount Street with outside hopes for seats in three marginal constituencies. Across the road in the Fine Gael offices the party general secretary, Finbar Fitzpatrick, was feeling strangely relieved despite the electoral debacle which had cost them 19 seats. It wasn't the rout which had been feared: as one party strategist put it, "that the PDs would drive right through" them; and there was the consolation of a new seat in Kerry North. As the counts in many constituencies continued into the early hours of Thursday morning, there was still a chance that Fianna Fáil would at least get the 84 seats needed for an actual working majority. In Kerry North a nail-biting recount was taking place with only four votes separating Labour leader, Dick Spring, and Tom McEllistrim of Fianna Fáil for the last seat; in Galway West Michael D. Higgins and Mark Killilea were battling it out for the fifth seat and in Dublin North East there was the hope that Sean Haughey, son of the party leader and an imposed candidate, might just take a seat over Pat McCartan of the Workers Party. A reporter for ABC News in Dublin dramatised the struggle between the two: "A wealthy Marxist lawyer is battling tonight with the son of the aspiring Prime Minister in a cliff-hanging contest that could give his father the crucial majority he needs to form the next Irish Government."

In the early hours of Thursday morning the recount in Kerry North ended; a very relieved Dick Spring held his seat by four votes and Fianna Fáil's chance of an overall majority was gone. By mid-morning it was clear that Michael D. Higgins of Labour would take the seat in Galway West and the "wealthy Marxist lawyer" was clearly the victor Dublin North East. When RTE's radio election programme came off air at five minutes to twelve the result of the election was called: Fianna Fáil had won just 81 seats; Fine Gael, 51; the Progressive Democrats, 14; Labour, 12; the Workers Party, 4; the Democratic Socialist Party, 1, and Independents, 3. Fianna Fáil were two seats short of a clear majority, but no other party could hope to form a government. While Charles Haughey reflected on the failure of Fianna Fáil to gain an overall majority, his most implacable political enemy, Desmond O'Malley, was enjoying the congratulations of his PD colleagues. The party had achieved a major breakthrough, winning fourteen seats and replacing Labour as the third largest party in the Dáil. As he contemplated the party's success O'Malley said they had not just broken the moulds, they had "smashed them".

On the other side of the ideological divide there was relief for Labour and celebration for the Workers Party. In addition to saving Dick Spring's seat the party had defied the prediction that they would be decimated. Although losing seats in Meath, Limerick East and Tipperary North they took consolation from the gains won by Brendan Howlin in Wexford, Emmet Stagg in Kildare and the party chairman, Michael D. Higgins, in Galway

West. The Workers Party had managed to double their representation from two to four seats thanks to the victories of Pat McCartan, and Joe Sherlock in Cork East. Absent from the list of returning TDs were some of the Fine Gael dissidents who had become famous over the previous 12 months. Both Alice Glenn and Liam Skelly, who contested the election as independents, were defeated, their votes having collapsed without the support of the party machine. Gone, too, was the former poll-topper from Limerick East, Tom O'Donnell, in one of the shock results of the election. Another who had been numbered with him in the conservative wing of the party, Liam Cosgrave, lost his seat as well. The most conservative voice of the party, Oliver J. Flanagan, was absent too; he had stepped down due to ill-health and his son Charles, a more liberal figure, was elected in his place. The only government minister to lose his seat, to a Fine Gael running mate, was Paddy O'Toole, the Minister for Defence from Mayo East.

On the Sunday before the count Charles Haughey had made a dramatic appeal to the electorate not allow a hung Dáil. It would, he said, be a nightmare for everybody. His warning had not been heeded and he must have felt a an unwelcome sense of *déjà vu* as the final tallies were presented by party officials. Yet again he would have to hope for the support of the Workers Party and/or the left-wing deputies, Gregory and Kemmy. His only other hope in the vote for election as Taoiseach was that Fine Gael would abstain, putting into practice their leader's promise of cooperation on the night of the count. During the campaign he had conceded the need, without giving specific details, for tough economic measures that would involve curtailing public expenditure. If he were to stand by this and by the inevitable cuts in health and social welfare, then the left would not vote for him. For Fine Gael the situation was also taxing. On the night of the count, when it appeared possible that Charles Haughey would get an overall majority, they had pledged to support Fianna Fáil if they tried to tackle the economic crisis. Now that Charles Haughey was unsure of election they had to decide whether to support him or to oppose him and, in concert with the other parties and the independents, bring about another general election. The PDs had made no commitment of support to Fianna Fáil, indeed quite the opposite. Their clear message on supporting a Fianna Fáil nominee was: "Get rid of Charlie and we'll talk about a deal to support you". In Labour's case the strong anti-Haughey line of Dick Spring, and Barry Desmond in particular, virtually ruled out any backing of Fianna Fáil on the vote. For Mr Haughey it was an unpalatable situation: during the campaign he had stressed the need for strong single-party government; repeatedly he had said that that too was the message coming through on the doorsteps to Fianna Fáil canvassers. Yet in the wake of the battle he found himself looking with uncertainty for support amongst the ranks of those who had taken power away from him before.

The prospect of a hung Dáil dependent on the support of the left reopened the debate about national government. It was a proposal which had long ago been suggested by Fine Gael's John Kelly and when he repeated it in the uncertain days following the election there was support from a fellow Fine Gael TD, Tom Enright. While there was no realistic chance of any such agreement between Fianna Fáil and Fine Gael there was a body of opinion within and outside of Leinster House which supported the idea.

Yet in spite of the uncertainty the media view was that somehow Charles Haughey would succeed. Commentators assumed that the Tipperary independant Sean Treacy would be offered the post of Ceann Comhairle, leaving Fianna Fáil three votes short of the total needed to win. It was also believed that Neil Blaney would supply one of those and there had been hints from the leader of the Workers Party, Tomas Mac Giolla, that if the terms were right they too would vote for Mr Haughey. Similarly in the case of Tony Gregory there was a view that he would "come on side" if a deal of some kind, perhaps a continuation of the deal of February '82, could be worked out. But speculation about another "Gregory Deal" was offset on the weekend after the election when Charles Haughey told the *Sunday Press* in most emphatic terms that there would be "no deals". There was simply no money in the state kitty for deals. He said privately that it would be impossible for him to govern if he had to make deals to remain in power. As Fianna Fáil pondered their position there were suggestions of a left-wing alliance from Tony Gregory and Jim Kemmy, and the Workers Party who proposed an alliance with Labour. A total of eighteen deputies represented the left in the Dáil. To an observer it would have seemed natural for them to agree a common approach. However, apart from sharing broad ideological similarities the parties of the left regarded each other with deep suspicion. The Workers Party wrote to Labour in the week after the election asking for a meeting to discuss an alliance or common front. Labour sources say the letter was not taken seriously by the leadership, who had no intention of entering an alliance with the Workers Party. The bitter electoral enmity between the two was not about to disappear overnight. A Labour minister told the authors:

> The reality is that these people tried to murder us on the ground for the last four years and they want the luxury of being able to say the Labour party wouldn't align with them on the left.

Similarly the efforts of Gregory and Kemmy to set up meetings came to nought with the Workers Party and Labour failing to respond to their advances. When Labour met to consider their position the week after the election the party voted overwhelmingly to oppose Charles Haughey and nominate Dick Spring as Taoiseach. Dick Spring has described it as a "good tactic", the idea of which was to force the Workers Party to declare against Charles Haughey as well. He also felt it was a signal to Fine Gael and the PDs that Labour were not going to help elect a right-wing government. Barry Desmond believed that a defeat for Haughey and all of the other candidates would lead to a constitutional crisis that would force Fianna Fáil to remove Mr Haughey and put forward another name, probably Albert Reynolds, which might win the support of a majority of deputies. The day after the Labour meeting the Árd Comhairle of the Workers Party announced they would vote against Mr Haughey. According to reliable sources there was a prolonged debate between the party leader Tomas Mac Giolla, who felt Charles Haughey should be supported, and a number of others, including the party press officer, Tony Heffernan, who felt he should be opposed. Heffernan denies that the party were "forced out of the closet" by Labour and points to the party's experience in February 1982 when they supported Fianna Fáil. "We didn't do a deal with Haughey in '82; we just said we'd support him. But the pressure was on every time there was a Dáil vote. People were asking us 'are you going to bring him down now?'" He says that the Workers Party political committee decided, on the Monday after the election, that they would oppose Fianna Fáil. An early decision would, they felt, shift the pressure from them onto Fine Gael, the PDs and the independents. Tony Gregory had called for an alliance of the left, but he flatly refused to support the nomination of Dick Spring, although he commented later that he would have supported Labour's chairman, Michael D. Higgins had he been nominated. Similarly there was never any realistic prospect of Gregory reaching agreement with the Workers Party. Gregory's former membership of Official Sinn Féin — from which the Workers Party evolved — and his admiration for Seamus Costello, who was shot dead by the Official IRA — the military wing of Official Sinn Féin — meant that there was a history of mutual suspicion. While Gregory waited for some form of alliance of the left Jim Kemmy took matters into his own hands and announced he'd be supporting Dick Spring's nomination. It was a shrewd move which removed the pressure from Kemmy who was a former member of the Labour Party. He had, ironically, gained his seat at the expense of the Labour Party in Limerick East.

The decision by Charles Haughey not to do any deals to secure power was endorsed by the Fianna Fáil parliamentary party when they met in the week after the election. That meeting endorsed the nomination of Charles Haughey as Taoiseach and ended after only half an hour. There was no discussion of the results and no speculation about the future.

Privately Charles Haughey was expressing confidence that he would be elected Taoiseach. But then the news of the Workers Party decision came through, altering the balance by making him dependent on winning the support of Tony Gregory or persuading one of the Fine Gael or Labour deputies to take the position of Ceann Comhairle and thereby give him a majority of one vote. The mood changed in Fianna Fáil. The discussions on a cabinet were broadened to include preparations for an early election which key figures like Ray Burke, Albert Reynolds, Bertie Ahern and Ray Mc Sharry believed was the only alternative if their leader was defeated in the Dáil. One leading Fianna Fáil figure told the authors at the time: "One half of me wants things to hold together and be sorted out, the other half, the black side of me, wants to hit the road and give it another lash."

If support wasn't to be gained from Gregory, then Fianna Fáil had only one card left: to persuade the outgoing Ceann Comhairle, Tom Fitzpatrick of Fine Gael, to stay on and thus reduce the strength of the opposition by a single vital vote. A formal approach was made to Fitzpatrick by the Fianna Fáil leadership two weeks before the vote was due to take place. The job held a number of attractions for Tom Fitzpatrick, the most obvious being the guarantee of re-election to the Dáil. At sixty-nine years of age, and with a long record of elections behind him, the prospect of having to take to the road again to seek election was not appetising. He may also have felt that by staying on he would guarantee the stability of government which so many politicians had talked about over the previous four weeks. He waited until four days before the Dáil was due to convene before announcing his decision and all through this time kept his counsel to himself.

The only remark attributed to him in the entire period was to a political correspondent whom he came across in the corridors of Leinster House. "How are ya doing?" he asked, "I thought you'd emigrated." "Why?" asked the journalist. "Well, because you're the only one that hasn't been bothering me to know what I'm going to do," Fitzpatrick replied. While he was considering his position there was a flurry of speculation around the Labour deputy for Louth, Michael Bell. On Tuesday 3 March — a week before the vote — Bell was quoted in *The Irish Times* as saying he would seriously consider taking the post of Ceann Comhairle if it were offered to him. It took less than 24 hours for that speculation to evaporate with Bell saying he would abide by the decision of the Labour parliamentary party which was to support the nomination of Dick Spring as Taoiseach. Three days later the assembled members of the Fine Gael parliamentary party met in the old College of Art building at Leinster House. Most of the three-hour meeting was taken up with discussion of the offer to Fitzpatrick. Dr FitzGerald and Peter Barry wanted him to reject the Fianna Fáil offer and a move to have a secret ballot on the question was defeated. Among those who argued that he should accept the job were Brendan McGahon, Gay Mitchell and Jim Mitchell, the outgoing Minister for Communications and a FitzGerald loyalist. It's believed that Jim Mitchell argued in favour of a national government arrangement, similar to that already proposed by John Kelly and Tom Enright. Others who supported the move to have Fitzpatrick stay on were ministers of state, John Donnellan and George Birmingham, who argued that the national interest would be best served by decreasing the influence of Blaney and Gregory. However, the motion was roundly defeated by 60 votes to 13 and four hours later Tom Fitzpatrick gave his decision: he would not be Ceann Comhairle of the 25th Dáil.

Fitzpatrick's refusal and the complete uncertainty over Gregory's position fuelled speculation that the Dáil would fail to elect any Taoiseach when it met on March 10. There were conflicting views about the constitutional implications of such a situation. The former Fianna Fáil Attorney General, John Murray, said the President would have no option but to call an immediate general election. The Fine Gael view, and that shared by Labour and the PDs, was quite different. It proposed that there was another option which would allow the acting Taoiseach, Dr FitzGerald, to seek an adjournment of the Dáil for 48 hours. In this time, it was suggested, there would be an onus on Fianna Fáil to come up with another candidate for the post of Taoiseach. Thus Charles Haughey would be removed from the forefront of Irish public life in one fell swoop. Whatever about the dissatisfaction expressed by some Fianna Fáil frontbenchers regarding the party's election performance there was little question of them agreeing to this scenario. As Ray Burke commented on ''This Week'' just two days before the vote.

Nobody will decide on the leadership of Fianna Fáil except Fianna Fáil and our leader is Charles J. Haughey. Let nobody outside Fianna Fáil have any feelings that since they've left the party they can influence our leadership. They tried that when they were on the inside and they're not going to do it from the outside. He will remain leader, and let there be no misunderstanding for any member of the Dáil, the only alternative to Mr Haughey being leader and being Taoiseach is a general election.

In fact it had been decided, between Mr Haughey and key frontbenchers like Bertie Ahern, Ray Burke and Ray McSharry, that in the event of the Dáil failing to elect a Taoiseach an immediate meeting of the parliamentary party would be convened to declare support for the continued leadership of Charles Haughey. The party would then proceed to seek a general election. A close supporter of Mr Haughey says of the plan: ''Those boys would have been marched up to the fifth floor so quickly to that meeting there would have been no time for people to get into huddles.'' As it happened the exact constitutional position was never properly established by any of the parties.

On the morning of the vote Charles Haughey was driven as usual from his home in Kinsealy to Leinster House. The possibility of defeat on his nomination as Taoiseach that afternoon was increasing by the hour. The night before he had been visited at Kinsealy by his old colleague Neil Blaney, the Donegal leader of Independent Fianna Fáil. Blaney was offering his support if Charles Haughey would agree to end the Anglo-Irish Agreement, scrap the Extradition Bill and make certain changes in the Supreme Court. He received the answer that had been repeated by party spokespersons over the previous fortnight: there would be no deals. Blaney left in an angry mood with a question mark hanging over his vote. And then there was Gregory. With the Fiannna Fáil leader sticking to his promise that no deals would be done, Gregory was being faced with a simple choice: abstain or support Charles Haughey and thereby ensure a tough budget, or vote against him and cause an election. On the morning of the vote he all but said to Fianna Fáil that he intended to vote against them. It caused panic among backbenchers who foresaw another election being called immediately and it shifted the pressure onto Fine Gael who were meeting to decide how they would vote. There was some hope in Fianna Fáil that Fine Gael would abstain, putting into practice Garret FitzGerald's wish for cooperation in the 25th Dáil. However, they decided to oppose Charles Haughey. There was a feeling among senior figures in the parliamentary party such as Dr FitzGerald, Peter Barry and Alan Dukes, that Tony Gregory would probably abstain. They argued cogently that it was not Fine Gael's job to elect Charles Haughey as Taoiseach whatever about helping to keep him there once elected. Among those who are believed to have argued against that position were Jim Mitchell and John Bruton.

With the situation becoming gradually more desperate Fianna Fáil floated a rumour that they would be nominating one of their own TDs to the position of Ceann Comhairle. The word was that it would be Denis Foley of North Kerry. It was what is known in political terms as a ''frightener'', designed to worry the Labour leader, Dick Spring, who would stand to lose his seat in the event of Foley's automatic re-election. There was also speculation that Fianna Fáil would nominate David Andrews of Dun Laoghaire for the chair, thus jeopardising the position of Barry Desmond, the deputy leader of the Labour Party. The Labour parliamentary party decided to counter this by proposing one of their own deputies to challenge the Fianna Fáil nominee. In the event that scenario did not come to pass. The rumour was thrown aside as quickly as it had been floated. There was a firm statement from Fianna Fáil shortly before lunch-hour that they were committed to giving the post to Sean Treacy, the Tipperary independent. About half-way through the morning Charles Haughey called in senior members of his frontbench and a number of key officials and told them to prepare for an election.

As Charles Haughey finished speaking to the frontbenchers the party press secretary, P.J. Mara was already making preparations for the campaign to come. Amongst the backbench TDs there was a mixture of dread and excitement. The younger and newer TDs had little stomach for an election; their older colleagues, veterans of the unstable Dáil years of 1981/82, were more philosophical about the prospect of a fresh poll. The deputies began filing into the chamber at about 3pm, the new TDs doing their best to settle in, regardless of the uncertainty. The first item on the agenda was the election of a Ceann Comhairle. Fianna Fáil immediately proposed Sean Treacy who was elected unopposed. The rumour of a nomination from within Fianna Fáil had been firmly quashed. It was time for the parties to nominate their contestants for the post of Taoiseach. Brian Lenihan was first on his feet to propose Charles Haughey. After him came Peter Barry who proposed Garret FitzGerald. Then came Barry Desmond, proposing Dick Spring; the last was Mary Harney who proposed her own party leader, Des O'Malley. Next to speak was the leader of the Workers Party Tomas Mac Giolla who explained their decision to vote against all of the candidates proposed. After him came the leader of the Democratic Socialist Party, Jim Kemmy who said he would be voting for Dick Spring because he was the leader of the largest left-wing party in the Dáil. But these were not the speeches the deputies or the thousands of people listening to RTE's live coverage were waiting for. They were the warm-up acts for the main player, Tony Gregory who sat above Charles Haughey to his right.

There was absolute stillness and silence as he stood up to speak. A tremor of excitement passed along the press bench. His voice, for all the importance of what he was about to say, sounded weak and nervous in the hushed chamber. He spoke of how his hopes for an alliance of the left had come to nothing and about how "the parties of the right" had created the economic crisis. He blamed FitzGerald, O'Malley and Haughey for making over "one million people dependant on social welfare" and for driving "over 300,000 people" onto the dole queues. He announced that he would not be voting for "the architects of the policies" which had created the problem. Neither would he be voting for Dick Spring who had "collaborated with a right-wing party" while in government. At this stage some of the journalists on the press gallery were mentally composing "election" stories. But then, as the tension seemed ready to explode, Gregory said he believed that another election would drive the country further into the grip of the "monetarist right". There was a responsibility for the parties of the left to combine to keep the right wing in check. And then he uttered the vital phrase: "It is in that context that I have decided to abstain..."

The words that followed were lost as the Fianna Fáil benches erupted in a tumult of cheering. It had the thrill and finish of a good Munster final and the team captain could justifiably smile. The victory was entirely his. He had weighed it up and waited it out with "divil a deal being done" as a Fianna Fáil supporter commented. As J.J. O'Molloy wrote in the *Sunday Tribune:* "It was eyeball to eyeball and Gregory blinked." Next on his feet was Neil Blaney who gave one of his best speeches ever before the house. The themes were familiar: support for the construction industry, the North and the problem of emigration, but there was a wit and passion which been absent in the other speeches. The highlight was Blaney's verbal battle across the benches with his old adversary Des O'Malley. In the course of his speech Blaney made it clear he would vote for Charles Haughey but warned that his support could not be taken for granted. He listed the things he wished to see changed, all of which had been rejected the previous Sunday night when he met the Fianna Fáil leader. When the votes were counted the Ceann Comhairle announced a tie — 82 votes to 82. He cast his vote in favour of the leader of Fianna Fáil and Charles Haughey became Taoiseach for the third time.

Later, as Charles Haughey prepared to release details of his cabinet, Tony Gregory defended himself against charges that he been engaged in brinkmanship. He told Charlie Bird of RTE on the steps of Leinster House that he had deliberately given the impression to Fianna Fáil that he would vote against them. It was a warning, said Gregory, that they could not count on his vote. The sense of relief within Leinster House was palpable. On the Fianna Fáil side there was delight but no triumphalism. The margin of victory was too narrow and the pitfalls too many for any flag waving or taunting of the opposition. More importantly a view was emerging that the time for party political games was over. Perhaps the best reflection of this was in the speeches of both Garret FitzGerald and Charles Haughey. The Fine Gael leader, while warning against any attempts to tamper with the Anglo-Irish Agreement, promised his party's support for action to tackle the economic crisis. Mr Haughey was generous in his thanks to Garret FitzGerald for his "help and cooperation" and thanked him for his efforts to solve the problems of the country. It was a moment of unique magnanimity between two men who had shared some bitter words in the lifetime of the last two Dáils. In his summing up the Fianna Fáil leader gave a portent of what his government's priorities would be.

> Deputies will have heard me say on other occasions that there is more to running a country than managing the economy. But I want to emphasise that at this stage in our affairs it is the effective managment of the economy that must take priority.

That night Charles Haughey announced the cabinet he had selected the previous weekend. There were no major surprises and very few new faces. The most significant appointment was that of Ray McSharry as Minister for Finance and the Public Service. He had last held the portfolio in the shortlived Fianna Fáil administration formed in March 1982. It was a highly significant move on Charles Haughey's part in both personal and political terms. There had been widespread media speculation, not discouraged by his supporters, that Albert Reynolds would get the Finance job while McSharry would be eased back into prominence with a portfolio like Agriculture. The view among a section of Fianna Fáil was that Ray McSharry was out of touch with the domestic political scene because of his involvement in the European Parliament. There had also been talk of a coolness between himself and the leadership ever since his resignation from government over the taping incident of 1982. However, the truth of the matter was that Haughey had a deep belief in McSharry's ability and felt that the Sligo TD needed an important ministry to restore his confidence.

From McSharry's own point of view it was a restoration to what he himself had always felt was his rightful place at Charles Haughey's right-hand side. There was less jubilation amongst Albert Reynolds' supporters who felt that their man should have been chosen. In the new cabinet he returned to the Department of Industry and Commerce which he had managed successfully in the last Fianna Fáil administration. Whatever about his alleged disappointment it was evident that he and McSharry would be to the fore of Charles Haughey's attempts to revive the economy. Apart from the selection of Ray McSharry in Finance the other surprise was Michael O'Kennedy as Minister for Agriculture. As party Finance spokesman he felt he should have been given the key job. The Agriculture portfolio is one of the hardest worked and most thankless in any government with its seemingly endless hours of negotiations and the pressure of representations from the numerous lobby groups. It wasn't what O'Kennedy had been expecting. Left out of the cabinet was Maire Geoghegan-Quinn, the Galway West TD, who had been expecting a senior ministry. There were rumours that she had been offered the Gaeltacht portfolio, a job she held in the last Haughey government, and had turned it down. The Gaeltacht ministry was kept within Mr Haughey's own brief.

Of the more experienced ministers Ray Burke was appointed to Energy, with responsibility for areas of Communications, having told the party leader that he would prefer not to return to the Department of the Environment, a post given to Padraig Flynn, the TD from Mayo West; John Wilson was appointed to Communications; Brian Lenihan, the deputy leader and Tanaiste, went back to his old post at Foreign Affairs, although it was clear that responsibility for Northern Ireland would remain with Mr Haughey; Gerry

Collins was returned to the Justice portfolio where he could be depended on to steer with a firm hand and keep controversy at bay; Michael Woods was given the task of handling Social Welfare, a difficult and bruising ministry in times of cutbacks; and Brendan Daly, a former Minister for Fisheries was given charge of the new Department of the Marine. Those appointed who had not served in senior ministries were: Mary O'Rourke, a sister of Brian Lenihan, who was given the Education portfolio; Dr Rory O'Hanlon, a conservative who spoke strongly against contraception and divorce, who became Minister for Health; Michael J. Noonan, a farmer from West Limerick who had been a rather low-key Agriculture spokesman, was made Minister for Defence; and there was Bertie Ahern, Lord Mayor of Dublin, former chief whip of Fianna Fáil and a rising star in the party, who was appointed to the Labour portfolio. With an affable manner and a streetwise political touch it was reasoned that he would be a good bridge-builder with the trade union movement.

The cabinet also featured a two-tiered system of ministers of state with four new ministries which would have offices attached to various departments. In essence it involved a beefing up of some of the junior ministries in areas like trade, new technology and agriculture. The idea, according to Mr Haughey, was to focus political attention on sectors where wealth and employment could be readily created. Two former dissidents who made it to the second tier but failed to gain promotion to the senior cabinet were Seamus Brennan and Joe Walsh, the poll topper from Cork South West. Brennan had gradually been restored to some kind of favour with the Fianna Fáil leadership after supporting the abortive heaves against Mr Haughey. He was appointed to the junior ministry of Trade and Marketing but was disappointed not to have made it to the cabinet table. There was speculation in political circles that his rumoured refusal of the frontbench post vacated by Bobby Molloy the previous year had damaged his chances of getting a senior cabinet seat. One famous face absent from the list of junior ministers was that of Sean Doherty, the controversial former justice minister. Over the previous 12 months there had been talk of his having been restored to a position of favour and that he would be rewarded with a cabinet post. From discussions with Fianna Fáil sources we can confirm that there was never any question of him being offered a ministry, junior or senior. Another face missing from the cabinet was Doherty's constituency colleague, Terry Leyden, the party's spokesman on communications.

The media concentration on the tasks facing Mr Haughey was abruptly terminated the following day, March 11, with dramatic news from Fine Gael. The bombshell came at a special meeting of the parliamentary party called by Dr FitzGerald for 11.30 am. The party press officer, Peter White, scoured the corridors of Leinster House to tell TDs about the meeting. Others were called at their homes and told: "It'll be an important meeting, you'd better turn up." In spite of the urgent tone of the calls the word of what was about to happen did not leak out. When he rose in the usual way to address the meeting Garret FitzGerald told the assembled TDs, Senators and MEPs that he was stepping down. According to those who were there the reaction was one of shock and surprise. It was generally believed that he would resign at some stage during the 25th Dáil, but few were prepared for such a quick announcement. His farewell was lengthy and emotional. He told the meeting that when he had become leader he had intended to stay for two elections and he had now been at the helm for 10 years. It was time to make way for a new force in Fine Gael. The first to pay tribute was his deputy, Peter Barry, who spoke "glowingly" of the former Taoiseach's record. The gathering, which had been growing all the time because of the late arrival of some members, became a highly-charged and emotional affair with practically everyone present contributing a personal eulogy to Garret FitzGerald. Many of them reminded Dr FitzGerald that he had brought them into politics. After hearing lengthy tributes the meeting turned finally to the logistical arrangements for electing a successor. In accordance with the party's constitution, election would be by secret ballot. The date set by the outgoing leader for the election of an heir was Saturday 21 March. The business of the meeting over, a happy looking Dr FitzGerald went to his home in Palmerstown Park for lunch, to a relieved wife Joan, who through the years had made little secret of the fact that she would have preferred him not to have entered politics.

That afternoon he explained his decision to the media at a news conference in Jury's Hotel in Ballsbridge. Even in the few short hours since his resignation he seemed to have shaken off a great burden. To a packed room the (soon to retire) Fine Gael general secretary, Finbar Fitzpatrick, gave his own verdict on the departing leader:

> History will judge Garret FitzGerald as one of the great influences on Irish politics in the latter half of the 20th century, as well as being the greatest single influence ever on the development of the Fine Gael party. On his accession to the leadership he inherited a party that was decimated and down-hearted, with a narrow base, very much to the right of centre and seemingly heading for a long winter of opposition. Within a few short years he changed all of that.

He said that, in spite of the election results, Garret FitzGerald was leaving the party with a "wider electoral base of support, more modern and youthful in its outlook and philosophy, better organised and better funded." Snatching the PDs' slogan of "breaking the mould in Irish politics," he declared that the only person actually to do that in 60 years was Dr FitzGerald because for the first time a political party had been led by a man who was both a strong nationalist and a committed European. Later Dr Fitzgerald revealed that he had made his final decision to step down two weeks before the parliamentary party meeting. It was obvious, however, with Fine Gael facing defeat at the polls, that it was a matter which had crossed his mind more than once since the beginning of the election campaign. Quite often during the campaign he seemed weary and close to exhaustion. One or two people had been told, but the secret had been well kept. In fact, as an operation the resignation was perfectly planned. Dr FitzGerald was leaving the country for the United States the next day, so he would not be around for the campaign to succeed him. He was to return only on the day his successor was to be chosen — then to act as teller for the ballot and, as he put it himself, "bring the figures to the grave with him". His decision to go, he told his audience, was not an easy one. Nor was it hasty.

> There have in the past, here and elsewhere, been people who have felt able to lead a political party in and out of government for long periods of time. Perhaps there may be others who will feel able to do so in the future. But for myself I do not believe that it would be beneficial for the party or for the country that I should remain on in my present position for the period of time that might be involved if I were to undertake the leadership of another Government after the expiration of the lifetime of the one just formed.

In the wake of his resignation he said that had Tony Gregory voted against Charles Haughey he would have resigned as Taoiseach, but he would have continued to carry out the duties of the office, seeking to resolve the constitutional deadlock. In all probability there would have been another election. In the course of the news conference he took a sideswipe at our multi-seat proportional representation system which he is most anxious to see reformed. It was, he said, one of the reasons why he had to change the Fine Gael constitution when he became leader, altering the balance of power towards the voluntary party workers rather than sitting TDs. There was for them a conflict "between their personal interest in securing the safety of their seats and the party's interest in maximising representation in the Dáil." He attributed Fine Gael's success in increasing their number of seats radically in the early eighties to that shift in power, "unwelcome" though it may have been to some members of the parliamentary party. He brushed off the defeat in the election saying that he left behind a far more formidable force than that which existed 30 years earlier, when its Dáil strength had been reduced to a figure in the twenties. Reflecting on the Fine Gael which had evolved from the era of the "Just Society" document of the sixties, he said the generation growing up in the seventies were seeking an Ireland in which the different traditions would be "accorded equal respect" and the "suffocating conservatism of traditional attitudes might be dissipated, without damage to the essential core of Christian values." He paid tribute to the loyalty of those who had served with him: "No leader," he declared "has ever had less reason than I to worry about his back!" His audience laughed. There was no need to include names in that sentence.

It was a moving event. On such occasions, the natural tensions between the politician and the reporter tend to dissolve. At the end of the conference, after Dr FitzGerald had fielded some routine questions about his future, including dismissing the notion of the Presidency, saying that in his future career he'd be looking for a good deal of freedom of speech, he received an impromptu presentation from *Irish Press* political journalist, John Wallace on behalf of the press corps. It was a reproduction of a famous *New Statesman* cartoon on the resignation of British Prime Minister, Harold Wilson. Wilson was dressed up as the children's storybook character Just William and was pictured addressing one of his mates in a regal manner. Garret read out the caption: "I'm sick of being Prime Minister. I'm fed up with politics altogether. There isn't any sense in 'em. I'd sooner be a red Indian anyday. You can get someone else to be Prime Minister and do things." "Not my sentiments — they're William's!" boomed Garret to the now dispersing reporters. Some left to file copy, some lingered to conduct interviews, which went on for another four hours.

Final assessments of the FitzGerald era will probably need a longer historical perspective, but on the central issue of the economy it is clear from discussions with some of the senior Fine Gael ministers that there was dissatisfaction with what had been achieved, and indeed with what had not been achieved. As one put it: "We took decisions — but they just weren't big enough." Those interviewed for this book were quick to point out the political circumstances of 1982/3 when the Government took power. Mr Haughey's last administration had been rocked by a number of very public scandals, not least the discovery of a double killer in the home of the Attorney General and the phone tapping revelations. According to one Fine Gael minister these were among the factors which "compelled the new partners in government to stick together."

> Everybody was conscious of the need for stability. We in Fine Gael would probably have taken stronger measures on our own, but there was an anxiety to stick together — not just to stay in power. The Taoiseach, who was not stupid, was conscious of this need. There was always an effort not to have a Fine Gael-Labour split in voting.

Another senior Fine Gael figure who felt strongly that the Taoiseach took the only road he could in presiding over a Coalition cabinet put it like this:

> Obviously if Labour said no on a breaking point issue his concern was to keep the government together. But you could exaggerate that. It wasn't a roller coaster with Labour all the time putting on the breaks and us trying to urge the thing ahead. There was an element of that in it. But it would be unfair to Labour and even unhistorical to portray the thing in those simplistic terms. First of all, we would have had constraints on our own side for some of the things proposed, and secondly, the real problem only arose in the last year, towards mid-May, when we saw our finances going wrong — and therefore our base for the coming year was going to be wrong to start with. You could write a history of the Coalition saying all would be well if Fine Gael did it on their own but it wouldn't be the truth.

However, there is controversy about the Coalition government's approach to budgetary policy in its first weeks in office. Fine Gael had at that stage fought two election campaigns essentially on the need to get the nation's finances right. It was part of Fine Gael's programme that the current budget deficit should be phased out in the period up to 1987. It was even included in the Joint Programme for Government, the agreement between Labour and Fine Gael, that this would be done taking into account prevailing economic circumstances. Yet when it came to drawing up the first budget, the Coalition stumbled into a very public disagreement. Alan Dukes, who was then Minister for Finance, revealed on "This Week" that the current budget deficit he was aiming for in 1983 was £750 million, which would entail very substantial cuts in public expenditure. The then Tanaiste, Dick Spring, attacked this statement fiercely from his hospital bed where was recovering from an injury sustained in a motor accident. He said loudly and clearly that this figure had not been agreed. It was one of those early shaky moments. It appears that the Taoiseach and Dick Spring had in private discussions talked about a figure of £900 million as tolerable, and the Taoiseach had been given the all-clear for this figure from his foreign financial advisors. The trouble seems to have been that no-one told the Minister for Finance about these discussions. According to a Fine Gael source, Alan Dukes' statement gave Dick Spring the impression that the Finance minister was "trying to pre-empt the situation".

When Alan Dukes was asked about this in his first interview as party leader on "This Week", he confirmed that international advice had been tendered at cabinet about the level of deficit which could be sustained by borrowing in 1983. However, he also agreed that part of the argument surrounding the affair was not "could we borrow" but "should we borrow". But the arguments against choosing the higher deficit figure lost out. As one of his cabinet colleagues put it, the Coalition had chosen the soft option then, and made the 1987 budget inevitable. Alan Dukes will not comment on those discussions between Dr FitzGerald and Dick Spring — "parallel" discussions as he called them, to those going on at the cabinet table. Some Fine Gael sources say that there is another explanation for cuts in public expenditure not being made in 1983. The decisions which should have been taken in the '83 budget were postponed because there was not enough time to agree them between the two parties before the budget was published. So the cuts were deferred until 1984. By the time they came to consider them in '84 the cabinet had been destabilised by the resignation of Frank Cluskey over the use of public funds for Dublin Gas. A senior Fine Gael minister says of the time:

> I was worried then. I felt we were not going to tackle the problem. The cuts to be faced then were essentially the same as those we came up with in 1987 and the government would not have held together then. We had to decide what was the best thing to do. As long as we were succeeding in bringing borrowing down — although this had been done in the first two years by cutting capital and not current spending — it seemed right to continue what we were doing. But I knew we'd be faced with the question of either not continuing to cut borrowing or doing it at the expense of current spending. I could see it looming up that we'd face problems in the end.

What the government did not foresee was the combination of economic setbacks which were to come with a huge burst in interest rates, the non appearance of the 2.5 per cent projected growth and a fall-off in tax and non-tax revenue. All of it combined to derail the National Plan.

> Everything went wrong on the revenue side. In 1984, while I was disturbed that we were not on course, we didn't seem to be that far off-course. I didn't feel that we were building up the leeway we would need to bring in a decent budget in '87. But I didn't think we were creating a situation where that budget would have to be harsh. That only became evident last year when all of these elements came on top of each other.

Another Fine Gael minister has told us that the crunch was inevitable in 1987. The '85 budget was neutral and the '86 document, with its several hundred million pounds worth of tax cuts, was "irrelevant and designed to make people happy". Although there were continuing differences over the need for cuts the cabinet only came to the verge of breakup once in its four year history. That was during the reshuffle of February 1986. In discussions with the authors the former Minister for Health Barry Desmond has confirmed that he refused to move to the Department of Justice at the Taoiseach's behest. The strategy was that Desmond would be moved to Justice and Alan Dukes would be made Minister for Education. Says Barry Desmond:

> My refusal to go to Justice completely upset the apple-cart. That day we came to within half an hour of leaving government. I decided I wasn't caving in. I might have considered the approach until I heard that a crowd of the Fine Gael backbenchers were out for my scalp. Once I heard that crowd were on the warpath the knives were out and there was no way I was going to be moved.

Desmond, who says he was fully supported by his party leader, Dick Spring, stuck to his guns. By 2.30 that afternoon there was still no agreement on the new cabinet which was to be announced to the Dáil at 4pm. Desmond stayed in Health although his other ministry, Social Welfare (a key cutting area) was given to Gemma Hussey of Fine Gael. She had been supposed to get a new ministry of European Affairs. Barry Desmond says he is not bitter about the affair and that at the time he did not regret being relieved of the strain of running two departments. Ministers on all sides of the government agree that the cabinet reshuffle was, as one of them put it to the authors, "a total botch job". However, in spite of their clash over the reshuffle Barry Desmond has described Dr FitzGerald to the authors as the "finest Taoiseach in the history of the modern Irish state, leaving aside the founding Taoisigh, W.T. Cosgrave and Eamon De Valera."

There is general agreement amongst political commentators that Garret FitzGerald's most substantial achievement in office was the Anglo-Irish agreement, though there are some who have doubts about its long-term chances of success and, of course, Mr. Haughey has maintained that he has constitutional reservations about it. It was certainly a diplomatic triumph. It came in the wake of the lowest ebb in Anglo-Irish relations, as Garret FitzGerald himself spelt out, in his major address on the North during the election campaign:

> At ministerial and official levels dialogue about the North between Dublin and London had stopped altogether. Public opinion in Britain was more hostile to our state than at any time in the previous forty years. The British Government, exhausted and bemused by the crisis of the hunger strikes, had even less positive ideas about what might be done than at any time since 1969. Its only policy seemed to be containment at the level of security.

The situation in the North was more desperate than ever, he said, traumatised by the IRA's exploitation of the hunger strikes, with a "new generation of gunmen, depraved and corrupted by bloodletting, determined both on vengeance and on seeking absolute power throughout Ireland." It was in this speech that he launched his most powerful attack yet on Sinn Féin, drawing on himself the confrontation with Gerry Adams described earlier. These men, he said, hoped that "despair and nihilism" would provoke an uncontrollable unionist backlash, and that the chaos would infect the south:

> Then as a tragedy on the Lebanese scale unfolded here — a tragedy to be stagemanaged by Adams, Morrison and the IRA — these men confidently hoped to ride to power throughout Ireland. That this was the strategy of the Provisional IRA and Sinn Féin is no mere political speculation. In Government it was confirmed to us in detail by our professional advisers both in the security forces and in the Department of Foreign Affairs.

Compounding all of that was Dr FitzGerald's disastrous meeting with Mrs Thatcher when the New Ireland Forum Report was discussed. Afterwards Mrs Thatcher gave her now infamous news conference, where she baldly rejected the three major suggestions: unity, a federal solution, and joint authority, with the phrase "Out, Out, Out." Dr FitzGerald referred to this episode obliquely in his speech when he said dealings with Britain were fraught with the "risk of recurring, unwitting, public humiliation, as the British Government cumbersomely and at times with painful clumsiness" tackled the problems of Ireland. However, Dr FitzGerald maintains that the basic breakthrough in Anglo-Irish relations had already been made at his Chequers meeting with the British Prime Minister in late 1983 when Downing Street decided that the situation in the North was so threatening that the policy of doing nothing would not serve. After the most intensive and exhaustive exchanges that have ever taken place between two countries, the Anglo-Irish Agreement was signed.

For Garret FitzGerald, it was a truly emotional experience, and he rememembers graphically the hour when he presented the results of his negotiations to the leadership of the SDLP, the people who as he puts it himself "stood squarely — unarmed but undaunted — on the very front line between the rest of us and anarchy." He takes up the story himself:

> The most moving moment of this dramatic experience came when on an evening very shortly before we went to Hillsborough, John Hume, Seamus Mallon, Eddie McGrady and Joe Hendron told us that they and their party were ready to back our efforts. I then went to Hillsborough: after the 15th November 1985, the nationalists of the North could at last raise up their heads.

For the future, Dr FitzGerald says the gain is that London now has a policy where before it had none — and Dublin has the same policy. The internationally binding agreement, lodged at the United Nations, is the "institutional framework" for the achievement of peace and stability. Its task, he says, is to create balance in Northern Ireland, not by taking away from unionists, but by giving nationalists a fair deal. Real progress, he feels, is being made in the implementation of the agreement with the Conference of Ministers meeting regularly and the Secretariat based in Belfast. Both of these give the Republic a voice in northern affairs, he says. Dr FitzGerald cites developments in the handling of provocative parades, the law on flags and emblems, voting rights, incitement to hatred, policy on the Irish language, the law on handling police complaints, supergrass trials, reform of the Emergency Provisions Act, and the commitment to have the UDR accompanied by the police.

He says his greatest hope is that the outright unionist hostility to the Agreement will give way to new thinking, and that devolved government can be achieved which commands cross-community support — a "central strategic objective" of the Hillsborough accord. As to the long term, it would essentially be up to the next generation. The agreement requires "consent" for any basic change in the status of Northern Ireland, and it requires the two Governments to provide for Irish unity if there is consent to unity. Garret FitzGerald has expressed as his "dearest wish" that in time such consent may emerge while "bitterly regretting" that the "murder campaign of the IRA has postponed the possibility of movement towards the coming together of the Irish people." That is how Dr FitzGerald sees the agreement himself.

There is an alternative view of the agreement among some northern nationalists. People like Fr Des Wilson of Ballymurphy, former SDLP member, Paschal O'Hare, and the Sinn Féin leadership have said that it has worsened the position of Northern nationalists. They point to the increase in the petrol bombing of Catholic homes during 1986 and the spate of sectarian murders as evidence to support this contention. There is also the view that some of the changes in the area of flags and emblems and the Irish language had already been implemented by nationalists, tired of waiting for the British to change things. During 1986 there were complaints of security force harrassment of people in the Strabane area while UDR patrols continued to patrol alone in many areas. Cardinal Tomás Ó Fiaich did however say that progress was being made in this and a number of other areas as a result of the agreement. There remains, at the time of writing, the unsolved question of the "Stalker affair" and the enquiry into the alleged "shoot to kill" policy of the RUC in the Armagh area in 1982. A proper resolution of this has been identified by Peter Barry, among others, as central to the establishment of trust between the security forces and nationalists. Ultimately, only time will tell if there are to be lasting benefits from the agreement. The final word is left to Charles Haughey, who was the agreement's harshest critic from the day it was signed, through to the election campaign. On his election he said that Dr FitzGerald's negotiation of the Anglo-Irish Agreement had won major recognition internationally for him, especially among nations friendly to Ireland. "Irish democracy has been served well by Dr FitzGerald," he said.

Yet, in terms of his own vision of a "new Ireland" the four years of government were, with the exception of the Anglo-Irish Agreement, a grave disappointment. The "Constitutional Crusade", which was intended to lead to a pluralistic and more tolerant, state was thrown off course by the devisive battles over the "Pro Life" and divorce amendments. Dr FitzGerald had on his resignation not gone anywhere near creating the kind of society he spoke about in that famous RTE interview with Gerald Barry in September of 1981.

> Most of my relatives are in fact Northern protestants. I was brought up with them, exchanging holidays with them from my childhood onwards. I know their attitudes. What I want to do is, if I may borrow a phrase from someone on television the other night, I want to lead a crusade, a republican crusade to make this a genuine republic on the principles of Tone and Davis. And if I can bring the people of this state with me on that path and get them to create down here the kind of state that Tone and Davis looked for, then I believe that we would have the basis on which many protestants in Northern Ireland would be willing to consider a relationship with us, who at present have no reason to do so. If I were a Northern protestant today I can't see how I would be attracted to getting involved with a state which is itself sectarian...the fact is that our laws and our constitution, our practices and our attitudes reflect those of the majority ethos and are not acceptable to protestants in Northern Ireland.

While there was progress in the liberalisation of the laws on contraception he found himself overwhelmed by those outside of, and within, his own party who did not share his vision of the Republic. There were some who felt that the crusade was attempted too far ahead of its time, that the nation was not ready for divorce and that Garret FitzGerald had misjudged the mood of the people. It is perhaps a harsh criticism given that successive opinion polls showed a growing number of people in favour of ending the ban on divorce.

The problem, as many in Fine Gael now agree, was in selling the message. On that score the government parties were comprehensively outmanoeuvered by the anti-divorce lobby who appealed successfully to basic human fears about the loss of land and property in their bid to defeat the amendment. With some of the Fine Gael TDs taking no part at all in the campaign, others announcing their support for the anti position, the party's approach was often seen as fractious and disorganised. Fianna Fáil TDs remained largely silent or encouraged the anti case. They could do so because they were not committed to any crusade to change the nature of the Republic. After the debacles of the "Pro Life" and divorce amendments the "crusade" petered out.

One of those closely involved with Dr FitzGerald at cabinet has expressed the view that his central weakness was a tendency to confuse the agenda.

> He was a great man for the confused agenda. He couldn't resist having forty-five items on the agenda and trying to deal with them all simultaneously. The difference between himself and Haughey on that score is that Charlie has a great capacity to get

down to the essentials very quickly. With Garret there was tendency to be sidetracked. At cabinet you could take a three-legged hare out of the bag and let it run around the room for half an hour before he would realise what you were up to. That is the essential difference between himself and Dukes. With Dukes you have to have your facts absolutely correct otherwise you get sidelined very quickly. He sees through the waffle straight away.

On the day of Garret FitzGerald's resignation the tributes flowed in from all quarters. On the News at 1.30 the people of his own constituency expressed their sorrow at his departure from the forefront of public life. On the programme the political correspondent of the *Sunday Tribune,* Gerald Barry, who had conducted the famous "crusade" interview while working with RTE, assessed Dr FitzGerald in the following terms:

He was a very tough politician despite everything else. He was capable of being quite ruthless. He did know about the ins and outs of politics. He gave the impression of being just this likeable, slightly fuzzy, decent uncle who had a job somewhere in academia but underneath this there was a tough politician, and he had to be.

The item which characterised Garret FitzGerald, according to Barry, was the famous £9.60 payment for housewives in the 1981 Fine Gael manifesto.

Like so much that is popularly associated with Garret it was good in theory but the practice fell a bit short. I think that is the kind of thing people will remember him by. I think the lasting impression both among people generally and in the media is that he was basically a very good and a decent man.

His relationship with Charles Haughey was by times corrosive and bitter and at best distant and formal. This appears to have changed in the wake of the election. The briefings between the two on economic matters were unusually cordial and unstuffy while their speeches in the Dáil on March 10 portrayed changed attidudes on both sides. Dr FitzGerald assured Mr Haughey that though he had become Taoiseach by the narrowest of margins, it was clear that there was a decisive majority in favour of economic action which would increase employment, lay the groundwork for lowering the tax burden, but would not add to the national debt. This was the formula which Fine Gael would use to support his first budget. He wished the new Taoiseach well "in the very difficult task he was now undertaking." Mr Haughey responded in warm tones, expressing his appreciation to Dr FitzGerald for his support and he added:

I would like to say to the outgoing Taoiseach that I appreciate the efforts he made to deal with the problems which confronted his government, which were unprecedented in severity during the last four years. Though I didn't always agree with the methods the Taoiseach and his colleagues used in their approach, they did as they saw best, in the best interests of the country. I hope myself and my colleagues do the same.

Speaking on "This Week" after his resignation, Dr. FitGerald said he welcomed that recognition, and went on to say: "It was a very gracious comment. There are moments like that when reality breaks through in Irish politics and the confrontational thing which has to go on in an adversarial system, to ensure there are alternatives, goes into the background." It was a rare moment for listeners and political observers as well. For years, they had seen these two political gladiators indulge only in bloodletting. In the United States during the St Patrick's Day celebrations the rapprochement between the two men went a stage further. During a lunch given by the speaker of the House of Representatives, Jim Wright, Charles Haughey spoke at length and in warm terms about his former opponent.

Others who were there said the Fianna Fáil leader went out of his way to involve Dr FitzGerald in conversation, introducing him as one would an honoured elder statesman.

Garret FitzGerald had only just resigned when the battle began to elect a successor. There were at any stage only three real contenders: John Bruton, the former Finance Minister, Peter Barry, the outgoing Minister for Foreign Affairs, and Alan Dukes, the former Justice Minister. Speculation that Michael Noonan, whose star had shone so brightly in the early days of the government, would be a contender evaporated within a day of the formal battle being declared. His popularity among backbenchers had waned over the previous three years. Similarly the speculation that Gemma Hussey, the only woman in the senior cabinet, would be a candidate was dismissed by herself within days of the contest beginning. The three candidates were markedly different in style. The most senior of them, Peter Barry, was one of the cabinet's elder statesmen; a Corkonian who listed among his favourite leisure activities walking greyhounds and drinking pints! He had served in previous coalition governments in the Ministries of Education, Environment, Transport and Power and latterly Foreign Affairs where he had been to the fore of Anglo-Irish Agreement negotiations. Barry, a statesmanlike figure in the party, had the support of senior cabinet members like Paddy Cooney, who had urged him strongly to run, and John Boland. The question of his age — he was fifty-eight — would not be a problem, he felt. He pointed out that he was only the "same age as Gorbachev".

There was no age problem for John Bruton. At forty he had served as Minister for Industry and Commerce and Minister for Finance in two coalition governments and had been a member of the Dáil since 1969. Bruton was regarded by the Labour Party as the right wing ideologue of the government, a man committed to the principle of free enterprise and firm financial managment. His blunt manner did not always make for plain sailing with Labour at cabinet level and his relationship with Frank Cluskey would take several pages to describe. One of his greatest ideological battles centred around the proposed National Development Corporation — the setting up of which had been identified by Labour as one of their key ambitions in government. When Dick Spring launched an attack on Bruton for a statement he had made about the role of the Corporation Bruton rang the newspapers from the lounge of Dublin airport to make a detailed point by point response to the Tanaiste. It was Bruton's style — direct and blunt. From the public's point of view he did have the albatross of two failed budgets around his neck but he himself saw the '82 and '87 budgets in a rather different light. They were, he felt, the only way to make people face the reality of the financial position. During the election campaign he had been at the forefront of the Fine Gael campaign, emerging as the best television performer of the four week campaign. To him it must have seemed that the time would never be more opportune.

To the backbenchers of Fine Gael the candidature of Alan Dukes, a forty-two year old former Finance and Justice Minister, was no surprise. Of all the Ministers he was the one who had assiduously courted them, the one who had always been available to travel to party functions and whose ministerial door was always open. As a spokesman he had been exceptional, going out to bat for the party and the government when reason would have suggested he keep his head down. An example of this was when he was accused of using political influence to secure a job in the Curragh camp for the son of a Kildare Fine Gael executive. When many other ministers might have avoided the publicity Dukes came on radio and delivered a sterling defence of himself. That was the end of the allegations of political interference. Although the divorce campaign was a political disaster for the coalition Dukes, who was the minister sponsoring the legislation, emerged without sustaining any damage to his image. At cabinet level his former colleagues pay tribute to his skills of logic. To many in the Fine Gael party he seemed the ideal successor to Garret FitzGerald. He described himself as a liberal, saying he would be proud to follow in the traditions of FitzGerald.

By the standards of recent political history the struggle for the leadership was subdued and private. The Fine Gael press office assured journalists at the outset: "It will be Marquess of Queensbury rules all the way." Dukes had an immediate head start in publicity terms. His right hand men, Gay Mitchell and Ivan Yates, put the word out to the newspapers that he had already sewn up enough votes to take the leadership. The newspapers took the bait and Dukes was installed as odds-on favourite. On the morning after the succession race had been declared John Bruton embarked on a punishing nationwide tour, visiting deputies in constituencies the length and breadth of the country. In the meantime Peter Barry's senior cabinet supporters were lobbying on his behalf with his position seemingly improving by the day. By the middle of the week the newspapers were focussing on Barry as a favourite with Dukes second and Bruton in third place. The truth was, however, that nobody in the media knew what was really going on, such was the secret nature of the election. There was in the Dukes camp, by the close of the week, a growing confidence. If the backbenchers were telling the truth their man had it in the bag. The worry was Peter Barry who seemed to be gaining with the help of his persuasive cabinet colleagues. However, it was made clear to the younger backbenchers that their chances of advancement and of a "new era" in Fine Gael would be substantially better if Dukes were elected. He would, they were told, sweep a new broom through Fine Gael.

On the morning of Saturday 21 March the parliamentary party assembled in Leinster House. The gates had been locked to all but TDs, senators, MEPs and a few selected Fine Gael officials. Outside the College of Art the three candidates stood shaking hands with the voters as they walked in in a scene reminiscent of the recent general election. The meeting, which had been scheduled for 11.30, didn't get underway until close to noon. Proposing Peter Barry were Sean Barret, the party chief whip, and Donal Creed, the deputy from Cork North West; for John Bruton the proposer was John Kelly and the seconder, John Donnellan. According to one of those at the meeting there was a gasp of surprise when Tom Enright, the Laois-Offaly deputy, stood up to propose Alan Dukes. A pivotal backbencher, Enright described Dukes as a man with a cool nerve who was a good listener. The party was at a crossroads, he said, and there was much to be done to project its separate identity into 1990s. Dukes was the man to do it, said Enright. The seconder was another rural backbencher, Dinny McGinley from Donegal South West. After the speeches, which were all relatively brief, the meeting moved to a vote. It was a secret ballot under the proportional representation system with Garret FitzGerald, who had only just returned from the United States, and Kieran Crotty as tellers. The votes would be known only to them. Outside in Kildare Street the crowds, mostly of Dukes' supporters, were beginning to gather and traffic was starting to back up. Shortly after 1pm the TDs trickled out for air having cast their votes in alphabetical order. By half past one they were all back in the room to hear the result. The news was delivered to a standing ovation inside and to the public by a delighted Ivan Yates, campaign manager for Alan Dukes. As he walked towards Buswells Hotel he gave a thumbs up sign and announced: "We have it". At exactly half past one, after the news had been flashed on RTE radio, the gates were opened and the journalists allowed in. Alan Dukes appeared with his wife Fionnuala. He smiled and smiled as most journalists had never seen him smile before. "I am thrilled," he said. Less delighted were Peter Barry and John Bruton. Said Bruton: "I wouldn't have gone forward if I hadn't hoped to win. I'm disappointed but not very…I'm delighted and I wish Alan Dukes well."

As Peter Barry, who was bitterly disappointed, went to shake his new leader's hand he joked about Dukes' impressive height: "The party voted by inches you know." Garret FitzGerald seemed relaxed and happy. He would not say who he favoured but the speculation is that he wanted Dukes to be his heir. As for the result, Garret was giving away nothing. Again the speculation was that Dukes had taken 46 of the first preference votes. Given that only two people know the actual result, Garret FitzGerald and Kieran Crotty, it is unlikely that we will ever know.

During the early years of his stewardship at the Department of Finance, the term of derision Fianna Fáil most liked to hurl at Alan Dukes was that of "bookkeeper", which was first used by Charles Haughey on RTE's radio budget programme in 1983, with Alan Dukes himself waiting to respond. Needless to say it is a description which he rejected then, and in interviews during the leadership election and since, he has been at pains to dispell that image which he feels is unfair and incomplete. He doesn't think the public think of him in that way at all.

Certainly the Fine Gael grassroots seem to find me a much more sympathetic person than that. They do like efficient politicians, I take that as a compliment. Bureaucratic — I don't think so — I just like to have things properly worked out when I'm talking about them. I think people who find me cold and bureaucratic are those who cross swords with me and lose arguments. But I can be quite a nice guy after that. I think it's a partial image. I feel sometimes a bit resentful, sometimes I worry about it. It usually arises in situations on TV or radio where you are being pursued to answer questions. You have to fight back, and concentrate on the issue in front of you.

The media image of an automated, programmed intelligence, he dismisses as "sloganeering by people in a hurry." He readily accepts the description of himself as a "liberal" which he defines as "very much a centrist in politics, with a social-democratic orientation." He believes moving to the far right is an "unjust" position to adopt because it discriminates against too many people, "particularly in a country like Ireland where there's a great deal of economic and social development still to be carried out."

Alan Dukes of course has his record in Finance for most of the term of the Coalition government to defend. He was in charge from 1983 to 1986 and as we have already seen, there are critics within Fine Gael who feel that a great deal more should have been done to put the nation's finances in order: As the race for the leadership of the party got under way, Alan Dukes told the authors:

There are people who would feel that. There are occasions when I feel that myself. We didn't do enough that's clear. Part of the difficulty there was not so much the will at government level, but the fact that political debate, particularly on economic issues in Ireland has for years been coccooned around catchphrases and mythology that pass for analysis. I think that one of the great things that Garret FitzGerald and Fine Gael have done is to strip away those skins of useless rhetoric and bring the argument down to the real issue. And at the end of the day in any group what emerges is the result of the merging of different points of view because nobody is going to get what he wants out of it.

But didn't that mean that the Coalition of Fine Gael and Labour had failed?

There is no doubt in my mind that that Coalition government over four years contributed more to the development of economic policy than a Fianna Fáil government would have over the period. It was a government that had a great degree of commitment and courage in the way it tackled problems. It's self evident that had there been a majority Fine Gael government, we would have done things differently — but we didn't have a majority Fine Gael government — that wasn't on offer.

In the Department of Justice, the job Barry Desmond wouldn't take, Alan Dukes feels proud, in particular, of bringing forward the Status of Children Bill with Nuala Fennell, and putting through the Extradition Act.

As we have seen, there are those in Labour who found Alan Dukes a man they could do business with in government, particularly Barry Desmond. Will the new leader then keep open a bridge to Labour, despite their policy of staying out of coalitions for a decade?

Alan Dukes feels that parliamentary politicians should have a degree of respect for each other despite their different views, reflecting the "committment most people in politics actually have." He has personal friendships with Labour party members but differs fundamentally with them on economic matters, and even on some social issues. But on closer ties to Labour: "To the extent that they're prepared to support us, I'd be happy to have that support — but in terms of policy accommodation I wouldn't set out to do that because Fine Gael must maintain and develop its own distinct personality as a party."

The Fine Gael front bench that was announced on 26 March contained two significant changes. Gone was Paddy Cooney, who had served in three coalition cabinets as a minister in Justice, Defence and Education. The other major change was the move of John Bruton from Finance to Industry and Commerce. He was also appointed deputy leader of the party. Other changes included: Michael Noonan to Finance and the Public Service; Austin Deasy from Agriculture to Transport and Tourism; Peter Barry retained Foreign Affairs; Jim Mitchell from Communications to Social Welfare; Gemma Hussey returned to Education. Sean Barrett, the outgoing chief whip and Minister for State, was promoted to Justice. Another to be promoted was Jim O'Keefe, who became Agriculture spokesman. John Boland retained Environment; Richard Bruton was appointed to Energy, George Birmingham to Labour; Avril Doyle moved to Marine, Paul Connaughton to Defence and Enda Kenny to Gaeltacht affairs. Bernard Allen was appointed to Health and Fergus O'Brien was made chief whip. One of those who had been predicted as a frontbench spokesman, Ivan Yates, was appointed junior spokesman for Trade and Marketing.

During the campaign for the leadership and immediately on taking over, Alan Dukes identified the tasks that he faced. He would have to begin again to broaden the base of support for the party, building up the organisation as Garret FitzGerald had done in 1977, not just electorally but also in policy terms. He promised to take on the PDs who he feels captured a large share of the floating vote which Fine Gael had won in the early '80s. The language he used was sharp. The PDs were a "disruptive factor in Irish politics...not a real party", they had taken up Fine Gael policies but had a "narrow focus in society." People who voted for them must feel "taken aback" that rather than providing stronger government, the PDs had made it more difficult to have "firmness and determination" in government. He declared that it was his ambition to get Fine Gael into government on their own. To those who would say that he will need the PDs to become Taoiseach, he replied that he would form no pre-election alliances with them, but he left open the prospect of some agreement afterwards, saying that after an election it was up to the Dáil to elect a Taoiseach. The PDs leader Desmond O'Malley was quick to counter-attack. He said the eagerness of others to attack the PDs showed their own growing irrelevance, and their fear of the electoral threat the new party posed to their "tired and outmoded politics". He described Alan Dukes' comments as "rather rash and silly."

> The Irish people are fed up with that brand of politics. We will continue to give a lead on the real social and economic issues facing the people and let the others blunder along with their spurious confrontational politics.

Thus were the battle lines drawn.

Now that they had become the third largest party in the Dáil within a year of being founded, the PDs were intent on proving to all comers that they were not a flash in the pan. With two bigger right-of-centre parties on either side of them the PDs say they are keenly aware of the dangers of entering alliances with either, though it is unlikely there would be any such arrangement with the present Fianna Fáil leadership.. The success which came out of the party's separateness has reinforced the view that the wisest course is the independent one. Both Des O'Malley and his general secretary, Pat Cox, have said there are more seats which the party can take in a future election. There are other signs which may give hope to those who wish to see a broader alliance in Irish political life in the future. One came in the "This Week" studio when Alan Dukes had finished his first major interview as party leader. There was a phone call for him. It was Ray McSharry, the new Fianna Fáil Minister for Finance, ringing from his office where he was working on the budget. He had been listening to the programme, and wanted to congratulate Alan Dukes and wish him well. Whatever the hopeful signs there are those who put the choices facing the country in very stark terms. We sought out two views from opposite poles of the political spectrum in the last cabinet. Barry Desmond, the former Minister for Health, gave this perspective:

There is still and there will be for two or three years a swing to the right in Irish politics. I think the groundwork for that was laid back in 1981/82. There has developed a view that says: 'Give us back our money. I'm healthy, I'm young, I'm not thinking of retiring so damn the old and the poor and the sick'. It is the kind of attitude that says 'damn unmarried mothers let them put their children in welfare homes'. Irish society has become mean, vicious, sectional and self interested. It will take two to three years of cuts actually affecting people in things like education and health and social welfare before there is a swing back to the politics of civilised compassion. The PDs captured that right wing swing and Fine Gael would like to but can't because of the 'Just Society' social democratic medal hanging around their necks. Garret to his eternal credit had no stomach for that. When the hardship backlash comes against the cutters they will run a mile.

A senior Fine Gael minister who sat at cabinet with Barry Desmond had this to say of the present state of Irish politics:

The national interest has to come first, full stop. It has to. The problem is the survival of the present political set-up over the next ten years. Is the present political class, Charlie Haughey, Des O'Malley and all the rest of us going to be bundled off to Mountjoy Jail? The whole lot of us? It's about time we faced up to our responsibilities. That's being a little bit apocalyptic about it...just a little bit.

On the left wing, the Labour Party's "Go it Alone" policy and the enmity between itself and the Workers Party has led political observers to conclude that a formal alliance between the two would be difficult to construct. According to Barry Desmond, Dick Spring and Michael D. Higgins it was a greatly revitalised Labour which returned to the Dáil, committed to following an independent course, despite gaining just over six per cent of the vote, their worst performance since 1933. The Workers Party doubled their representation to four deputies and it was clear they intended to build on that base. For Sinn Féin the result was a severe disappointment, but they hoped for better next time.

For the new Taoiseach, Charles Haughey, there were no illusions about the problems he faced entering the first year of his government. The massive debt and deficit problems and the record unemployment levels had been a growing feature of political life over two decades. In discussions with the authors Charles Haughey has spoken in passionate terms of his desire to get the country going again. He spoke in the United States about catching the country "by the scruff of the neck". His ambition, he said, was to tackle unemployment by creating jobs and wealth. It was, he said, his vision for the future. Everything else came second to that. It was also made clear that Northern Ireland would not be to the fore of his government's attentions, for the short term at least. The message was that Fianna Fáil would forge ahead, regardless of the uncertain situation in the Dáil. The uncertainty of that situation was underlined by Albert Reynolds on the day Mr Haughey was elected Taoiseach when he said: "We've got to expect that sooner or later real politics will return to the Dáil and when that happens we will be faced with a very difficult situation." Among many TDs there was a feeling in those first weeks that sooner or later, to borrow Neil Blaney's phrase, it would be time to "clear the pitch and play again".

PART TWO

How the Nation Voted

THE DISTRIBUTION OF VOTES
by Brendan M. Walsh

The last opinion poll published before the election, and the only one conducted after the television debate, revealed that 15 per cent of the electorate still had not decided which party to support. This unusually high level of uncertainty, more than twice that recorded before earlier elections, suggested that there might be a low turnout, but in fact 73.3 per cent of the registered voters actually voted on 17 February, a slightly higher proportion than in the November 1982 election.

The distribution of voting intentions revealed in the opinion poll clearly indicated that it would be a close-run thing. It was apparent that Fianna Fáil were losing the lead they had enjoyed in earlier polls, and were not likely to obtain sufficient support to be sure of a clear majority in the new Dáil. However, despite this evidence, there was a fairly widespread expectation that a significant swing to Fianna Fáil compared with the November '82 result would ensure them a comfortable majority of the 165 seats to be contested in the election.

In the event, the polls provided a very accurate guide to the way first-preference votes were cast (see Table 1). There was a fall of 1.1 per cent of Fianna Fáil's share of the vote from the level of 1982, reducing it to the lowest recorded since 1961. The partners in the outgoing government fared much worse. Fine Gael's vote fell by almost one-third, to the lowest share of the national total the party had received in any election since 1951. The long-term decline of the Labour Party's vote continued at an accelerated pace and its share of the vote fell to its lowest level since 1933.

The main gainer was, of course, the Progressive Democrats party, which received almost 12 per cent of the vote in the first election it contested. It won 14 seats, 9 of them obtained by new TDs. The party fielded candidates in 33 constituencies, where it obtained an average of 13.8 per cent: Support was strongest in the suburban areas and weakest in the handful of western rural constituencies in which it entered candidates.

It is striking that the PDs obtained almost exactly the number of votes lost by the Fine Gael party. But their support was not simply a disaffected Fine Gael vote. This is obvious in constituencies such as Galway West, Limerick East and Cork South Central, where former prominent members of Fianna Fáil took their large personal vote with them to the new party. (Mary Harney in Dublin South West, however, left the Fianna Fáil vote undiminished and gained her support mainly at the expense of Fine Gael.) A rough indication of the effect of the PDs on the votes obtained by Fianna Fáil and Fine Gael is provided by looking at the swing in their votes in constituencies with and without a PD candidate. In the 8 constituencies in which there was no PD candidate, the FG vote fell by an average of 5.4 per cent, compared with an average decline of 12.9 per cent in constituencies with a PD candidate. This suggests that the presence of a PD candidate accounted for an average swing of about 7.5 per cent against Fine Gael. Its effect on the Fianna Fáil vote, while appreciable, was much smaller (See Table 2).

The other newcomer in this election was Sinn Féin, who entered candidates in 24 constituencies. Outside of the border constituencies, they received an average of only 2.4 per cent of the valid poll. In the five border constituencies, however, they averaged 6.1 per cent of the vote. Their second preferences tended to transfer predominantly to Fianna Fáil candidates and proved decisive in winning Dr FitzPatrick his seat in Dublin Central.

Because of the absence of an agreement between Fine Gael and Labour on transfers, and the large number of Independents and candidates from small parties that stood for election, the distribution of second and lower preferences votes was very important in deciding the distribution of seats. Fianna Fáil won 6 seats more than they did in November 1982, despite the fact that their share of the first-preference vote fell by 1.1 per cent. Table 3 displays the percentage distribution of votes and seats. It may be seen that Fianna Fáil, Fine Gael and Labour gained a larger proportion of seats than of votes, whilst the PDs, the small parties and the Independents lost out.

In the closing days of the election campaign Dr FitzGerald urged Fine Gael supporters to exercise their lower preferences in favour of the PDs. This advice was followed by a large majority of Fine Gael voters. In Dr FitzGerald's own constituency, Dublin South East, on the elimination of the Fine Gael candidate, Joe Doyle, 60 per cent of his transfers went to the PD candidate, Michael McDowell, and clinched his election. Transfers from the PDs went predominantly to Fine Gael candidates and this proved quite important in deciding the distribution of seats. The striking reciprocal transfer of lower preferences between Fine Gael and the PDs will undoubtedly have a significant bearing on these parties' future electoral strategies.

An exciting feature of all recent Irish elections has been the large number of seats decided by a handful of votes after numerous counts. In this election these long struggles meant that the suspense regarding whether Fianna Fáil would gain the 84 seats needed for a majority was maintained not only through the night of Wednesday but until almost noon on Thursday. There were 12 cases where a seat was decided between candidates from two different parties by less than 1,000 votes. All these cases are listed in Table 4.

It is therefore fair to say that Fianna Fáil were deprived of a clear majority in the new Dáil by the narrowest of margins and the intricacies of the proportional representation system. But it is also true that they owe it to the PR system that they managed to win almost half the seats that were contested by obtaining only 44 per cent of the votes.

TABLE 1

Results of general elections in the 1980s

Share of first preference votes

	FF	FG	PD	Lab	WP	OTH (incl. SF when standing
1981	45.3	36.5	—	9.9	1.7	6.6
1982 (Feb)	47.3	37.3	—	9.1	2.3	4.0
1982 (Nov)	45.2	39.2	—	9.4	3.3	3.0
1987 (Feb)	44.1	27.1	11.8	6.4	3.8	6.7

Number of candidates elected
(excluding outgoing Ceann Comhairle)

	FF	FG	PD	Lab	Others
1981	77	65	—	15	8
1982 (Feb)	81	63	—	15	6
1982 (Nov)	75	70	—	16	4
1987 (Feb)	81	50	14	12	8

Distribution of voting intentions in opinion poll published by IMS/Sunday Independent on 15 Feb 1987 (distributing "don't knows")

FF	FG	PD	Lab	Others	Total
45	30	13	5	7	100

TABLE 2

Average swing (Nov 1982–Feb 1987) in share of first preference vote

	FF	FG
33 constituencies with PD candidates	−1.0%	−12.9%
8 constituencies with no PD candidate	+1.2%	−5.4%

TABLE 3

Comparison of percentage distribution of first prefernece votes and seats won

	FF	FG	PD	Labour	Others
Seats*	49.1	30.3	8.5	7.3	4.8
Votes	44.1	27.1	11.8	6.4	10.5

*Excluding outgoing Ceann Comhairle.

TABLE 4

Constituencies in which a seat was decided between two candidates from different parties by less than 1,000 votes

Constituency	Winning Party	Margin (votes)	Losing Party
Kerry North	Labour	4	Fianna Fáil
Dublin Central	Fianna Fáil	78	Fine Gael
Dublin North East	Workers' Party	235	Fianna Fáil
Wexford	Labour	350	Fianna Fáil
Wicklow	Fianna Fáil	430	Fine Gael
Laois-Offaly	Fine Gael	493	PDs
Cork North West	Fine Gael	548	Fianna Fáil
Cork South Central	Labour	569	Fine Gael
Carlow-Kilkenny	Prog. Democrats	718	Fine Gael
Galway East	Fianna Fáil	883	PDs
Clare	Fine Gael	888	Fianna Fáil
Dublin North Central	Fine Gael	958	Fianna Fáil

TRANSFERS

For the election to the 25th Dáil the country was divided into 15 five-seat, 13 four-seat, and 13 three-seat constituencies. Apart from minor adjustments the constituencies were those drawn up by the Walsh Commission, used for the first time in 1981. Bigger constituencies make the destination of lower preferences more important — especially if the voting is close. So, with the outcome of the election for the last seat in 12 constituencies this time being decided with a margin of less than 1,000 votes, transfers were extremely important.

In the February 1987 context there were additional factors which make an analysis of the transfer pattern very interesting. The Fine Gael-Labour coalition had broken up, and for the first time in 14 years it was clear to the electorate that the same combination was no longer on offer. The Labour Party's electoral commission had ruled out coalition for the foreseeable future, and this approach was endorsed by the party leader Dick Spring well in advance of the election. Since the formal coalition pact of 1973 the possibility of such an alliance has always been present at election time, reinforcing the transfer pattern between Fine Gael and Labour Party supporters established when the parties won power in the early seventies. In the eighties the formula for the Labour Party was to hold a special delegate conference after the election to decide on the possibility of coalition. With the formal and informal alliance ended, and indeed with tough attacks by the former coalition paterners on each other's policies during the election, the strong traditional transfer pattern was bound to come under strain.

On top of all this, in the last days of the election campaign the outgoing Taoiseach Dr FitzGerald asked Fine Gael voters to cast their succeeding preferences for Progressive Democrat candidates, as potential allies or supporters in the formation of a government. After that, Dr FitzGerald indicated that Fine Gael voters might wish to continue their traditional support for Labour. The gesture was not reciprocated by the Progressive Democrats' leader, Des O'Malley. However, it was generously reciprocated by Progressive Democrat voters, resulting in Fine Gael winning an additional five seats, according to Garret FitzGerald.

Table 1 shows the destination of final transfers for all constituencies, including those from Fianna Fáil, Fine Gael, Progressive Democrats, Labour, the Workers Party and Sinn Féin. Smaller groups and Independents are not included. The basis for inclusion is the destination of final transfers from candidates of these parties WHEN THERE IS NO OTHER CANDIDATE OF THAT PARTY IN THE FIELD. Transfers may be on the basis of elimination, or the distribution of a surplus. Care must be used in extrapolating from these figures, but they are a useful guide to the destination of votes when the party in possession can no longer make use of them. (Mayo West is not included in the table because there were only two counts, the second for the elimination of a Fianna Fáil candidate while two others from the party were still in the count.)

Table 2 compiles the final transfers nationally for each party. The Progressive Democrat final transfer to Fine Gael is the highest at 53.2 per cent, while the final transfer from Fine Gael to the PDs is 31.4 per cent. The table shows that old traditions die hard in Irish politics, with Fine Gael still giving Labour 25.9 per cent of final transfers and receiving 28.6 per cent of Labour's in return, in spite of everything. The transfers were vital for Labour in saving a number of its seats, with the party's national vote down three points to 6.4 per cent. The outgoing Minister for Labour Ruairi Quinn was a beneficiary in Dublin South East where he held his seat with 9.1 per cent of first preferences, having failed to gain a seat in June '81 with 12 per cent. He gained an additional 6.7 per cent in final transfers from Fine Gael and the PDs; the PD candidate, Michael McDowell, on election passed on transfers from Fine Gael in the distribution of his surplus. Labour's Mervyn Taylor benefitted similarly in Dublin South West where he relied on 2,562 transfers from Fine Gael in order to pass out the Workers Party and be elected on the 13th count. Michael D. Higgins received a large final transfer of 1,330 from Fine Gael's losing TD Fintan Coogan; in Dublin South Central, Frank Cluskey, perceived as a strong left-winger in the Labour movement, got a transfer of 1,163 from the PDs to put him ahead of Fianna Fáil, and 820 from Fine Gael to keep him ahead and give him a seat.

In Clare, Dublin North Central, and Meath PD transfers enabled Fine Gael to win the last seat from Fianna Fáil. In the case of Dublin North Central Fine Gael were also dependent on the remnants of the old traditional Labour transfer — nearly two to one in their favour against Fianna Fáil. The PD transfer was five to one for Fine Gael against Fianna Fáil, and both of these factors ensured that the party pulled off what appeared an impossible feat: holding two seats out of four with 24 per cent of the first-preference vote. In Kildare Fine Gael received 48 per cent of PD transfers from two candidates, enabling the party to retain its two seats and hold off the Fianna Fáil challenge for three. In Wexford 2,260 PD transfers were critical for Fine Gael, while in Tipperary North PD support was also important. Again in Cork North West, and South West, the PD transfer to Fine Gael at rates of two and three to one allowed the party to fight off strong challenges from Fianna Fáil in each case. Obviously, in many cases throughout the country strong evidence is available to support the Fine Gael contention that much of the PD vote is simply a disaffected Fine Gael vote which they lost through leading an unpopular government. It remains to be seen if it returns in the future, as Fine Gael suggests, or if the new party, having made such a successful breakthrough, can retain and build on its support.

The PDs benefitted from the strong Fine Gael transfer as well. Apart from Michael McDowell receiving more than 60 per cent of Fine Gael transfers in Dublin South East, Pat O'Malley took 2,820 Fine Gael transfers in Dublin West to assure him of a seat. In Galway East and Louth, Fine Gael transfers helped PD candidates turn in strong performances. It is obvious that in Limerick, Galway and Cork, the high profile PD TDs, who were former members of Fianna Fáil, took substantial personal votes with them, damaging Fianna Fáil to that extent. However, it is worth noting that on the evidence available from final transfers (which admittedly is scant because few Fianna Fáil candidates are eliminated without another in the field to benefit) that the PDs are lowest on the scale of preference for transfer by Fianna Fáil voters, apart from Sinn Féin. Ahead are Fine Gael, Labour and the Workers Party in that order. The breakdown reveals a well-known truism about many Fianna Fáil voters; they are plumpers who vote for the party ticket and then stop — 41.6 per cent. Also, the biggest share of Sinn Féin votes passed on to Fianna Fáil — 39 per cent. In this election, the former Tánaiste and Labour Party leader, Dick Spring, had cause to reflect on the possibility that his father Dan Spring's roots in the Republican Labour tradition back in the forties helped save his seat. He defeated Fianna Fáil's Tom McEllistrim by four votes, and during the count he received 189 final transfers from Sinn Féin.

The vagaries of the PR system are legendary, but of the elections of this decade, February '87 might well be remembered for the result in Dublin North East. There the PD transfers, favouring the Workers Party before Fianna Fáil, saw to it that Pat McCartan rather than the Taoiseach's son, Sean Haughey, was elected to the Dáil, thus denying Mr Haughey the extra vote he needed to govern without undue hazard.

TABLE 1

		FF	FG	PD	LAB	WP	SF	OTH	NT
Carlow-K	LAB		325	209					232
	WP	300	200	306	638				250
	FF		1,090	760	1,385				3,357
Cavan-M	WP	214	136				85	129	39
	SF	2,195	668						1,810
Clare	LAB	105	183	104				175	33
	PD	1,013	2,885						1,685
Cork East	PD	522	1,916			629			450
Cork N/C	SF	177	49	35	80	158		133	100
	FF		218		239	210			543
	WP	776			1,102				1,785
Cork N/W	PD	1,130	2,379						287
Cork S/C	WP	859	236	261	1,000				584
	PD	929	2,471		751				1,017
Cork S/W	PD	708	2,642						354

		FF	FG	PD	LAB	WP	SF	OTH	NT
Donegal N/E	FG	351					127		1,392
Donegal S/W	FF		860			518	426		
	FF		250			435	107		
	SF		259			620			930
Dublin C	LAB	91	169	197		429	135	71	144
	WP	366	210	312			495	128	530
	PD	65	138				9		
	SF	1,427	290						1,862
Dublin N	LAB	763	1,211	682					902
Dublin N/C	SF	276	21	21	103	211		99	139
	WP	450	224	197	972				444
	PD	594	2,530		729				376
	LAB	1,395	2,367						1,496
Dublin N/E	SF	275	30	26	83	214			92
	LAB	748	473	191		937			112
	PD	707	3,044			514			706
	FG	403				751			1,523
Dublin N/W	WP	168	71		157		53	52	173
	WP	28	23		32		12	18	13
	SF	383	72		180				498
	LAB	388	913						682
Dublin S	PD	267	1,743		149	39		203	
	WP	281	156		457			393	113
	FF		575		509				1,607
Dublin S/C	SF	433	88	36	134	414			238
	WP	971	673	386	1,930				678
	PD	827	3,211		1,163				641
	FG	65			87				
	FG	294			820				
Dublin S/E	SF	271	18	23	72	196		148	117
	WP	523	151	170	839				632
	FG	187		2,837	876				763
	PD	152			1,704				261
Dublin S/W	PD	18	75		28	15	1		
	SF	394	33		152	384			357
	FG				2,566	608			1,645
Dublin W	SF	337	68	37	34	392		112	216
	LAB	121	300	137		581	193		116
	WP	81	83	71					
	FG	231		2,820					173
Dun Laoghaire	SF	419	88	55	86	480			125
	WP	844	868	660	1,543				957
	PD	216	1,491						2
Galway E	FG	134		1,189					

		FF	FG	PD	LAB	WP	SF	OTH	NT
Galway W	WP	268	283	94	877			87	132
	PD	602	1,045		546			138	554
	FG	252			1,330				
Kerry N	FG	478			816		101		
	SF	578			189				294
Kerry S	WP	317	81	163	266				71
	PD	1,227	1,161		981				285
	FF		350		365				194
Kildare	WP	204	129	107	728		108		85
	SF	611	126	126	473				192
	PD	1,023	3,691						999
Laois Offaly	SF	816	335	153					225
	FF		366	324					1,808
Limerick E	PD	76	380		113	7	3	253	
	WP	13	28		24		24	179	27
	SF	169	32		52			274	137
	LAB	306	933					1,025	443
Limerick W	LAB		236	182					121
Longford Westmeath	LAB	372	303	251					152
Louth	SF	1,137	301	138	312			282	523
	FG	42		508	125				
Mayo E	SF	431	133						104
Meath	WP	216	70	77	244		154	79	98
	SF	627	64	71	123			100	213
	LAB	1,429	1,185	636					973
	PD	1,714	2,337						1,608
Roscommon	FF		853						
	FF		715						
Sligo Leitrim	PD	391	1,677				71	315	116
	SF	1,356	539					419	408
Tipp N	PD		1,505		897				585
Tipp S	PD	912	1,461		383			728	261
	LAB	1,473	1,444					1,153	469
	FG	1,522							472
Waterford	WP	1,028	368	434	925				653
	FG	289		1,781	433				286
	LAB	2,066		1,498					1,505
	PD	652							152
Wexford	WP	182	172	96	500			247	58
	PD	849	2,260		493				399
	FG	148			473				461
Wicklow	WP	923	514	541	1,589				512
	PD	542	3,121						1,268
	LAB	428	390						227

TABLE 2

Read from left-hand, PD transfers to FF, FG, LAB, WP, etc.

	FF	FG	PD	LAB	WP	SF	OTH	NT	TOT
PD	15,136	43,163	—	7,831	1,197	84	1,637	12,006	81,054
	18.7%	53.2%		9.7%	1.5%	0.1%	2.0%	14.8%	
FG	4,396	—	9,135	7,526	1,359	228	—	6,429	29,073
	15.1%		31.4%	25.9%	4.7%	0.7%		22.2%	
LAB	9,685	10,432	4,087	—	1,947	328	2,424	7,607	36,510
	26.5%	28.6%	11.2%		5.3%	0.9%	6.7%	20.8%	
WP	9,012	4,676	3,875	13,799	—	931	1,312	7,834	41,439
	21.7%	11.3%	9.4%	33.3%		2.2%	3.2%	18.9%	
SF	12,312	3,214	721	2,073	3,069	—	1,567	8,580	31,536
	39.0%	10.2%	2.3%	6.6%	9.7%		5.0%	27.2%	
FF	—	5,277	1,084	2,498	1,163	533	—	7,509	18,064
		29.2%	6.0%	13.8%	6.4%	3.0%		41.6%	
TOT	50,541	66,762	18,902	33,727	8,735	2,104	6,940	49,965	237,676
	21.3%	28.1%	8.0%	14.2%	3.7%	0.8%	2.9%	21.1%	

TABLES: HOW THE NATION VOTED

DUBLIN

Constituency Name	Members	FF	FG	PD	LAB	WP	OTH
Dublin Central	5	3		1			1
Dublin North	3	2	1				
Dublin North-Central	4	2	2				
Dublin North-East	4	2	1			1	
Dublin North-West	4	2	1			1	
Dublin South	5	2	2	1			
Dublin South-Central	5	2	2		1		
Dublin South-East	4	1	1	1	1		
Dublin South-West	4	2			1	1	
Dublin West	5	2	1	1		1	
Dun Laoghaire	5	1	2	1	1		
Total Seats	48						

1987 RESULTS

	1st Pref	Seats	Nov 1982 Seats
FF	199,946	21	18
FG	116,989	13	22
PD	66,942	6	
LAB	35,001	4	4
WP	36,838	3	2
SF	10,699		
OTHERS	27,044	1	2

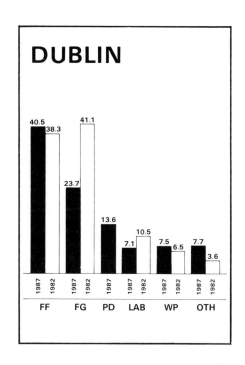

1st Pref	FF	FG	PD	LAB	WP	SF	OTH
Dublin Central	19,993	5,973	6,361	1,399	1,463	2,501	9,766
Dublin North	16,542	8,878	4,008	3,433			1,157
Dublin North-Central	21,344	10,397	3,582	2,973	1,643	779	2,206
Dublin North-East	19,663	7,243	4,655	2,227	3,297	655	539
Dublin North-West	16,737	6,493		1,370	7,480	1,065	1,476
Dublin South	20,496	17,704	11,957	2,684	1,308		3,182
Dublin South-Central	21,149	14,267	5,212	4,701	3,946	1,266	1,151
Dublin South-East	12,522	12,251	5,961	3,480	1,910	811	1,335
Dublin South-West	16,004	5,250	8,169	5,065	5,086	1,379	501
Dublin West	20,920	11,456	6,014	1,185	6,651	1,041	4,445
Dun Laoghaire	14,576	17,077	11,023	6,484	4,054	1,202	1,286
	199,946	116,989	66,942	35,001	36,838	10,699	27,044

REST OF LEINSTER

Constituency Name	Members	FF	FG	PD	LAB
Carlow-Kilkenny	5	2	1	1	1
Kildare	5	2	2		1
Laois-Offaly	5	3	2		
Longford-Westmeath	4	3	1		
Louth	4	2	1		1
Meath	5	3	2		
Wexford	5	2	2		1
Wicklow	4	2	1		1
Total Seats	37				

1987 RESULT

	1st Pref	Seats	Nov 1982 Result: Seats
FF	189,046	19	16
FG	112,851	12	16
PD	45,345	1	
LAB	39,457	5	5
WP	9,021		
SF	6,436		
*OTHERS	11,237		

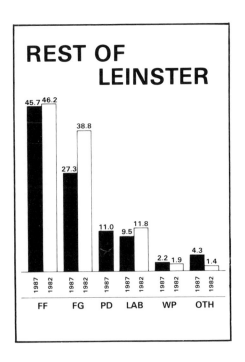

1st Pref	FF	FG	PD	LAB	WP	SF	OTH
Carlow-Kilkenny	25,527	14,873	8,063	7,358	1,664		
Kildare	22,913	14,124	6,320	7,567	1,238	1,420	123
Laois Offaly	30,204	17,479	5,353	818		1,405	863
Longford/Westmeath	26,017	12,416	5,401	1,038			280
Louth	18,470	10,820	5,219	6,205	570	2,599	2,926
Meath	27,694	14,172	4,831	3,631	790	1,012	3,065
Wexford	23,233	16,783	4,708	5,086	1,250		1,862
Wicklow	14,988	12,184	5,450	7,754	3,509		2,118
	189,046	112,851	45,345	39,457	9,021	6,436	11,237

MUNSTER

Constituency Name	Members	FF	FG	PD	LAB	WP	OTH
Clare	4	2	2				
Cork East	4	2	1			1	
Cork North-Central	5	2	2	1			
Cork North-West	3	1	2				
Cork South-Central	5	2	1	1	1		
Cork South-West	3	1	2				
Kerry North	3	1	1		1		
Kerry South	3	2	1				
Limerick East	5	1	1	2			1
Limerick West	3	2		1			
Tipperary North	3	2	1				
Tipperary South	4	2	1				1
Waterford	4	2	1		1		
Total Seats	49						

1987 RESULT

	1st Pref	Seats	Nov 1982 Seats
FF	224,682	22	22
FG	141,830	16	20
PD	78,952	6	
LAB	35,824	2	7
WP	16,758	1	
SF	4,643		
*OTHERS	23,843	2	

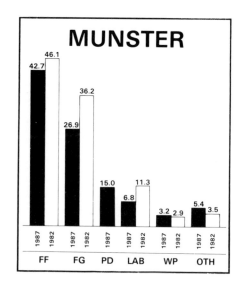

1st Pref	FF	FG	PD	LAB	WP	SF	OTH
Clare	25,022	13,274	5,603	600			2,874
Cork East	16,347	12,739	4,276	888	6,986	534	
Cork N.C.	16,127	11,372	7,245	3,720	2,628	681	1,570
Cork N.W.	15,120	14,488	3,796				
Cork S.C.	18,460	12,254	14,047	4,862	2,349		4,287
Cork S.W.	15,132	14,566	3,570				134
Kerry North	16,712	10,087		6,739		1,227	
Kerry South	17,926	5,946	3,215	4,559	735		830
Limerick East	12,633	8,881	18,427	2,201	246	565	6,660
Limerick West	17,443	9,464	6,580	519			
Tipperary North	17,099	7,859	2,444	4,558		878	453
Tipperary South	17,661	8,480	4,402	3,820	407		
Waterford	19,000	12,420	5,347	3,358	3,407	758	304
	224,682	141,830	78,952	35,824	16,758	4,643	23,843

CONNACHT/ULSTER

Constituency Name	Members	FF	FG	PD	LAB	OTHERS
Cavan/Monaghan	5	3	2			
Donegal North-East	3	1	1			1
Donegal South-West	3	2	1			
Galway East	3	2	1			
Galway West	5	2	1	1	1	
Mayo East	3	2	1			
Mayo West	3	2	1			
Roscommon	3	2	1			
Sligo/Leitrim	4	3	1			
Total Seats	32					

1987 RESULT

	1st Pref	Seats	Nov 1982 Seats
FF	170,874	19	19
FG	109,457	10	12
PD	19,344	1	
LAB	4,271	1	
WP	4,656		
SF	11,155		
OTHERS	24,027	1	1

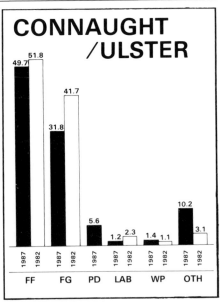

CONNAUGHT/ULSTER

1st Pref	FF	FG	PD	LAB	WP	SF	OTH
Cavan/Monaghan	31,747	18,927			577	4,219	2,342
Donegal N.E.	9,512	8,734		393		2,365	8,416
Donegal S.W.	18,384	9,403			2,512	1,276	
Galway East	17,056	10,419	5,463				
Galway West	19,979	9,600	11,360	3,878	1,567		6,378
Mayo East	17,224	13,028				668	
Mayo West	17,197	13,093					
Roscommon	16,201	12,093					4,067
Sligo/Leitrim	23,574	14,160	2,521			2,627	2,824
	170,874	109,457	19,344	4,271	4,656	11,155	24,027

NATIONAL SUMMARY

1st Pref	FF	FG	PD	LAB	WP	SF	OTHERS
Dublin	199,946	116,989	66,942	35,001	36,838	10,699	27,044
Rest of Leinster	189,046	112,851	45,345	39,457	9,021	6,436	11,237
Munster	224,682	141,830	78,952	35,824	16,758	4,643	23,843
Connacht/Ulster	170,874	109,457	19,344	4,271	4,656	11,155	24,027
	784,548	481,127	210,583	114,553	67,273	32,933	86,151
	44.1%	27.1%	11.8%	6.4%	3.8%	1.9%	4.9%

Total 1,777,168 Valid Poll

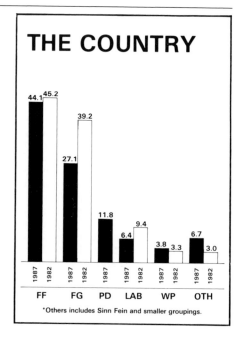

THE COUNTRY

*Others includes Sinn Fein and smaller groupings.

Proportional Representation:

Theory and Practice

Senator Michael Yeats

The system of proportional representation used in Irish elections (the single transferable vote) was invented in the middle of the 19th century by an English barrister called Thomas Hare. It was intended to remedy the distortions caused by the "straight vote" system under which the candidate coming top of the poll in any constituency will be elected, even though he might have the support of only a minority of the voters. This new concept led to a good deal of discussion at the time, but was never adopted in Britain. While most people were perhaps willing to admit that STV would lead to a parliament more representative of all shades of public opinion, the view that prevailed was that the object of an election was, in essence, to elect a government. Whatever its faults might be, the "straight vote" system was clearly best adapted to this object.

So far as Ireland was concerned, British attitudes to the electoral system began to change after the Sinn Féin landslide in the 1918 election that destroyed the old Home Rule Party: only one Home rule candidate was elected in the 26-county area. Such a clean sweep would have been impossible under a system of proportional representation, as the total Sinn Féin vote in the contested constituencies was only 47 per cent. (It is perhaps fair to say that at least part of the Sinn Féin victory was due to the total collapse in certain areas of the Home Rule party organisation. I was told once by a respected senator from the west of Ireland that in the 1918 election he had voted 167 times for Sinn Féin in the Wexford constituency.)

Even before the 1918 election there had been talk about the possibility of using the single transferable vote (STV) as a safeguard for the Unionist minority in Ireland. The first practical experiment was made just after the election, in January 1919, when a local election in Sligo Town was conducted under the STV system. The Ratepayers Association (largely Unionist) came first, with Sinn Féin in second place, and establishment circles as a result proclaimed that Sligo had been given a "model council".

This desire to placate the Unionist minority was in part the reason for the inclusion of a provision for proportional representation in the Free State Constitution of 1922. The system of the single transferable vote then adopted is essentially that in force today, some 65 years later. It is unique to Ireland, and has never been introduced in any other country in the form used here, though other countries have different systems of proportional representation.

The theory behind the STV system is that each vote should be given its full weight, that none should be wasted. Under the "straight vote" system a vote for a weak candidate is wasted; under STV the voter has the chance to give a preference vote that will be handed on to another candidate on the elimination of his own favourite. This is the first basic principle of the system. The second principle is more complicated: in order that no successful candidate will have a surplus of votes beyond what he actually needs to get elected, the concept of the "quota" is introduced. During the course of the count, once any candidate has reached this quota, then he is deemed to be elected and any surplus votes he may have can be distributed amongst other candidates.

How is a quota fixed? To find the quota in any constituency, one is added to the number of seats to be filled, this number is divided into the total valid poll and, finally, one is added to the result. Take, for example, a four-seat constituency with a total valid poll of 50,000. In this instance the quota will be 10,001, as this is the smallest number of votes that just four candidates can reach, but no more. In other words in a four-seat constituency anyone who gets one-fifth of the votes (plus one) is sure of election. In practice less than this will do, as a strong candidate can expect to receive a certain number of additional preferences as the count proceeds.

In a five-seat constituency, then, the quota will be one-sixth of the total valid poll, and one-quarter in the case of a three-seater; in each case plus one vote. The result of this rule, therefore, is that the larger the constituency, the smaller the proportion of the total poll needed in order to get a seat. In the early years after 1922, constituencies were much larger than they are now: some of them had seven, eight or even nine seats. In a nine-seat constituency the quota would be one-tenth of the total poll, so it was not surprising that in those days the membership of the Dáil was scattered amongst a large number of parties and independents. Though Cumann na nGaedheal were in office for ten years, from 1922 to 1932, at no time did they hold more than 63 seats out of a total of 153.

The tendency since then has been for there to be a constant fall in the average size of constituencies: not for 40 years has any constituency held morethan five seats. This trend culminated in the redistribution carried out shortly after the 1973 election, by Jim Tully, Minister for Local Government in the new coalition government. More than half the total membership of the Dáil was now to be elected in 26 three-seat constituencies, and the number of five-seat constituencies was cut to six. One effect of these changes — and one certainly not intended by Mr Tully — was to enable Fianna Fáil to win an enormous and unprecedented 20-seat overall majority in the 1977 general election.

Since that result there have been a number of indecisive elections. There are, of course, political reasons for this, but an essential factor has been the major changes made in the size of the constituencies. These were brought about by an independent commission set up after the 1977 election. As a result of the proposals of this commission, the number of 3-seat constituencies was cut from 26 to 13: where there had been 13 three-seaters in Dublin city and county, there was now only one. The number of five-seat constituencies, on the other hand, was increased from six to 15.

In each of the four elections held since then, the influence of these changes has been clearly felt. There is no doubt, for example, that their effect in February 1987 was to prevent Fianna Fáil from gaining an overall majority. It has long been known that it is much more difficult for any party to obtain a majority of the seats in a five-seat constituency than in a three-seater, and this has been proven conclusively by the results of the recent election. Whereas Fianna Fáil gained a majority of the seats in nine out of the 13 three-seaters, they only gained a majority in four out of the 15 five-seaters. It was these large constituencies that led to the inconclusive result of the election.

The problems posed to political stability by the single transferable vote led in earlier years to two attempts (both by Fianna Fáil) to eliminate it from the Constitution, in 1959 and again in 1966. Their referendum proposal was rejected by a fairly narrow margin on the first occasion but when it was put to the people a second time, in 1966, it was heavily defeated. There was a number of reasons for these defeats. The electorate was used to the existing electoral system and felt that a sudden change-over to the straight vote system would be a leap in the dark. The voters were unwilling to lose their wide choice of candidates, each of whom could be given a preference, whereas under the proposed straight vote system they would be limited to putting an X in front of one candidate only. The arguments in favour of the need for political stability were weakened by the fact that in 1959 Fianna Fáil had a safe over-all majority, while by the time the second referendum was under way the party had already spent seven consecutive years in office. However, the really decisive factor in the double defeat of the straight vote was the general feeling (buttressed by some rather garbled statistics) that the introduction of the new system of election would lead to the permanent retention of Fianna Fáil in government with an enormous majority.

What then, of the future? It is obvious that there will never again be a proposal to introduce the straight vote into Irish elections. It is, on the other hand, possible that at some time in the future the main parties might agree to ask the people to amend the Constitution to allow the creation of single-seat constituencies, while retaining the single transferable vote. This is effectively the system now used for by-elections. It would have the advantage of making it very much easier to elect a stable government, while maintaining the electoral chances of minority parties.

The elimination of multi-member constituencies would end the wasteful rivalries between the various deputies sharing the constituency (and not least amongst those deputies belonging to the *same* party). Complaints are often made about the excessive clientilism of Irish politics — but this is largely caused by the existence of these multi-member constituencies. If someone is described as a ''good deputy'', it is not his parliamentary activities that are referred to but his efficiency as a sort of full-time ombudsman in his constituency.

Realism suggests, however, that any new proposal to change the election system is very unlikely to be introduced in the near future. There is, on the other hand, a general agreement that the nation is going through a grave social and economic crisis. There is a universal feeling that it may be some years before we finally emerge from this crisis, and that it is therefore essential that whatever governments are elected should have sufficient strength in the Dáil to enable them to govern. As a first step to ensuring this, should not something, then, be done about all those five-seat constituencies?

Simple Guide to the Count

The rules for the conduct of an election count are of a stupefying complexity, so what follows is a highly simplified account of what takes place:

1. All the valid first-preference votes are counted and the quota is fixed (see main text).

2. If any candidate reaches the quota on the first count, he or she is deemed to be elected. In order to transfer any surplus of votes he/she has received above the quota, *all* ballot papers are gone through again. The second-preference votes given to each of the other candidates are counted and placed in separate sub-parcels. Ignoring non-transferable votes, each of the other candidates is then given a share of this surplus in proportion to the percentage of second preference votes cast in their favour. The actual ballot papers to be handed on must in each case be taken from the *top* of the relevant sub-parcel.

3. If no further candidate reaches the quota after this procedure, then the candidate with the least votes will be eliminated and their (transferable) votes will be handed on to the recipients of their second or later preferences. This process will be continued, count by count, until someone else reaches the quota. This candidate in turn will now be deemed to be elected and their surplus will be distributed (as above), though in this case only the *last* sub-parcel of votes received by him or her will be considered. For example, if candidate A has 9,000 votes, the quota is 10,000, and he receives 2,000 votes on the elimination of candidate B, then he is deemed to be elected with a surplus of 1,000 votes. For the purpose of distributing this surplus only the ballot papers received by him from B will be considered.

4. The count will continue until all the seats allotted to that constituency have been filled. One or more candidates may on occasion be elected without reaching the quota: this happens if the point is reached that the number of seats still remaining to be filled is equal to the number of candidates still in the race if another elimination takes place.

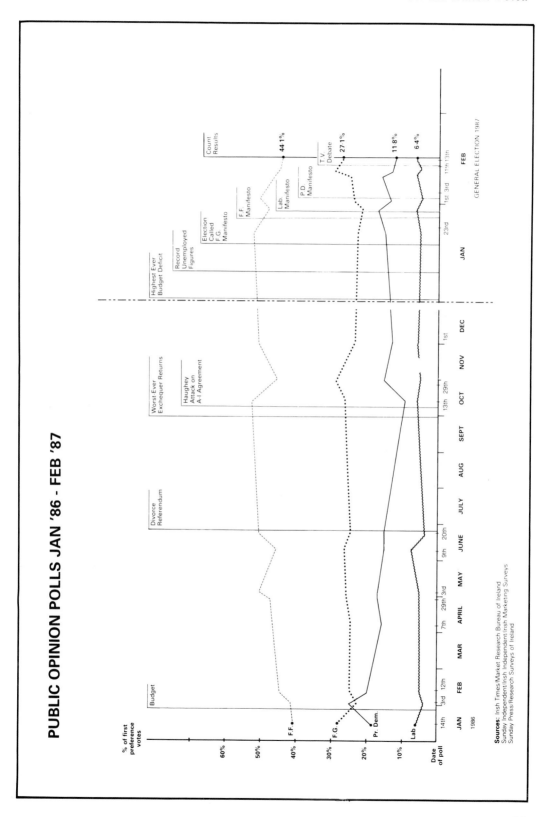

PUBLIC OPINION POLLS JAN '86 - FEB '87

Sources: Irish Times/Market Research Bureau of Ireland
Sunday Independent/Irish Independent/Irish Marketing Surveys
Sunday Press/Research Surveys of Ireland

The 25th Dáil: A Directory

---

*Denotes a re-elected sitting TD;
Bold type indicates the stage in the count at which a candidate was elected.
NT denotes non-transferable.

CARLOW KILKENNY (5)

Elected: *Liam Aylward (FF) **1st Count**; *M.J. Nolan (FF) **3rd Count**; *Seamus Pattison (LAB) **6th Count**; *Kieran Crotty (FG), Martin Gibbons (PD) **7th Count**.

Targeted by FF for a possible three seats, the gambit began to come unstuck as early as the selection convention. Party HQ wanted agricultural journalist Jimmy Brett on the ticket but they ended up with the two sitting TDs, and 48-year-old farmer Pat Millea from Tullaroan outside Kilkenny city. Fine Gael also had convention problems which played into the hands of the PDs and Lab, battling to retain Seamus Pattison's seat. Their South Kilkenny TD, Dick Dowling, was beaten for nomination by a 26-year-old insurance broker, Phil Hogan, and he refused FG's blandishments to be added to the ticket, leaving the way clear for FF's Liam Aylward to sweep up the vote in South Kilkenny.

This constituency provided rich pickings for the new PDs. They had strong candidates in both counties; Martin Gibbons, a farmer and son of long-serving TD for the constituency Jim Gibbons, in Kilkenny, and former FF member Michael Kearns in Carlow. Kearns had resigned from FF in protest at the expulsion of Des O'Malley and topped the poll as an Ind in the 1985 local elections. The big question was, would the PD vote transfer across the notoriously difficult hurdle of the county boundary? In the event it did handsomely, at a rate of 55 per cent when Michael Kearns was eliminated after the 3rd count, putting Martin Gibbons clear of Pat Millea and the Fine Gael candidates in a position to benefit from further transfers from FG's Senator John Browne and Millea on elimination. He was elected with Kieran Crotty on the 7th count.

Seamus Pattison defied the pundits once again, and justifiably gave them a tongue lashing on RTE radio's election special for writing him off in every election. He has mastered the art of survival, picking up vital transfers from all parties. This time he stood on his own, chalking up 1,700 extra votes on his first-preference total in Nov 1982, more or less taking all of the first-preference share which had gone to his Carlow running mate on that occasion.

FEB 87 % Poll		NOV 82 % Poll		Electorate:	78,410	
FF	44.4	FF	44.6	Total poll:	58,134	(74.1%)
FG	25.9	FG	36.1	Spoiled votes:	649	
PD	14.0	—	—	Total valid poll:	57,485	
LAB	12.8	LAB	13.5	Quota:	9,581	
WP	2.9	WP	3.9			
OTH	—	OTH	1.9	10 Candidates		

COUNTS	1st	2nd Aylward Surplus (1,192)	3rd Butleir Votes (1,694) (NT) (250)	4th Kearns Votes (3,675) (NT) (143)	5th Browne Votes (5,221) (NT) (337)	6th Millea Votes (6,592) (NT) (3357)	7th Pattison Surplus (766) (NT) (232)
Aylward L. (FF)	**10,773**						
Nolan M. (FF)	9,319	+210 9,529	+105 **9,634**				
Pattison S. (Lab)	7,358	+65 7,423	+638 8,061	+357 8,418	+544 8,962	+1,385 **10,347**	
Millea P. (FF)	5,435	+720 6,155	+195 6,350	+143 6,493	+99 6,592		
Hogan P. (FG)	5,376	+30 5,406	+73 5,479	+114 5,593	+1,107 6,700	+720 7,420	+184 7,604
Crotty K. (FG)	5,107	+46 5,153	+91 5,244	+126 5,370	+2563 7,933	+370 8,303	+141 **8,444**
Gibbons M. (PD)	4,511	+58 4,569	+197 4,766	+2016 6,782	+571 7,353	+760 8,113	+209 **8,322**
Browne J. (FG)	4,390	+19 4,409	+36 4,445	+776 5,221			
Kearns M. (PD)	3,552	+14 3,566	+109 3,675				
Butleir J. (WP)	1,664	+30 1,694					

LIAM AYLWARD (FF) First elected in 1977 when FF took three seats in Carlow Kilkenny, the only time the party had taken three of the five since 1957. He is a son of Councillor and Senator Bob Aylward (died 1974).
Home address: Aghaviller, Hugginstown, Co Kilkenny.
Tel: 056 28703; 01 606663.
Born: Knockmoylon, Mullinavat, Sept 1952.
Married: Kathleen Noonan. 2 sons, 2 daughters.
Education: St Kieran's College, Kilkenny.
Occupation: Public representative. Former laboratory technician. Member Kilkenny County Council since 1974; South Eastern Health Board; General Council of County Councils; GAA.

M.J. NOLAN (FF) First elected Nov 1982, the first time he contested the Dail. Taoiseach's nominee to Senate 1981-82. His father, Tom Nolan, was a long-serving TD for the area, Minister for State at Health and Social Welfare 1980, and Minister for Labour 1980-81.
Home address: Athy Road, Carlow; business address: Industrial Estate, Strawhall, Carlow.
Tel: Home 0503 42371; Business 0503 31777.
Born: Bagenalstown, Jan 1951.
Married: Mary Forde. 2 sons, 1 daughter.
Education: De La Salle, Bagenalstown; Mount St Joseph, Roscrea.
Occupation: Manufacturing confectioner. Public representative. Member Muine Bheag Town Commissioners 1972-85; Carlow County Council since 1979; Carlow UDC since 1985; GAA.

SEAMUS PATTISON (LAB) First elected 1961 after unsuccessfully contesting 1960 by-election. MEP from 1981-83 when he took the seat held by Liam Kavanagh in Leinster, upon the latter's appointment as Minister for Labour in Garret FitzGerald's first government. Minister of State at the Department of Social Welfare 1983-87.
Home address: 6 Upper New Street, Kilkenny.
Tel: 056 21295.
Born: Kilkenny, 1936.
Marital status: Single.
Education: St Kieran's College, Kilkenny; UCD.
Occupation: Public representative. Member Kilkenny County Council; Kilkenny Corporation since 1964.

MARTIN GIBBONS (PD) First elected Feb 1987. Son of Jim Gibbons, former FF TD for Carlow Kilkenny, and Minister for Defence and Agriculture. Elected to Kilkenny County Council in June 1985 as a FF councillor. He joined the PDs in Jan 1986.
Home address: Dunmore, Kilkenny.
Tel: 056 67818
Born: Kilkenny, Mar 1953.
Married: Catherine Hughes. 2 sons, 1 daughter.
Education: Dunmore NS; Colaiste na Rinne; Cistercian College, Roscrea.
Occupation: Farmer and public representative.

KIERAN CROTTY (FG) First elected 1969, succeeding to the seat held by his father, P.J. Crotty (1948-69). Parliamentary Secretary to the Minister for Industry and Commerce 1954-57. Chairman of the FG parliamentary party since 1977. Chairman of the Public Accounts Committee 1982.
Home address: Ayrefield, Granges Road, Kilkenny; business address: P.J. Crotty and Son, Rose Inn Street, Kilkenny.
Tel: Home 056 21626; Business 056 21099/21063
Born: Kilkenny, Aug 1930.
Married: Margaret Mulrooney. 1 son, 4 daughters.
Education: CBS, Kilkenny; St Kieran's College, Kilkenny.
Occupation: Public representative and baker.

CAVAN MONAGHAN (5)

Elected: *Rory O'Hanlon (FF), *John Wilson (FF) 4th Count; *Jim Leonard (FF), Andrew Boylan (FG) 5th Count. *Tom Fitzpatrick (FG) was the Ceann Comhairle of the outgoing Dáil and was automatically re-elected.

The constituency was effectively a four-seater because of the return of the Ceann Comhairle, and this made FG confident of taking two seats. But it turned into a particular disaster area for FG. The party's share of the first-preference vote fell more than 12 per cent and ignominiously succeeded only in electing one of the FG candidates in the field on the day, Andrew Boylan. Without even a PD challenge in this constituency the unpopularity of the government handed a sweet victory to the three outgoing FF TDs — one of whom was widely predicted would lose out because of the automatic return of Tom Fitzpatrick. Fine Gael's performance here was the worst for nearly twenty years. In 1969 and 1973 FG outpolled FF in the area, and even in the dark days of 1977 the first-preference share was 43.5 per cent. In all of the elections in the early eighties FG stayed above 40 per cent. Boylan, a farmer from Butlersbridge outside Cavan town, took most of Tom Fitzpatrick's Cavan vote as expected, but failed to add on a surplus to pass over the county boundary to John F. Conlan in Monaghan, a weaker area for FG. So first-timer Boylan took the sole FG seat won on the day, and veteran campaigner, John F. Conlan, who has held a seat in Monaghan since 1969 when he took over from James Dillon, was the loser. Fianna Fail's Jimmy Leonard took 47 per cent of SF's transfers (the SF candidate and Jimmy Leonard are both based in North Monaghan) to take three out of four on the fifth count. Fianna Fail's strategy of dividing up the constituency paid off — and anger in border areas about price differentials with the North helped to keep their share of the first-preference vote at 54.9 per cent, equalling the Nov 1982 performance which itself was a record. Fianna Fail workers were convinced that the Taoiseach's visit to the constituency, when he was alleged to have spoken of peoples' "right" to shop in the North, helped them.

FEB 87 % Poll		NOV 82 % Poll				
				Electorate:	75,742	
FF	54.9	FF	54.9	Total poll:	58,540	(77.3%)
FG	32.7	FG	44.9	Spoiled votes:	728	
PD	—	—	—	Total valid poll:	57,812	
LAB	—	LAB	—	Quota:	11,563	
WP	1.0	WP	—			
SF	7.3	—	—			
OTH	4.1	OTH	0.2	9 Candidates		

COUNTS	1st	2nd Duffy Votes (474)	3rd Rodgers Votes (603)	4th McKiernan Votes (2,051)	5th O Caolain Votes (4,673)
		(NT) (42)	(NT) (39)	(NT) (183)	(NT) (1810)
O'Hanlon R. (FF)	11,265	+41 11,306	+88 11,394	+263 **11,657**	
Wilson J.P. (FF)	11,163	+15 11,178	+72 11,250	+349 **11,599**	
Boylan A. (FG)	10,132	+43 10,175	+78 10,253	+393 10,646	+283 **10,929**
Leonard J. (FF)	9,319	+125 9,444	+54 9,498	+292 9,790	+2195 **11,985**
Conlan J.F. (FG)	8,795	+80 8,875	+58 8,933	+250 9,183	+385 9,568
O Caolain C. (SF)	4,219	+48 4,267	+85 4,352	+321 4,673	
McKiernan P. (TRL)	1,868	+54 1,922	+129 2,051		
Rodgers O. (WP)	577	+26 603			
Duffy P. (Ind)	474				

RORY O'HANLON (FF) First elected 1977. Appointed Minister of Health Mar 1987. Minister of State Department of Health and Social Welfare 1982. Member Dáil Public Accounts Committee.
Home address: Carrickmacross, Co Monaghan.
Tel: Home 042 61530; Business 042 61227.
Born: Dublin 1934.
Married: Teresa Ward. 4 sons, 2 daughters.
Education: St Mary's College, Dundalk; Blackrock College Dublin; UCD.
Occupation: Public representative, doctor. Member Monaghan County Council since 1979. Medical representative of the North-Eastern Health Board; Fellow of the Royal Academy of Medicine.

JOHN WILSON (FF) First elected 1973. Appointed Minister for Communications March 1987. Minister for Transport and Minister for Posts and Telegraphs 1982; Minister for Education 1977-81. Opposition spokesman on Education and the Arts 1973-77.
Home address: The Bungalow, Kilgolah, Co Cavan.
Tel: 049 31299.
Born: Callanagh, Kilcogy, Co Cavan 1923.
Married: Ita Ward. 1 son, 4 daughters.
Education: St Mel's College, Longford; University of London; National University of Ireland.
Occupation: Public representative. Former secondary teacher and university lecturer. Past President Association of Secondary Teachers of Ireland; Member European Association of Teachers. Member GAA. Former footballer; 5 Ulster Championship medals, 2 All-Ireland medals, 1 National League medal.

JIM LEONARD (FF) First elected in 1973, he was re-elected in Feb 1982 after losing his seat in Jun 1981. Senator 1981-82. He was opposition frontbench spokesman on Tourism 1975-77. Lost Dail seat to hunger striker Kieran Doherty, H-Block candidate in 1981 general election.
Home address: Stranagarvagh, Smithborough, Co Monaghan; business address: 3, Park Street, Monaghan.
Tel: Home 047 57020; Business 047 82288.
Born: Stranagarvagh, June 1927.
Married: Tess Goodwin. 3 sons, 2 daughters.
Education: Magherarney NS, Smithborough.
Occupation: Public representative, farmer and auctioneer. Member Monaghan County Council since 1974; North Eastern Health Board; Federation of Health Boards; Acot County Committee of Agriculture and General Council of Committees of Agriculture. Member Council of Europe; New Ireland Forum.

ANDREW BOYLAN (FG) First elected 1987. Member Cavan County Council since 1974.
Home address: Derrygarra, Butlersbridge, Co Cavan.
Tel: 049 31747.
Born: Butlersbridge 1939.
Married: Margo Galligan. 4 boys, 1 girl.
Education: Butlersbridge NS; Rockwell College, Tipperary.
Occupation: Public representative and farmer. Chairman Cavan Vocational Education Parents' Committee; Vice Chairman of Killeshandra Co-Op. Chairman Spina Bifida Organisation Cavan Monaghan since 1970.

TOM FITZPATRICK (FG) First elected 1965. Ceann Comhairle 1982-87. Senator 1961-65. Minister for Lands 1973-76; Minister for Transport and Power 1976-77; Minister for Fisheries and Forestry 1981-82.

Home address: Rathanna, Drumleis, Co Cavan.

Tel: Home 049 31451; Business 01 789911.

Born: Scotshouse, Clones, Co Monaghan, 1918.

Married: Betty Cullen (dec.). 2 daughters. Carmel McDonald. 1 son.

Education: St Macartan's College, Monaghan; Incorporated Law Society; UCD.

Occupation: Public representative. Former solicitor. Chairman Civil Service and Local Appointment Commission since 1982; Committee on Procedure and Privileges since 1982; Comhairle na Mire Gaile. Member Incorporated Law Society of Ireland since 1939.

CLARE (4)

Elected: Sile de Valera (FF), *Donal Carey (FG), *Brendan Daly (FF) 6th Count; *Madeleine Taylor-Quinn (FG) 8th Count.

A major upset for FF here. The party confidently expected to return three deputies in this stronghold. But the wily FG defenders, Carey and Taylor-Quinn, managed to fight off the challenge with just 28 per cent of the first-preference vote. The PDs pulled in an impressive 11.8 per cent and helped save Madeleine Taylor-Quinn's seat by passing on 52 per cent of their transfers. Fine Gael conceded before the election that it was the most marginal constituency, and could be lost by "a puff of wind". However, with FF needing just a tiny swing on their Nov '82 result to take three out of four, the party in fact dropped 3.3 per cent. Fianna Fail may have been mistaken in running four candidates. It was close. On the 7th count, Madeleine Taylor-Quinn was 984 votes behind FF's Frank Barrett and only 274 ahead of the PD's O'Keeffe. The Barrett name did not carry the day for young Frank after his father Sylvester opted for Europe. Sylvester Barrett had held a seat for FF in Clare since the by-election in 1968.

FEB 87 % Poll		NOV 82 % Poll		Electorate:	64,303	
FF	52.8	FF	56.1	Total Poll:	47,736	(74.2%)
FG	28.0	FG	32.8	Spoiled votes	363	
PD	11.8	—	—	Total valid poll:	47,373	
LAB	1.3	LAB	5.2			
OTH	6.1	OTH	5.9	Quota:	9,475	
				11 Candidates.		

COUNTS	1st	2nd O'Shaughnessy Votes (600) (NT) (33)	3rd Makowski Votes (716) (NT) (76)	4th Brennan Votes (2,514) (NT) (180)	5th Meaney Votes (2,870) (NT) (38)	6th O'Rourke Votes (4,060) (NT) (86)	7th DeValera Surplus (856)	8th O'Keeffe Votes (5,583) (NT) (1,685)
De Valera S. (FF)	8,530	*+36* 8,566	*+127* 8,693	*+277* 8,970	*+62* 9,032	*+1299* **10,331**		
Carey D. (FG)	8,045	*+84* 8,129	*+63* 8,192	*+742* 8,934	*+303* 9,237	*+435* **9,672**		
Daly B. (FF)	7,897	*+31* 7,928	*+50* 7,978	*+320* 8,298	*+90* 8,388	*+1144* **9,532**		
Taylor-Quinn M. (FG)	5,229	*+99* 5,328	*+20* 5,348	*+147* 5,495	*+162* 5,657	*+157* 5,814	*+43* 5,857	*+2885* **8,742**
Barrett F. (FF)	4,799	*+22* 4,821	*+51* 4,872	*+330* 5,202	*+59* 5,261	*+791* 6,052	*+789* 6,841	*+1013* 7,854
O'Rourke J. (FF)	3,796	*+16* 3,812	*+46* 3,858	*+131* 3,989	*+71* 4,060			
O'Keeffe D. (PD)	3,069	*+65* 3,134	*+54* 3,188	*+138* 3,326	*+2085* 5,411	*+148* 5,559	*+24* 5,583	
Meaney T. (PD)	2,534	*+39* 2,573	*+48* 2,621	*+249* 2,870				
Brennan T. (Ind)	2,230	*+103* 2,333	*+181* 2,514					
Makowski B. (NLJAG)	644	*+72* 716						
O'Shaughnessy T. (Lab)	600							

SILE DE VALERA (FF) First elected in 1977 as the youngest ever member of Dáil Éireann 1977-81. She was also the youngest member elected to the European Parliament 1979-84. Member Procedure and Privileges Committee; Joint Committee on EEC Legislation.
Home address: Charton, Kerrymount Ave, Dublin 18.
Born: 1955.
Marital status: Single.
Education: Loreto Convent Foxrock, Co Dublin. UCD.
Occupation: Public representative and student. Grand-daughter of the late President De Valera.

BRENDAN DALY (FF) First elected 1973, when he won the Clare FF seat previously held by President Hillery. Appointed Minister for Tourism, Fisheries and Forestry Feb 1987. Minister for Fisheries and Forestry 1982.
Home address: Cooraclare, Kilrush, Co Clare.
Tel: 065 59040.
Born: Cooraclare, Co Clare, Feb 1940.
Married: Patricia Carmody. 2 sons, 1 daughter.
Education: Kilrush CBS.
Occupation: Public representative.
Member Clare Tourist Council; Clare Fisheries Development Committee; West Clare Industrial Development Committee.

DONAL CAREY (FG) First elected Feb 1982. Member Oireachtas Joint Services Committee; Joint Committee on Legislation. Member Clare County Council since 1974.
Home address: Thomond Villas, Clarecastle, Ennis; business address: Friary Bow, Ennis, Co Clare.
Tel: Home 065 22191; Business 065 29683.
Born: Ennis, October 1937.
Married: Evelyn Forde. 2 sons, 1 daughter.
Education: St Flannan's College, Ennis; UCD.
Occupation: Public representative. Former cost controller. Member Muintir na Tíre; Ennis and District Round Table; GAA.

MADELEINE TAYLOR-QUINN (FG) First elected 1981. Senator 1982. Member Oireachtas Joint Committees on Women's Rights and Marriage Breakdown. Member Clare County Council since 1979.
Home address: Francies Street, Kilrush, Co Clare.
Tel: 065 51656.
Born: Kilkee, Co Clare, Jun 1951.
Married: George Quinn.
Education: Convent of Mercy Secondary School, Kilrush; UCD; Law School of the Incorporated Law Society of Ireland.
Occupation: Public representative. Former secondary school teacher.
Member Mid-Western Regional Development Organisation; West Clare Tourist Development Association. Joint Honorary Secretary of Fine Gael 1979-81; founder member Young Fine Gael.

CORK EAST (4)

Elected: *Michael Ahern (FF) 2nd Count; *Ned O'Keeffe (FF), *Paddy Hegarty (FG), Joe Sherlock (WP) 4th Count.

The scene was set here for the re-election of the WP's Joe Sherlock when, back in the 1985 local elections, he headed the poll in the Mallow area with a massive vote, more than 1,000 over the quota. That, combined with FG's loss of their poll-topper, Myra Barry, who resigned from politics aged just 30 after seven years in the Dáil, gave the WP their opening. Before the election, FG were worried about defending her seat without a Barry — her father Dick Barry held a seat in the area from 1973-81. Their fears were justified. On the 1st count Joe Sherlock was over 1,000 votes ahead of FG's Paul Bradford, and he stayed ahead throughout. He took 629 of PD John Guinevan's transfers to reach the quota on the 4th count with O'Keeffe and Hegarty.

FEB 87 % Poll		NOV 82 %Poll		Electorate:	55,767	
				Total poll:	42,160	(75.6%)
				Spoiled votes:	390	
FF	39.1	FF	39.4	Total valid poll:	41,770	
FG	30.5	FG	42.5	Quota:	8,355	
PD	10.2	—	—			
LAB	2.1	LAB	2.9			
WP	16.7	WP	14.9			
SF	1.3	—	—			
OTH	—	OTH	0.3	9 Candidates		

COUNTS	1st	2nd Hobbs McCarthy Votes (1,422)	3rd Hall Votes (2,090)	4th Guinevan Votes (3,517)
		(NT) (105)	(NT) (82)	(NT) (450)
O'Keeffe N. (FF)	8,178	+75 8,253	+87 8,340	+522 **8,862**
Ahern M. (FF)	8,169	+188 **8,357**		
Sherlock J. (WP)	6,986	+561 7,547	+181 7,728	+629 **8,357**
Hegarty P. (FG)	6,831	+233 7,064	+400 7,464	+965 **8,429**
Bradford P. (FG)	5,908	+76 5,984	+193 6,177	+951 7,128
Guinevan J. (PD)	2,340	+30 2,370	+1,147 3,517	
Hall H. (PD)	1,936	+154 2,090		
Hobbs T. (Lab)	888			
McCarthy K. (SF)	534			

MICHAEL AHERN (FF) First elected in Feb 1982. Member of Select Committee on Public Accounts since 1982.
Home Address: Libermann, Barryscourt, Carrigtwohill, Co Cork; business address: 114 North Main St, Youghal, Co Cork. Tel: 021 883592.
Born: Dungourney, Co Cork, Jan 1949.
Married: Margaret Monahan. 3 daughters.
Education: Rockwell College, Cashel, Co Tipperary; UCD.
Occupation: Public representative, auditor and accountant. Son of the late Liam Ahern, Senator 1957-73 and Deputy for Cork North East 1973-74. Grand-nephew of John Dineen, Farmers' Party Dáil Deputy 1922-27. Member GAA.

NED O'KEEFFE (FF) First elected Nov 1982. Fianna Fáil deputy spokesman on Industry.
Home address: Ballylough, Mitchelstown, Co Cork.
Tel: 022 25255.
Born: Mitchelstown, Aug 1942.
Married: Ann Theresa Buckley. 3 sons, 2 daughters.
Education: Ballindangan NS; Darra Agricultural College, Clonakilty, Co Cork; UCC.
Occupation: Public representative, company director and farmer.
Director Mitchelstown Co-Operative Society 1974-82; Agricultural Credit Corporation 1980-82. Member Macra na Feirme 1958-71; Irish Farmers' Association 1969-82; GAA.

JOE SHERLOCK (WP) First elected in June 1981. Re-elected in Feb 1982 but narrowly lost his seat in Nov '82.
Home address: 20 Blackwater Drive, Mallow, Co Cork.
Tel: 022 21053.
Born: Kildorrery, Co Cork, Sept 1935.
Married: Ellen Spillane. 2 sons, 1 daughter.
Educated: Graigue Kildorrery NS.
Occupation: Public representative. Former Irish Sugar Company employee. Member Mallow Urban District Council since 1967; currently Chairman. Member Cork County Council since 1974; Southern Health Board; County Cork VEC. Part-time branch secretary of the Mallow No. 2 Branch of the ITGWU.

PADDY HEGARTY (FG) First elected 1973. Fine Gael spokesman on Tourism, 1979-81; on Agriculture 1982. Minister of State at Departments of Agriculture, Industry and Commerce 1982-87.
Home address: Ballinvoher, Cloyne, Co Cork.
Tel: Home 021 652578; Business 01 789911.
Born: Ballinvoher, Co Cork, Dec 1926.
Married: Eileen Burns. 5 sons, 2 daughters.
Education: St Colman's College, Fermoy.
Occupation: Public representative, farm owner. Member Cork County Council 1974-85. Member IFA since 1960; Cork County Committee of Agriculture since 1974.

CORK NORTH CENTRAL (5)

Elected: *Dan Wallace (FF) 1st Count; *Denis Lyons (FF), Mairin Quill (PD) 10th Count; *Bernard Allen (FG), *Liam Burke (FG) 12th Count.

From the time of the Nov '86 poll in the *Cork Examiner* showing the PDs with 23 per cent in North Central, it was on the cards that the new party would take a seat here. The question was, at whose expense? In the event the widely predicted victim, Lab, was the party to suffer. The party's former TD in this constituency, Toddy O'Sullivan, no doubt seeing the writing on the wall, emigrated to South Central and the torch was carried by two candidates who divided the Lab vote. One, the Lord Mayor, Gerry O'Sullivan, survived to the 12th count. Then, however, nearly 50 per cent of the WP's vote proved non-transferable, ensuring the return of Liam Burke (FG) with his party colleague Bernard Allen, both without reaching a quota. With one candidate, Lab might have stood a better chance of holding their seat at FG's expense. Fianna Fáil had hopes of taking three seats, but their vote dropped 5.3 per cent. The party is still a long way off returning to the days of Jack Lynch in Cork city when they won over half the vote and a majority of the seats. In the Cork city and county area, FF took just 8 seats — the same result as in Nov 1982. It is generally felt that FF should take at least 10 out of the 20 seats in the area to be on the way to an overall majority.

FEB 87 % Poll		NOV 82 % Poll		Electorate:	63,517	
FF	37.2	FF	42.5	Total poll:	43,970	(69.2%)
FG	26.2	FG	36.0	Spoiled votes:	627	
PD	16.7	—	—	Total valid poll:	43,343	
LAB	8.6	LAB	13.1	Quota:	7,224	
WP	6.1	WP	4.3			
SF	1.6	—	—			
OTH	3.6	OTH	4.0	17 Candidates.		

COUNTS	1st	2nd Wallace Surplus (285)	3rd M Murphy N Murphy O'Connell Votes (311) (NT) (19)	4th Tobin Votes (603) (NT) (47)	5th O'Leary Votes (732) (NT) (100)	6th B. Murphy Votes (917) (NT) (208)	7th O'Callaghan Votes (1,295) (NT) (75)	8th Whyte Votes (1,397) (NT) (81)	9th McCarthy Votes (2,356) (NT) (73)	10th Black Votes (3,158) (NT) (224)	11th Lyons Surplus (1,210) (NT) (543)	12th Kelleher Votes (3,663) (NT) (1,785)
Wallace D. (FF)	**7,509**											
Allen B. (FG)	5,934	*+16* 5,950	*+15* 5,965	*+70* 6,035	*+31* 6,066	*+89* 6,155	*+118* 6,273	*+51* 6,324	*+207* 6,531	*+132* 6,663	*+119* 6,782	*+510* **7,292**
Burke L. (FG)	5,438	*+8* 5,446	*+5* 5,451	*+35* 5,486	*+18* 5,504	*+58* 5,562	*+42* 5,604	*+34* 5,638	*+139* 5,777	*+70* 5,847	*+99* 5,946	*+266* **6,212**
Quill M. (PD)	5,046	*+13* 5,059	*+10* 5,069	*+89* 5,158	*+18* 5,176	*+82* 5,258	*+75* 5,333	*+98* 5,431	*+1665* 7,096	*+140* **7,236**		
Lyons D. (FF)	5,039	*+94* 5,133	*+19* 5,152	*+28* 5,180	*+69* 5,249	*+38* 5,287	*+98* 5,385	*+517* 5,902	*+124* 6,026	*+2,408* **8,434**		
Kelleher J. (WP)	2,628	*+6* 2,634	*+91* 2,725	*+84* 2,809	*+158* 2,967	*+172* 3,139	*+116* 3,255	*+51* 3,306	*+48* 3,354	*+99* 3,453	*+210* 3,663	
O'Sullivan G. (Lab)	2,553	*+14* 2,567	*+24* 2,591	*+49* 2,640	*+48* 2,688	*+78* 2,766	*+685* 3,451	*+49* 3,500	*+74* 3,574	*+85* 3,659	*+239* 3,898	*+1,102* 5,000
Black P. (FF)	2,435	*+58* 2,493	*+9* 2,502	*+27* 2,529	*+44* 2,573	*+39* 2,612	*+29* 2,641	*+491* 3,132	*+26* 3,158			
McCarthy J. (PD)	2,199	*+3* 2,202	*+5* 2,207	*+28* 2,235	*+17* 2,252	*+45* 2,297	*+34* 2,331	*+25* 2,356				
O'Callaghan J. (Lab)	1,167	*+4* 1,171	*+15* 1,186	*+22* 1,208	*+32* 1,240	*+55* 1,295						
Whyte A. (FF)	1,144	*+60* 1,204	*+3* 1,207	*+50* 1,257	*+64* 1,321	*+53* 1,374	*+23* 1,397					
Murphy B. (Ind)	684	*+4* 688	*+39* 727	*+57* 784	*+133* 917							
O'Leary D. (SF)	681	*+2* 683	*+32* 715	*+17* 732								
Tobin D. (Ind)	576	*+2* 578	*+25* 603									
Murphy N. (CPI)	182	*+0* 182										
O'Connell C. (Ind)	75	*+1* 76										
Murphy M. (Ind)	53	*+0* 53										

MAIRIN QUILL (PD) First elected in 1987. Member of Cork Corporation since 1979. Member of the Housing Committee; Environmental Committee; Fota Wildlife Committee; City of Cork VEC. Former member FF.
Home address: 1 Wellesley Terrace, Wellington Road, Cork.
Tel: 021 502099.
Education: UCC.
Occupation: Public representative and secondary school teacher. Alderman Cork Corporation. Member of the Board of Management North Infirmary; Board of Management Mayfield Community School; Regional Committee Rehabilitation Institute. Regional Chairman of Rehabilitation Inst. 1982-84.

DENIS LYONS (FF) First elected in 1981. Appointed Minister of State at the Department of Tourism Feb 1987. Deputy spokesman on Education 1983-84. Frontbench spokesman on Industry and Employment since 1984.
Home address: Tower, Blarney, Co Cork.
Tel: 021 85299.
Born: Cork, Aug 1935.
Married: Catherine McCarthy. 2 sons, 4 daughters.
Education: North Monastery, Cork.
Occupation: Public representative. Formerly self-employed. Member Cork County Council since 1972; Joint Committee Cork Corporation and Cork County Council since 1983; Management Board of Cork North and South Infirmaries (current Chairman of South Infirmary); South-West Regional Development Board. Former Trade Union Officer. GAA member.

DAN WALLACE (FF) First elected Nov 1982. Lord Mayor of Cork 1985-86. Member Cork Corporation since 1979. Chairman of the Housing Committee. Member Environment; Community; Finance Planning and Development Committees. Member Southern Health Board; North Infirmary Board of Management; Cork Voluntary Hospitals Board.
Home address: 13 Killeen's Place, Farranree, Cork.
Tel: 021 507465.
Born: Cork, Jun 1942.
Married: Ethel Sutton. 2 sons, 3 daughters.
Education: North Presentation Convent; North Monastery; School of Commerce, Cork.
Occupation: Public representative.

LIAM BURKE (FG) First elected 1969. Senator 1977-79. Member Cork City Council since 1967. Member Joint Oireachtas Committee on Secondary Legislation of the European Communities.
Home address: The Grove, Douglas Hall, Cork.
Tel: 021 292707.
Born: Cork 1928.
Married: Noreen Casey. 2 daughters.
Education: Christian Brothers Secondary School, Cork.
Occupation: Public representative. Member Cork Health Authority since 1967; South West Regional Development Authority since 1974.

BERNARD ALLEN (FG) First elected 1981. Alderman Cork City Council since 1979. Member Joint Oireachtas Committee on Public Expenditure. Fine Gael spokesman on Environmental Protection 1982.
Home address: 27 Halldene Grove, Bishopstown, Cork.
Tel: 021 46689.
Born: Cork 1944.
Married: Marie Dorney. 3 daughters.
Education: North Monastery, Cork; Cork Technical College; UCC.
Occupation: Public representative. Former laboratory technologist.

CORK NORTH WEST (3)

Elected: *Frank Crowley (FG) 2nd Count; *Donal Creed (FG), *Donal Moynihan (FF) 3rd Count.

This was one of the key marginal constituencies, and FF expected their candidate Jack Roche would pick up a second seat for the party. There was no Lab candidate, and FF only had two candidates, instead of three as in the last election. Their candidates this time were also strategically placed. But FG's strong organisation held off the challenge. The party general secretary, Finbar Fitzpatrick, was a former organiser here and before the election he defied the pundits, predicting that the party would retain its two seats. The FG man considered at risk was Frank Crowley, but the party push, including 1,000 canvassers according to local organiser John Donegan, some from Britain, worked well for Crowley and he ended up nearly 374 votes ahead of his party colleague and former poll-topper Donal Creed on the 1st count. But with just 548 votes separating FF and FG on the last count this constituency must still be considered a marginal.

FEB 87 % Poll		NOV 82 % Poll		Electorate:	41,441	
				Total poll:	33,688	(81.3%)
FF	45.3	FF	44.4	Spoiled votes:	284	
FG	43.4	FG	48.9	Total valid poll:	33,404	
PD	11.4	—	—	Quota:	8,352	
LAB	—	LAB	6.6	5 Candidates.		

COUNTS	1st	2nd O'Riordan Votes (3,796)	3rd Crowley Surplus (166)
		(NT) 287	
		+566	+12
Moynihan D. (FF)	7,777	8,343	8,355
		+1,087	
Crowley F. (FG)	7,431	8,518	
		+564	+24
Roche J. (FF)	7,343	7,907	7,931
		+1,292	+130
Creed D. (FG)	7,057	8,349	8,479
O'Riordan S. (PD)	3,796		

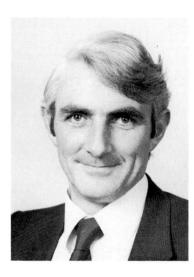

DONAL MOYNIHAN (FF) First elected 1982. Member Cork County Council since 1970.
Home address: Gortnascorty, Ballymakeera, Co Cork.
Tel: 026 45019.
Born: Ballymakeera, Oct 1941.
Married: Catherine Twomey. 4 sons, 5 daughters.
Education: Coolea NS; Ballyvourney Vocational School.
Occupation: Public representative and farmer. Member Cork VEC; Southern Health Board; General Council of County Councils; ACOT.

FRANK CROWLEY (FG) First elected 1981. Member Cork County Council since 1974. Member Joint Oireachtas Committee on Co-Operation with Developing Countries 1982-87.
Home address: Derrygowna, Banteer, Co Cork; business address: Main St, Kanturk, Co Cork.
Tel: Home 022 27157; Business 029 50392.
Born: Cork, May 1939.
Married: Winifred MacCarthy. 1 son, 1 daughter.
Education: Mungret College, Limerick.
Occupation: Public representative. Member Cork VEC since 1974; Cork County Committee of Agriculture since 1974.

DONAL CREED (FG) First elected 1965. Minister of State Department of Education 1982-87; Department of Health 1981; Department of the Environment 1981-82. Fine Gael Chief Whip 1977-79. Frontbench spokesman on Defence 1979-81; on Agriculture 1969-71; on Social Welfare 1971-73. Member European Parliament 1973-77. Member Dáil and Seanad Joint Committee on Secondary Legislation of the European Parliament 1973-77.
Home address: Codrum House, Macroom, Co Cork.
Tel: Home 026 41177; Business 01 789911.
Born: Macroom, Co Cork 1924.
Married: Madeleine Kelleher. 1 son, 6 daughters.
Education: De la Salle School, Macroom; UCC.
Occupation: Public representative and farm owner.

CORK SOUTH CENTRAL (5)

Elected: *Pearse Wyse (PD) 1st Count; John Dennehy (FF), *Peter Barry (FG) 9th Count; Batt O'Keeffe (FF), *Toddy O'Sullivan (LAB) 10th Count.

Here in Peter Barry's base, the FG vote dropped by a huge 18.2 per cent, and Hugh Coveney lost his seat. FF were down 6.9 per cent. Both of the major parties lost to the PDs who took a 25 per cent share of the poll. However the PDs were never in the reckoning for a second seat because of a totally unbalanced vote. Former FF TD Pearse Wyse had nearly 11,000 first preferences while his running mate, Owen Curtin, had only 3,100. This allowed Hugh Coveney to benefit from Curtin's transfers and come within 569 votes of Lab's Toddy O'Sullivan for the last seat. However, O'Sullivan's move to the South city constituency to hold Eileen Desmond's seat paid off. He held it with a party vote reduced by 4.5 per cent, aided by 1,000 transfers from the WP. Fianna Fáil took two seats, holding Gene Fitzgerald's (he had opted for Europe) and regaining the seat they lost when Pearse Wyse defected to the PDs. But the party has a long way to go to recover the ground they've lost since 1977 when FF won 58.6 per cent of the vote in the Cork city area.

FEB 87 % Poll		NOV 82 % Poll		Electorate:	75,322	
FF	32.8	FF	39.7	Total poll:	56,703	(75.3%)
FG	21.8	FG	40.0	Spoiled Votes:	444	
PD	25.0	—	—	Total valid poll:	56,259	
LAB	8.6	LAB	13.1	Quota:	9,377	
WP	4.2	WP	3.0			
SF	—	—	—			
OTH	7.6	OTH	4.2	16 Candidates		

COUNTS	1st	2nd M Murphy B Murphy O'Donovan	3rd Wyse	4th Dunphy	5th Hennessy	6th Lynch	7th Martin	8th Curtain	9th Cogan	10th Dennehy
		Votes (1,473)	Surplus (1,558)	Votes (1,402)	Votes (1,969)	Votes (2,940)	Votes (4,219)	Votes (5,168)	Votes (5,723)	Surplus (2,736)
		(NT) (88)		(NT) (107)	(NT) (179)	(NT) (584)	(NT) (251)	(NT) (1017)	(NT) (458)	
Wyse P. (PD)	**10,935**									
Barry P. (FG)	7,328	+121 7,449	+121 7,570	+123 7,693	+267 7,960	+129 8,089	+118 8,207	+1,136 9,343	+198 **9,541**	
Dennehy J. (FF)	6,099	+86 6,185	+79 6,264	+54 6,318	+107 6,425	+313 6,738	+1,733 8,471	+360 8,831	+3,282 **12,113**	
Coveney H. (FG)	4,926	+97 5,023	+94 5,117	+128 5,245	+285 5,530	+107 5,637	+80 5,717	+1,335 7,052	+356 7,408	+92 7,500
O'Sullivan T. (Lab)	4,862	+183 5,045	+114 5,159	+178 5,337	+270 5,607	+1,000 6,607	+315 6,922	+751 7,673	+279 7,952	+117 **8,069**
O'Keeffe B. (FF)	4,437	+70 4,507	+45 4,552	+33 4,585	+56 4,641	+122 4,763	+950 5,713	+321 6,034	+1,150 7,184	+2,527 **9,711**
Cogan B. (FF)	4,305	+62 4,367	+36 4,403	+111 4,514	+207 4,721	+114 4,835	+640 5,475	+248 5,723		
Martin M. (FF)	3,619	+91 3,710	+44 3,754	+57 3,811	+98 3,909	+310 4,219				
Curtain E. (PD)	3,112	+183 3,295	+950 4,245	+179 4,424	+351 4,775	+261 5,036	+132 5,168			
Lynch K. (WP)	2,349	+190 2,539	+27 2,566	+225 2,791	+149 2,940					
Hennessy C. (Ind)	1,585	+154 1,739	+23 1,762	+207 1,969						
Dunphy M. (Ind)	1,229	+148 1,377	+25 1,402							
Beausang S. (Ind)	756									
Murphy B. (Ind)	441									
O'Donovan C. (Ind)	245									
Murphy M. (Ind)	31									

PEARSE WYSE (PD) First elected in 1965 for FF. Parliamentary secretary to the Minister for Finance 1977-78 and Minister of State at the Department of Finance 1978-79. Opposition frontbench spokesman on Youth and Community Care 1973-77. Member Committee on Procedure and Privileges 1969-77. Member Cork Corporation since 1960; Lord Mayor of Cork 1967-68 and 1974-75. Member Southern Health Board since 1971.
Home address: Shanoon, Dunmore Lawn, Boreenmanna Road, Cork.
Tel: 021 295493.
Born: March 1928.
Married: Theresa Lucey. 1 son.
Education: Cork School of Commerce.
Occupation: Public representative. Former printing works manager. Member Irish Bookbinder's and Allied Trader's Union. Vice President of Cork County Board. President Cork Community Games since 1972. Member Advisory Committee Southern Health Board; Vice-Chairman Cork/Kerry Regional Development Authority.

BATT O'KEEFFE (FF) First elected 1987. Elected to Cork County Council in June, 1985.
Home address: 8 Westcliffe, Balincollig.
Tel: 021 871393
Married: Mary Murphy. 1 son, 3 daughters.
Occupation: Public representative and lecturer in General studies and Communication in Cork Regional College. Member of Cork County VEC Sports Advisory Body. Cork footballer and holder of Munster Medals at under-21, junior and senior levels. Cork County intermediate handball champion 1980.

TODDY O'SULLIVAN (LAB) First elected for Cork North Central in 1981. Former Lord Mayor of Cork. Junior Minister at the Department of the Environment 1986-87. Spokesman for Labour on Communications, particularly local radio. Member Cork Corporation since 1974.
Home address: 92 Barrack Street, Cork.
Tel: 021 962788.
Born: Cork, Nov 1935.
Married: Esther Chandley. 2 daughters, 1 son.
Education: Greenmount NS; School of Commerce and Domestic Science, Cork.
Occupation: Public representative.

JOHN DENNEHY (FF) First elected 1987. Lord Mayor of Cork 1983-84.
Home address: "Avondale", Westside Estate, Togher, Cork.
Tel: 021 962908.
Born: Togher 1941.
Married: Phil Martin. 5 boys, 2 girls.
Education: Scoil Chríost Rí (Turners Cross); Sharman Crawford Technical School, Cork; Municipal School of Commerce.
Occupation: Public representative and engineering supervisor. Alderman Cork Corporation 1985. Chairman Southern Health Board since 1985. Chairman Cork Corporation Community Development Committee. Member Cork Enterprise Board and its executive committee. One of the initiators of the "Cork 800".

PETER BARRY (FG) First elected 1969. Minister for Foreign Affairs 1982-87; Minister for the Environment 1981-82; Minister for Education 1976-77; Minister for Transport and Power 1973-76. Frontbench spokesman on Environment 1982; on Finance 1977-80; on Labour 1972-73. Deputy leader of Fine Gael since 1979. Co-Chairman Intergovernmental Conference set up under Anglo-Irish Agreement Nov 1985-Mar 1987.
Home address: Sherwood, Blackrock, Cork.
Tel: Home 021 292242; Business 01 789911
Born: Cork 1928.
Married: Margaret O'Mullane. 4 sons, 2 daughters.
Education: Christian Brothers College, Cork.
Occupation: Public representative. Former tea importer and wholesaler, tea-taster. Alderman Cork City Council 1969-73; Lord Mayor of Cork 1961-62 and 1970-71. Senator 1957-61. Son of Anthony Barry, TD for Cork 1954-57 and 1961-65.

CORK SOUTH WEST (3)

Elected: *Joe Walsh (FF) 1st Count; *Jim O'Keeffe (FG) 2nd Count; *P.J. Sheehan (FG) 4th Count.

Fianna Fáil devised a strategy of dividing the constituency between Denis O'Donovan in the west and sitting TD Joe Walsh in the east, in an effort to prise an extra seat out of this area. However, despite out-polling FG, they failed. There were reports of poaching by the respective FF candidates which would undermine the vote management strategy — and by all accounts the two ran separate campaigns. Joe Walshe had a surplus of 1,100 first preferences and most of these went to his running mate. But FG divided up the constituency and balanced the vote of their two men. They scooped nearly 75 per cent of the PD transfers and saw P.J. Sheehan and Minister of State Jim O'Keeffe back to the Dáil.

FEB 87 % Poll		NOV 82 % Poll		Electorate:	42,956	
				Total poll:	33,679	(78.4%)
FF	45.3	FF	41.7	Spoiled votes:	277	
FG	43.6	FG	49.8	Total valid poll:	33,402	
PD	10.7	—	—	Quota:	8,351	
OTH	0.4	OTH	8.4	6 Candidates.		

COUNTS	1st	2nd O'Neill Davies Votes (3,704)	3rd Walsh Surplus (1,137)	4th O'Keeffe Surplus (1,063)
		(NT) (354)		
Walsh J. (FF)	**9,488**			
O'Keeffe J. (FG)	7,814	*+1,600* **9,414**		
Sheehan P.J. (FG)	6,752	*+1,042* 7,794	*+178* 7,972	*+925* **8,897**
O'Donovan D. (FF)	5,644	*+708* 6,352	*+959* 7,113	*+138* 7,449
O'Neill R. (PD)	3,570			
Davies S.G. (Ind)	134			

JOE WALSH (FF) First elected in 1977. Appointed Minister of State Department of Agriculture (Food Industry) Mar 1987. He has held his seat since then with the exception of the period Jun 1981 to Feb 1982. Senator 1981-82.

Home address: 5 Emmett Square, Clonakilty, Co Cork; business address: Strand Dairy, Clonakilty, Co Cork.

Tel: Home 023 33575; Business 023 33324.

Born: Balineen, Co Cork, May 1943.

Married: Marie Donegan. 3 sons, 2 daughters.

Education: St Finbar's College, Farranferris, Cork; UCC.

Occupation: Public representative. Former dairy manager. Member Cork County Council since 1974; Cork County VEC since 1979. Member Cork County Committee of Agriculture since 1974; Irish Creamery Managers' Association; Society of Dairy Technology.

PATRICK J. SHEEHAN (FG) First elected in 1981. Member Oireachtas Joint Committee on Small Businesses. Member Cork County Council since 1967; Cork County Committee of Agriculture since 1962.
Home address: Main Street, Goleen, Co Cork.
Tel: 028 35236.
Born: Kilbrown, Goleen, Mar 1933.
Married: Elizabeth Frances Collins. 1 son, 3 daughters.
Education: Kilroy's College, Dublin.
Occupation: Public representative. Member Muintir na Tire; IFA; Munster Agricultural Society Show Committee. Member Institute of Professional Auctioneers, Valuers and Livestock Salesmen.

JIM O'KEEFFE (FG) First elected in 1977. Minister of State Department of Foreign Affairs (Development Co-operation) Jun 1981-Mar 1982; 1982-86; Departments of Public Service and Finance 1986-87. Opposition frontbench spokesman on Law Reform 1977-79; Foreign Affairs 1979-80; Security 1980-81; Health 1982. Chairman Dáil Consolidation Committee 1977-81.
Home address: New Road, Bandon, Co Cork.
Tel: Home 023 41399; Business 01 789911.
Born: Skibbereen, Co Cork, Mar 1941.
Married: Maeve O'Sullivan.
Education: St Fachtna's High School, Skibbereen; UCD; Law School of the Incorporated Law Society of Ireland.
Occupation: Public representative. Former solicitor. Founder-President Skibbereen Junior Chamber of Commerce 1967. Member Muintir na Tire since 1958; Irish Council of the European Movement since 1973. Member GAA; Skibbereen Rugby Football Club (past captain and past president and member of Munster Junior inter-provincial team); Bandon Rugby Football Club.

DONEGAL NORTH EAST (3)

Elected: *Neil Blaney (IND FF) 1st Count; *Hugh Conaghan (FF) 2nd Count; *Paddy Harte (FG) 3rd Count.

The return of the three sitting TDs was a foregone conclusion with the real interest centring on the order of election. In Nov 1982, Paddy Harte topped the poll with 37 per cent of the vote, but this time it was Donegal's best-known politician, Neil Blaney, who was elected on the 1st count. Re-election confirmed him as the father of the Dáil, with 39 years of unbroken service. As usual he received a huge personal vote from his base in the Fanad peninsula, and his performance improved slightly on Nov '82. His poll-topping position probably helped make up for the loss of his Euro-seat in 1984 to Ray McSharry. FG's vote dropped by 7.3 per cent, and FF's by 2.4 per cent. Sinn Féin failed to improve significantly on their performance in the local elections, and Lab suffered the ignominy of trailing behind the Bible-wielding Ulster Protestant candidate, Michael Boomer-Brookes, a charity worker from Belfast who surprised everyone — including himself — by polling 696 votes.

FEB 87 % Poll		NOV 82 % Poll				
				Electorate:	44,853	
				Total poll:	29,836	(66.5%)
FF	32.3	FF	34.7	Spoiled votes:	416	
FG	29.7	FG	37.0	Total valid poll:	29,420	
PD	—	—	—	Quota:	7,356	
LAB	1.3	LAB	1.8			
SF	8.0	—	—			
OTH	28.6	OTH	26.4	8 Candidates.		

COUNTS	1st	2nd Blaney Surplus (364)	3rd Brooks Monaghan Votes (1,104) (NT) (332)	4th Loughrey Votes (1,870) (NT) (1,392)
Blaney N. (Ind FF)	**7,720**			
Conaghan H. (FF)	7,324	+131 **7,455**		
Harte P. (FG)	6,997	+44 7,041	+440 **7,481**	
Fullerton E. (SF)	2,365	+73 2,438	+98 2,536	+127 2,663
Sweeney R.(FF)	2,188	+81 2,269	+121 2,390	+351 2,471
Loughrey J. (FG)	1,737	+20 1,757	+113 1,870	
Brooks M. (Ind)	696	+9 705		
Monaghan K. (Lab)	393	+6 399		

HUGH CONAGHAN (FF) First elected in 1977 for the Donegal constituency. Re-elected for Donegal North East in Jun 1981. Member Donegal County Council; North-Western Health Board since 1974.
Home address: Monfad, Newtowncunningham, Lifford, Co Donegal.
Tel: 074 56297.
Born: Newtowncunningham, May 1926.
Married: Jean McGrory. 3 sons, 2 daughters.
Education: Newtowncunningham, Lifford, Co Donegal.
Occupation: Public representative. Former transport official (traffic controller). Member Transport Salaried Staff Association for over thirty years.

PADDY HARTE (FG) First elected 1961. Minister for State at the Department of Posts and Telegraphs 1981-82. Opposition spokesman Office of Public Works 1965-69; Security and Northern Ireland 1977-80; Social Welfare 1980-81; Posts and Telegraphs 1982.
Home address: The Diamond, Raphoe, Co Donegal.
Tel: 074 45187.
Born: Lifford 1931.
Married: Rosaleen McGoldrick. 5 sons, 4 daughters.
Education: St Eunan's College, Letterkenny.
Occupation: Public representative. Former auctioneer. Chairman All-Party Committee on Irish Relations 1973-77. Member Committee on Procedure and Privileges 1973-77. Member New Ireland Forum. Member Donegal County Council since 1960; North Western Health Board since 1971.

NEIL BLANEY (IND) First elected 1948 for FF. Minister for Posts and Telegraphs 1957; Minister for Local Government 1957-66; Minister for Agriculture and Fisheries 1966-70. MEP since 1979. Independent FF TD since 1973.
Home address: 485 Howth Road, Raheny, Dublin 5; Rossnakill, Co Donegal.
Tel: Dublin 01 313085; Donegal 074 59014
Born: Rossnakill, Co Donegal, Oct 1922.
Married: Eva Corduff. 5 sons, 2 daughters.
Education: St Eunan's College, Letterkenny, Co Donegal.
Occupation: Public representative, farmer and publican. Member Donegal County Council 1948-57. Chairman Donegal VEC since 1985. President Football Association of Ireland 1968-73. Son of Neal Blaney, FF TD for Donegal 1927-37, and Donegal East 1937-38 and 1943-48.

DONEGAL SOUTH WEST (3)

Elected: Mary Coughlan (FF), *Pat the Cope Gallagher (FF) 1st Count; *Dinny McGinley (FG) 5th Count.

There were no surprises in this traditional two FF, one FG constituency. Prior to the election there were only two sitting TDs owing to the death of Cathal Coughlan (FF) in June 1986. His daughter, 21-year-old Mary Coughlan, surprised old hands at the count by topping the poll with nearly 9,700 first preferences. Her party colleague, the hard-working Pat the Cope Gallagher, was also elected on the 1st count. It went to the 5th count before sitting FG TD Dinny McGinley was elected. The FG vote was down nearly 10 per cent. Young Mary Coughlan's candour was totally disarming during the campaign. When asked why she was going into politics, she said: "I need the job". In that, she spoke for young Ireland.

FEB 87 % Poll		NOV 82 % Poll		Electorate:	45,871	
				Total poll:	31,958	(69.7%)
FF	58.2	FF	54.8	Spoiled votes:	383	
FG	29.8	FG	39.1	Total valid poll:	31,575	
WP	8.0	WP	6.1	Quota:	7,894	
SF	4.0	—	—	6 Candidates.		

COUNTS	1st	2nd Coughlan Surplus (1,804)	3rd Gallagher Surplus (792)	4th Monaghan Votes (1,809) (NT) 930	5th O'Kelly Votes (3,614) (NT) 692
Coughlan M. (FF)	**9,698**				
Gallagher The Cope (FF)	**8,686**				
McGinley D. (FG)	6,331	+480 6,811	+197 7,008	+150 7,158	+2,663 **9,821**
O'Kelly F. (FG)	3,072	+380 3,452	+53 3,505	+109 3,614	
Rodgers S. (WP)	2,512	+518 3,030	+435 3,465	+620 4,085	+259 4,344
Monaghan E. (SF)	1,276	+426 1,702	+107 1,809		

PAT THE COPE GALLAGHER (FF) First elected in Jun 1981. Appointed Minister of State at the Department of the Marine, Mar 1987. Deputy spokesman on Fisheries & Forestry in the last Dáil. Member Donegal County Council since 1979 (Chairman 1985-86); Council's General Purposes, Housing and Roads Committees. Grandson of "Paddy the Cope", a pioneer of the Irish Co-Operative Movement.
Home address: Dungloe, Co Donegal.
Tel: Home 075 21364; Constituency Office 075 21133.
Born: Burtonport, Co Donegal, Mar 1948.
Education: Roshine NS; Luinnagh National School; Dungloe High School; St Enda's College, Galway; UCG.
Occupation: Public representative and fish exporter. Member Regional Development Organisation; Local Advisory Health Committee; VEC; Board of Management RTC Letterkenny.

DINNY MCGINLEY (FG) First elected Feb 1982. Member Oireachtas Joint Services Committee; Joint Services Committee on the Irish Language; Committee on Procedure and Privileges.
Home address: Bunbeg, Letterkenny, Co Donegal.
Tel: 075 31025.
Born: Gweedore, Co Donegal, Apr 1945.
Marital status: Single.
Education: St Patrick's Teacher Training College Drumcondra, Dublin; UCD.
Occupation: Public representative. Former national school teacher. Chairman Gweedore Social Services Committee. Member GAA; Comhaltas Ceoltóirí Éireann.

MARY COUGHLAN (FF) First elected in 1987.
Home address: The Lodge, Cranny, Inver, Co Donegal.
Tel: 073 36002.
Born: May 1965.
Marital Status: Single.
Education: Keelog's NS; Frosses National School; Ursuline College, Sligo, UCD.
Occupation: Public representative. Vice-chairperson and secretary of Kevin Barry Cummann UCD 1984-85, 1985-86. Daughter of Cathal Coughlan (dec.), FF TD for Donegal South West 1983-86.

DUBLIN CENTRAL (5)

Elected: *Bertie Ahern (FF) 1st Count; *Tony Gregory (IND) 2nd Count; *Michael Keating (PD) 9th Count; John Stafford (FF), Dermot Fitzpatrick (FF) 12th Count.

This was one of the most interesting constituencies in the run-up to the election, with the defection of Michael Keating to the PDs and Alice Glenn's expulsion/resignation from FG before Christmas 1986. Fine Gael was left without a sitting TD before the contest — and that was the way it remained at the end of the 12th count as well, when FG's Dr Pat Lee was pipped by FF's Dermot Fitzpatrick with a margin of 78 votes. Fianna Fáil carried off three seats in a victory that reflected great credit on Dublin's Lord Mayor, Bertie Ahern, who led the FF team — and who, incidentally, out-polled his party leader Charles Haughey in neighbouring North Central with a massive 13,635 first preferences. The FF strategy was that Fitzpatrick would receive a proportionately higher percentage of Bertie Ahern's surplus than John Stafford so that they would both creep up together. The plan worked well: Fitzpatrick got 2,717 and Stafford got 1,737.

Fine Gael's lack of clear strategy and co-ordination resulted in their failure to regain even one of their former two seats. Three candidates were probably too many; they were bunched too closely together on the 1st count, and then over 300 of Shane Byrne's votes leaked away when he was eliminated after the 6th count. More than 180 of Luke Belton's transfers leaked away on the 11th count, to ensure that the party was not in any position to capitalise on the 290 transfers Pat Lee received from SF's Christy Burke on the 12th count.

Alice Glenn's campaign, based largely on her public defence of the family and conservative morality and values, won her less than 2,000 votes. It was a salutary lesson to those elected on a party ticket who may be tempted to believe that notoriely as a party dissident is better insurance of re-election than the party machine. Tony Gregory showed his strength in the constituency once again by increasing his first-preference vote by 1,500 over Nov 1982. The turnout was up 5 per cent on the last time — but on an electorate which had dropped by 1,000.

FEB 87 % Poll		NOV 82 % Poll		Electorate:	74,679	
				Total poll:	47,916	(64.2%)
FF	42.1	FF	41.7	Spoiled votes:	460	
FG	12.6	FG	31.9	Total valid poll:	47,456	
PD	13.4	—	—	Quota:	7,910	
LAB	2.9	LAB	7.5			
WP	3.1	WP	4.9			
SF	5.3	—	—			
OTH	20.6	OTH	14.0	14 Candidates.		

COUNTS	1st	2nd Ahern Surplus (5,725)	3rd Gregory Surplus (294)	4th Hyland Votes (98) (NT) (9)	5th Freehill Votes (673) (NT) (22)	6th Costello Votes (1,236) (NT) (144)	7th Byrne Votes (1,384) (NT) (37)	8th Jennings Votes (2,041) (NT) (530)	9th Glenn Votes (2,366) (NT) (289)	10th Keating Surplus (212)	11th Belton Votes (3,042) (NT) (314)	12th Burke Votes (3,579) (NT) (1,862)
Ahern B. (FF)	**13,635**											
Gregory T. (Ind)	7,721	+483 **8,204**										
Keating M. (PD)	6,361	+210 6,571	+50 6,621	+18 6,639	+83 6,722	+197 6,919	+207 7,126	+312 7,438	+684 **8,122**			
Stafford J. (FF)	3,966	+1737 5,703	+93 5,796	+4 5,800	+18 5,818	+44 5,862	+16 5,878	+205 6,083	+459 6,542	+36 6,578	+47 6,625	+848 **7,473**
Lee P. (FG)	2,643	+58 2,701	+11 2,712	+4 2,716	+25 2,741	+76 2,817	+468 3,285	+137 3,422	+195 3,617	+86 3,703	+2491 6,194	+290 6,484
Burke C. (SF)	2,501	+169 2,670	+39 2,709	+6 2,715	+11 2,726	+135 2,861	+15 2,876	+495 3,371	+106 3,477	+9 3,486	+93 3,579	
Fitzpatrick D. (FF)	2,392	+2,717 5,109	+46 5,155	+4 5,159	+9 5,168	+47 5,215	+25 5,240	+161 5,401	+456 5,857	+29 5,886	+47 5,983	+579 **6,562**
Belton L. (FG)	2,034	+66 2,100	+4 2,104	+6 2,110	+11 2,121	+53 2,174	+566 2,740	+73 2,813	+177 2,990	+52 3,042		
Glenn A. (Ind)	1,951	+148 2,099	+12 2,111	+8 2,119	+17 2,136	+71 2,207	+31 2,238	+128 2,366				
Jennings M. (WP)	1,463	+44 1,507	+21 1,528	+17 1,545	+48 1,593	+429 2,022	+19 2,041					
Byrne S. (FG)	1,296	+25 1,321	+4 1,325	+1 1,326	+18 1,344	+40 1,384						
Costello J. (Lab)	767	+45 812	+7 819	+6 825	+411 1,236							
Freehill M. (Lab)	632	+21 653	+5 658	+15 673								
Hyland B.	94	+2 96	+2 98									

BERTIE AHERN (FF) First elected in 1977 for the constituency of Dublin Finglas. Appointed Minister for Labour Mar 1987. Minister of State at the Department of the Taoiseach and at the Department of Defence Mar-Dec 1982. Government Assistant Whip 1980-81; Chief Whip Mar-Dec 1982. Fianna Fáil spokesman on Youth 1981; on Labour and the Public Service 1983-87. Lord Mayor of Dublin since 1986.

Home address: 25 Church Avenue, Drumcondra, Dublin 9.

Tel: Home 01 374267; Business 01 374129.

Born: Dublin, Sept 1951.

Married: Patricia Kelly.

Education: St Aidan's CBS Secondary School, Dublin; Rathmines College of Commerce; UCD.

Occupation: Public representative and accountant. Former Member Federated Workers' Union of Ireland. Governor of UCD. Member of Dublin Port & Docks Board; Eastern Health Board; Dublin Chamber of Commerce. Chairman of the Dublin Millennium Committee to organise and celebrate 1,000 years of Dublin's history in 1988.

DERMOT FITZPATRICK (FF) First elected in 1987. Elected Dublin Corporation 1985. Member of the Eastern Health Board. Governor Rotunda Hospital. Governor Royal Irish Academy of Music.
Home address: 80 Navan Road, Dublin 7; business address: 145 Navan Road, Dublin 7.
Tel: Home 01-304663; Business 01-300580.
Born: 1941
Married: Mary Wallace. 1 son, 3 daughters.
Education: NS, Phoenix Park; Colaiste Mhuire, Parnell Square; UCD, Dental and Medical Schools.
Occupation: Public representative. Dentist and doctor. Member The Old Dublin Society; Royal Canal Amenity Group.

JOHN STAFFORD (FF) First elected in 1987. Member Dublin Corporation since Jun 1985. Member of Fianna Fáil National Executive; Vice-Chairman of Cairde Fáil. Vice-Chairman of Dublin Port and Docks Board. Son of Tom Stafford a former Lord Mayor of Dublin.
Home address: 60 North Strand Road, Dublin 3.
Tel: 01 741373.
Born: Dublin, May 1944.
Married: Phyl O'Dwyer. 3 boys.
Education: William Street and O'Connell's CBS.
Occupation: Public representative and funeral director.

MICHAEL KEATING (PD) First elected for FG in 1977. Minister of State at the Department of Education 1981-82. Fine Gael spokesman on Urban Affairs; Law Reform and Human Rights. Former Lord Mayor of Dublin. Elected to the City Council for North Inner City in 1985. Patron Liffey Trust Co-Operative, East Wall.
Home address: 149 Phibsboro Road, Dublin 7.
Tel: Home 01 259718; Business: 01 792599; 789911; 303100.
Born: Dublin 1947.
Married: Kathryn Keaveney. 2 children.
Education: St Canice's CBS; O'Connell's CBS; UCD; St Patrick's College Maynooth.
Occupation: Public representative. Former school teacher.

TONY GREGORY (IND) First elected Feb 1982. Member Dublin City Council since 1979.
Home address: 5 Sackville Gardens, Dublin 3.
Tel: 01 729910.
Born: Dublin 1947.
Education: O'Connell Schools, North Richmond Street, Dublin; UCD.
Occupation: Public representative. Former secondary school teacher.
Chairman North City Centre Community Action Association.
Secretary Tosach (Inner City Training Project). Former Member Official Sinn Féin. Member ASTI.

DUBLIN NORTH (3)

Elected: *Ray Burke (FF) 1st Count; *John Boland (FG), G.V. Wright (FF) 8th Count.

At noon on the day of the count in Dublin North, FF's Ray Burke went over the party's tally, looked up and smiled: "I think we can be confident of our two seats here". And so it was — a particularly sweet victory for FF because this is the home constituency of the party leader. The riding instructions for all of the elections in the eighties have been to go for two out of three. But this is the first time that that result has been achieved. Fianna Fáil took the second seat with an increase in their vote of 3.2 per cent, a massive drop in the FG vote of 16.1 per cent, and with the PD candidate, Vincent Gaul, taking 11.8 per cent. The unknown Vincent Gaul was 547 votes ahead of the outgoing FG TD, Nora Owen, on the 1st — she was eliminated on the 7th count — while Gaul remained on for the next, and last count. G.V. Wright finally took the seat he had been chasing since Feb 1982. In advance of the election FG knew they were in trouble in this constituency. FF needed a swing of just 2.7 per cent to pick up two seats. G.V. Wright had topped the poll in the 1985 local elections while, in the same election, Nora Owen trailed both Wright and Lab's Bernie Malone.

FEB 87 % Poll		NOV 82 % Poll		Electorate:	46,545	
				Total poll:	34,337	(73.8%)
FF	48.6	FF	45.4	Spoiled votes:	319	
FG	26.1	FG	42.2	Total valid poll:	34,018	
PD	11.8	—	—	Quota:	8,505	
LAB	10.1	LAB	12.4			
OTH	3.4	OTH	—	10 Candidates.		

COUNTS	1st	2nd Burke Surplus (1,060)	3rd Hyland Votes (97)	4th Malone Votes (1,103)	5th Sargent Votes (1,165)	6th Gilbride Votes (3,285)	7th Ryan Votes (3,558)	8th Owen Votes (4,355)
			(NT) (4)	(NT) (15)	(NT) (130)	(NT) (114)	(NT) (902)	(NT) (249)
Burke R. (FF)	**9,565**							
		+38	*+1*	*+61*	*+116*	*+210*	*+662*	*+3,134*
Boland J. (FG)	5,417	5,455	5,456	5,517	5,633	5,843	6,505	**9,639**
		+347	*+6*	*+86*	*+118*	*+2641*	*+763*	*+220*
Wright G. (FF)	4,402	4,749	4,755	4,841	4,959	7,600	8,363	**8,583**
		+36	*+9*	*+90*	*+201*	*+99*	*+682*	*+752*
Gaul V. (PD)	4,008	4,044	4,053	4,143	4,344	4,443	5,125	5,877
		+14	*+7*	*+139*	*+135*	*+50*	*+549*	
Owen N. (FG)	3,461	3,475	3,482	3,621	3,756	3,806	4,355	
		+554	*+0*	*+23*	*+133*			
Gilbride S. (FF)	2,575	3,129	3,129	3,152	3,285			
		+52	*+10*	*+643*	*+332*	*+171*		
Ryan S. (Lab)	2,350	2,402	2,412	3,055	3,387	3,558		
		+12	*+8*					
Malone B. (Lab)	1,083	1,095	1,103					
		+6	*+52*	*+46*				
Sargent T. (GA)	1,061	1,067	1,119	1,165				
		+1						
Hyland B.	96	97						

RAY BURKE (FF) First elected 1973. Appointed Minister for Energy Mar 1987. Minister for the Environment 1982; 1980-81. Minister of State at the Department of Industry, Commerce and Energy, 1978-80. Opposition spokesman on the Environment 1982-87. Chairman Dublin County Council since July 1985. Son of the late Patrick J. Burke, Dáil Deputy for Dublin County constituencies 1944-73.
Home address: Briargate, Malahide Road, Swords, Co Dublin.
Tel: 01 401734.
Born: Dublin, Sept 1943.
Married: Anne Fassbender. 2 daughters.
Education: Christian Brothers' O'Connell School, Dublin.
Occupation: Public representative.

JOHN BOLAND (FG) First elected in 1977. Minister for the Environment 1986-87; Minister for Health Jan-Feb 1987; Minister for the Public Service 1982-86; Minister for Education Jun 1981-Mar 1982; Opposition frontbench spokesman on Health and Social Welfare 1977-81; on Environment, Jan-Jun 1981; on Industry 1982. Fine Gael Leader of the House 1982. Senator 1969-77.
Home address: 14 Shenick Drive, Holmpatrick, Skerries, Co Dublin.
Tel: Home 01 491503; Business 01 789911
Born: Dublin, Nov 1944.
Married: Kay Kennedy. 1 son, 1 daughter.
Education: CBS; Synge Street, Dublin; UCD.
Occupation: Public representative. Member Dublin County Council 1967-85. Chairman 1973-74, 1976-77 and 1979-80. Member County Dublin VEC 1974-81. Chairman Adult Education Sub-Committee 1975-76. Chairman Youth and Sport Sub-Committee 1978-81.

THOMAS (GV) WRIGHT (FF) First elected 1987. Senator 1982. Member Dublin County Council.
Home address: 58 The Moorings, Malahide, Co Dublin.
Tel: 01 450710
Born: Malahide, Aug 1947.
Married: Monica Kane. 2 boys, 1 girl.
Education: Malahide NS; Chanel College, Dublin.
Occupation: Public representative and businessman. Chairman Dublin County Committee of Agriculture. Member Bord Iascaigh Mhara. Former Dublin County and Fingal footballer.

DUBLIN NORTH CENTRAL (4)

Elected: *Charles J. Haughey (FF) 1st Count; *Vincent Brady (FF), *Richard Bruton (FG), *George Birmingham (FG) 10th Count.

In recent general elections FF had been hoping to take a third seat by relying on Mr Haughey's very large personal vote. Their strategy on this occasion appeared to be to one of reducing Mr Haughey's vote, thereby increasing the vote of the other two candidates, Vincent Brady and Ivor Callely. While the party had some success in doing this, it failed to get the transfers from other parties that were needed to keep Callely ahead of the two FG candidates, George Birmingham and Richard Bruton, on the final count. In the 1982 elections, Birmingham and Bruton worked well together, splitting the FG vote. However, with everyone predicting a FG loss on this occasion, there wasn't the same level of co-operation between them. On the day before polling, leaflets distributed throughout the constituency said: "In order to save George Birmingham's seat, it is vital that FG supporters vote as follows: No 1 George Birmingham and (equally important) No 2 Richard Bruton". When FG headquarters heard about the leaflet, the general secretary, Finbar Fitzpatrick, rushed out a second one that said: "A leaflet has been dropped to Fine Gael voters today indicating: vote No 1 Birmingham, No 2 Bruton. This leaflet was a false directive and has not been issued with the knowledge of the Fine Gael Director of Elections. Richard Bruton should be fully supported". At the end of the day, FG held onto its two seats with the help of large transfers from the PDs and Lab.

FEB 87		NOV 82		Electorate:	57,167	
% Poll		% Poll				
FF	49.7	FF	48.7	Total poll:	43,300	(75.7%)
FG	24.2	FG	36.6	Spoiled Votes:	376	
PD	8.4	—	—	Total valid poll:	42,924	
LAB	6.9	LAB	7.6	Quota:	8,585	
WP	3.8	WP	3.6			
SF	1.8	—	—			
OTH	5.1	OTH	3.4	13 Candidates.		

COUNTS	1st	2nd Haughey Surplus (4,401)	3rd Hyland Votes (79)	4th McCoy Votes (122)	5th O'Connor Votes (745)	6th McCormaic Votes (870)	7th Loftus Votes (1,581)	8th Dooney Votes (2,287)	9th O'Hanrahan Votes (4,229)	10th O'Mahony Votes (5,258)
			(NT) (3)	(NT) (4)	(NT) (25)	(NT) (139)	(NT) (123)	(NT) (444)	(NT) (376)	(NT) (1496)
Haughey C.J. (FF)	**12,986**									
Birmingham G. (FG)	5,201	+51 5,252	+1 5,253	+11 5,264	+61 5,325	+7 5,332	+173 5,505	+89 5,594	+1258 6,852	+1,002 **7,854**
Bruton R. (FG)	5,196	+77 5,273	+3 5,276	+7 5,283	+76 5,359	+14 5,373	+180 5,553	+135 5,688	+1,272 6,960	+1,365 **8,325**
Brady V. (FF)	4,454	+2,558 7,012	+7 7,019	+30 7,049	+22 7,071	+129 7,200	+265 7,465	+214 7,679	+316 7,995	+659 **8,654**
Callely I. (FF)	3,904	+1362 5,266	+8 5,274	+8 5,282	+49 5,331	+147 5,478	+168 5,646	+236 5,882	+278 6,160	+736 6,896
O'Hanrahan J. (PD)	3,582	+41 3,623	+6 3,629	+8 3,637	+87 3,724	+21 3,745	+287 4,032	+197 4,229		
O'Mahony F. (Lab)	2,973	+110 3,083	+7 3,090	+14 3,104	+156 3,260	+103 3,363	+194 3,557	+972 4,529	+729 5,258	
Dooney T. (WP)	1,643	+51 1,694	+7 1,701	+5 1,706	+179 1,885	+211 2,096	+191 2,287			
Loftus S. (Ind)	1,341	+51 1,392	+27 1,419	+21 1,440	+42 1,482	+99 1,581				
McCormaic C. (SF)	779	+36 815	+4 819	+3 822	+48 870					
O'Connor P. (DSP)	681	+52 733	+1 734	+11 745						
McCoy A. (Ind)	111	+6 117	+5 122							
Hyland B	73	+6 79								

VINCENT BRADY (FF) First elected 1977. Appointed Minister of State Departments of the Taoiseach and Defence and Government Chief Whip Mar 1987. Opposition Chief Whip Oct 1985. Member Oireachtas Committee on Crime, Lawlessness and Vandalism; Oireachtas Committee on Procedure and Privileges. Member Dublin City Council since 1979. Re-elected as Alderman 1985. Member City Council Finance, Planning and Development Committees. Chairman Special Committee for Bull Island. Member Council of Europe 1982-84.
Home address: 59 Seafield Road East, Clontarf, Dublin 5.
Tel: 01 333590.
Born: Dublin, Mar 1936.
Married: Mary Neville. 2 sons, 1 daughter.
Education: O'Connell School, Dublin; College of Commerce, Rathmines, Dublin.
Occupation: Public representative and company director. Member Board of Governors of St Vincent's Psychiatric Hospital, Fairview; Incorporated Orthopaedic Hospital of Ireland.

CHARLES J HAUGHEY (FF) First elected 1957. Elected Taoiseach Mar 1987; Taoiseach 1979-81; Taoiseach Mar-Dec 1982. Leader of the Opposition 1981-82; 1982-87. Minister for Justice 1961-64; Minister for Agriculture 1964-66; Minister for Finance 1966-70; Minister for Health and Social Welfare 1977-79. Parliamentary Secretary to the Minister for Justice 1960-61. Chairman Joint Committee on Secondary Legislation of the European Community 1973-77. Member Dublin Corporation 1953-55.
Home address: Abbeyville, Kinsealy, Co Dublin.
Tel: 01 450111.
Born: Castlebar, Co Mayo, Sept 1925.
Married: Maureen Lemass. 3 sons, 1 daughter.
Education: Scoil Mhuire, Marino; St Joseph's CBS, Fairview; UCD; Kings Inns, Dublin.
Occupation: Public representative. Former accountant.

RICHARD BRUTON (FG) First elected Feb 1982. Senator 1981-1982. Minister of State Department of Industry 1986-87. Member Oireachtas Committees on Public Expenditure and Women's Rights 1982-87. Member Meath County Council 1979-82.
Home address: 90 Elm Mount Avenue, Beaumont, Dublin 9.
Tel: 01 316895.
Born: Dublin 1953.
Married: Susan Meehan. 2 sons.
Education: Clongowes Wood College; UCD; Nuffield College, Oxford.
Occupation: Public representative. Former economist. Author *Irish Public Debt* (1979); joint author *Irish Economy* (1985); joint author *Drainage Policy in Ireland* (1982). Brother of John Bruton, Dáil deputy for Meath since 1969 and Minister for Finance 1986-87.

GEORGE BIRMINGHAM (FG) First elected in 1981. Minister of State Department of Foreign Affairs 1986-87; Department of Labour 1982-86. Opposition spokesman on Urban Affairs 1982. Member Dublin City Council 1979-8. Member City Council Planning and Cultural Committees.
Home address: 13A Kincora Court, Clontarf, Dublin 3.
Tel: 01 338744.
Born: Dublin, Aug 1954.
Married: Myra Delaney.
Education: St Paul's College, Raheny; TCD; Kings Inns, Dublin.
Occupation: Public representative. Former barrister-at-law. Former Chairman Raheny Community Council. Member An Taisce; Irish Association for Civil Liberties.

DUBLIN NORTH-EAST (4)

Elected: *Liam Fitzgerald (FF) 7th Count; *Michael J. Cosgrave (FG), *Michael Woods (FF) 10th count; Pat McCartan (WP) 12th Count.

This constituency provided some of the major excitement of the general election, both during the campaign and in the course of the count. It was the scene of a very public row within FF when the National Executive imposed Charles Haughey's son, Sean, as a fourth candidate. The selection convention had chosen the two sitting TDs plus the colourful conservative and old-campaigner, Councillor Ned Brennan, and they were deeply upset by Sean Haughey's imposition. There were fears that one of the sitting TDs might lose a seat to Sean Haughey and that FF would fail to gain their objective of a third seat. In the event, the sitting FF TDs held their seats and Sean Haughey narrowly missed taking the last seat which went instead to the WP's Pat McCartan, with 235 votes separating them. The count illustrated both the vagaries of the PR system and some of the oddities and cruelties of Irish politics. Micky Joe Cosgrave, perhaps the only survivor of the deeply conservative wing of FG, saw his vote collapse on the first count — down 42 per cent on Nov 1982. According to RTE's reporter at the count, Myles Dungan, he had more or less given up the ghost until the distribution of Ned Brennan's votes on the 7th count put him 52 votes ahead of his party colleague Maurice Manning. The distribution of Manning's votes still left Cosgrave less than 400 short of a quota — but at this stage all the excitement centred on the placings of Pat McCartan (WP) and Neil Holman (PD). McCartan was just 24 votes ahead and the count was treated to the spectacle of FF calling for a recount on the PDs' behalf; they knew that if the order was the other way around, McCartan's transfers would probably elect Sean Haughey. However, the order remained unchanged, and Pat McCartan edged home without reaching a quota, on his fourth attempt at a Dáil seat. At the count there were interesting alliances — WP and FG tallymen side by side ensuring that FF did not get ballots disallowed in the recount, and Neil Holman of the PDs reassuring Pat McCartan not to worry about the destination of the PDs' transfers — they would not go Sean Haughey's way. In the event, only 157 went to Haughey leaving him just 4 votes ahead of McCartan who took 514; Cosgrave's surplus gave McCartan a lead of 344 and Michael Wood's surplus on the 12th could not close the gap.

FEB 87 % Poll		NOV 82 % Poll		Electorate:	50,848	
				Total poll:	38,704	(76.1%)
FF	51.4	FF	42.8	Spoiled votes:	425	
FG	18.9	FG	33.0	Total valid poll:	38,279	
PD	12.2	—	—	Quota:	7,656	
LAB	5.8	LAB	9.5			
WP	8.6	WP	9.4			
SF	1.7	—	—			
OTH	1.4	OTH	5.3	13 Candidates.		

COUNTS	1st	2nd Hyland Votes (109) (NT) (4)	3rd Healy Votes (458) (NT) (21)	4th Kane Votes (720) (NT) (92)	5th McGettigan Votes (1,996) (NT) (17)	6th Kenny Votes (2,461) (NT) (112)	7th Brennan Votes (3,370) (NT) (39)	8th Fitzgerald Surplus (583)	9th Manning Votes (4,139) (NT) (93)	10th Holman Votes (4,971) (NT) (706)	11th Cosgrave Surplus (2,677) (NT) (1,523)	12th Woods Surplus (528) (NT) (255)
Fitzgerald L. (FF)	6,378	+1 6,379	+27 6,406	+78 6,484	+64 6,548	+260 6,808	+1,431 **8,239**					
Woods M. (FF)	5,927	+3 5,930	+25 5,955	+54 6,009	+91 6,100	+205 6,305	+949 7,254	+276 7,530	+104 7,634	+550 **8,184**		
Haughey S. (FF)	4,222	+0 4,222	+15 4,237	+98 4,335	+27 4,362	+154 4,516	+539 5,055	+259 5,314	+42 5,356	+157 5,513	+403 5,916	+191 6,107
Cosgrave M.J. (FG)	3,658	+4 3,662	+23 3,685	+19 3,704	+113 3,817	+184 4,001	+183 4,184	+10 4,194	+3095 7,289	+3,044 **10,333**		
Manning M. (FG)	3,585	+9 3,594	+23 3,617	+11 3,628	+172 3,800	+289 4,089	+43 4,132	+7 4,139				
McCartan P. (WP)	3,297	+14 3,311	+143 3,454	+214 3,668	+48 3,716	+937 4,653	+128 4,781	+25 4,806	+189 4,995	+514 5,509	+751 6,260	+82 **6,342**
Brennan N. (FF)	3,136	+4 3,140	+15 3,155	+45 3,200	+41 3,241	+129 3,370						
Holman N. (PD)	2,691	+9 2,700	+24 2,724	+17 2,741	+1,359 4,100	+191 4,291	+58 4,349	+6 4,355	+616 4,971			
Kenny S. (Lab)	2,227	+14 2,241	+73 2,314	+83 2,397	+64 2,461							
McGettigan M. (PD)	1,964	+8 1,972	+15 1,987	+9 1,996								
Kane P. (SF)	655	+11 666	+54 720									
Healy P. (Ind)	430	+28 458										
Hyland B	109											

MICHAEL WOODS (FF) First elected 1977. Appointed Minister for Social Welfare Mar 1987. Minister for Health and Social Welfare 1979-81; 1982. Minister of State Department of the Taoiseach; Department of Defence 1979. Fianna Fáil Chief Whip 1979. Opposition spokesman on Justice; Chairman of the Select Committee on Crime, Lawlessness and Vandalism 1982-87. Member Dublin Corporation 1979.
Home address: 13 Kilbarrack Grove, Raheny, Dublin 5.
Tel: 01 323357.
Born: Bray, Co Wicklow, Dec 1935.
Married: Margaret Maher. 3 sons, 2 daughters.
Education: Synge Street CBS; UCD; Institute of Public Administration; Harvard Business School.

LIAM FITZGERALD (FF) First elected Jun 1981. Elected Dublin City Council 1985. Chairman City of Dublin VEC. Member Joint Oireachtas Committee on Public Expenditure. Opposition deputy spokesman on Education 1982-87.
Home address: 117 Tonlegee Road, Raheny, Dublin 5.
Tel: 01 470632
Born: Doon, Co Limerick, Sept 1949.
Married: Brid Lynch. 3 sons, 2 daughters.
Education: Doon CBS, Limerick; St Patrick's Training College, Drumcondra; UCD.
Occupation: Public representative. Former national school teacher.

PAT McCARTAN (WP) First elected Feb 1987. Member of Dublin City Council since 1985.
Home address: 32 Smithfield, Dublin 7.
Tel: 01 723836.
Born: Gorey, Co Wexford, May 1953.
Married: Felicity Hogan. 1 child.
Education: St Peter's College, Wexford; UCD.
Occupation: Public representative and solicitor. Member of the General Purposes and Cultural Committees of Dublin City Council; Board of the Royal Orthopaedic Hospital, Clontarf; Board of Advisers of the Municipal Art Gallery.

MICHAEL J. COSGRAVE (FG) First elected 1977. Member Joint Oireachtas Committee on Legislation. Member Dublin City Council since 1974. Member of the Council's Finance and Planning Committees. Member Dublin Port and Docks Board.
Home address: Mangerton, 22 College Street, Baldoyle, Dublin 13.
Tel: 01 322554.
Born: Baldoyle, Dublin, Feb 1938.
Married: Mary McMunn. 2 sons, 2 daughters.
Education: St Joseph's CBS, Fairview; School of Management Studies, Rathmines; UCD.
Occupation: Public representative. Former company director and farmer.

DUBLIN NORTH-WEST (4)

Elected: *Proinsias De Rossa (WP) 5th Count; *Michael Barrett (FF) 8th Count; *Jim Tunney (FF) 9th Count; *Mary Flaherty (FG) 13th Count.

This was one of the most predictable constituencies in the country. The WP's hard-working deputy, Prionsias de Rossa, topped the poll for the first time, as expected, and it took 13 counts to fill all the seats, largely because there were seven candidates who, with less than 1,000 votes each, all had to be eliminated. The FG vote was down by 11.5 per cent, reflecting the massive national swing against the party. Most of it was mopped up by FF, a fact reflected in Michael Barrett's share of the first-preference vote which was up more than 60 per cent on his Nov 1982 performance. Jim Tunney has topped the poll on the previous six outings — but he had to be content with third place this time, behind de Rossa and Barrett. Mary Flaherty had to wait until the 13th count for election on the transfers of her party colleague. The result confirmed the view that this is the safest WP seat. It is probably one of the strongest working-class constituencies in the country, taking in the sprawling housing estates of Finglas and the Ballymun tower blocks and almost totally dominated by FF and the WP. The PDs did not run a candidate.

FEB 87 % Poll		NOV 82 % Poll		Electorate:	52,182	
				Total poll:	35,087	(67.2%)
FF	48.3	FF	40.2	Spoiled votes:	466	
FG	18.8	FG	30.3	Total valid poll:	34,621	
PD	—	—	—	Quota:	6,925	
LAB	4.0	LAB	6.4			
WP	21.6	WP	19.8			
SF	3.1	—	—			
OTH	4.3	OTH	3.3	14 Candidates.		

COUNTS	1st	2nd Hyland Votes (33)	3rd Doolin Votes (100)	4th Donnelly Votes (426)	5th Larkin Votes (521)	6th Donnelly Votes (674)	7th DeRossa Surplus (126)	8th Cox Votes (1,006)	9th Fleming Votes (1,133)	10th Barrett Surplus (145)	11th Tormey Votes (1,983)	12th Tunney Surplus (26)	13th Farrell Votes (2,299)
(NT)		(NT) (1)	(NT) (1)	(NT) (2)	(NT) (26)	(NT) (173)	(NT) (13)	(NT) (190)	(NT) (498)		(NT) (682)	(NT) (1)	(NT) (120)
De Rossa P. (WP)	6,866	+1 6,867	+27 6,894	+22 6,916	+135 **7,051**								
Barrett M. (FF)	6,698	+3 6,701	+3 6,704	+12 6,716	+33 6,749	+76 6,825	+11 6,836	+234 **7,070**					
Tunney J. (FF)	6,591	+1 6,592	+6 6,598	+14 6,612	+28 6,640	+45 6,685	+12 6,697	+80 6,777	+174 **6,951**				
Flaherty M. (FG)	4,662	+0 4,662	+9 4,671	+5 4,676	+83 4,759	+44 4,803	+18 4,821	+101 4,922	+42 4,964	+14 4,978	+642 5,620	+1 5,621	+2,088 **7,709**
Carey P. (FF)	3,448	+1 3,449	+4 3,453	+6 3,459	+23 3,482	+47 3,529	+5 3,534	+75 3,609	+209 3,818	+109 3,927	+388 4,315	+24 4,339	+91 4,430
Farrell T. (FG)	1,831	+1 1,832	+9 1,841	+5 1,846	+27 1,873	+27 1,900	+5 1,905	+84 1,989	+30 2,019	+9 2,028	+271 2,299	+0 2,299	
Tormey B. (Lab)	1,370	+3 1,373	+4 1,377	+2 1,379	+63 1,442	+157 1,599	+32 1,631	+159 1,790	+180 1,970	+13 1,983			
Cox A. (Ind)	844	+7 851	+23 874	+10 884	+52 936	+52 988	+18 1,006						

Fleming H. (SF)	642	*+0* 642	*+3* 645	*+327* 972	*+13* 985	*+53* 1,038	*+12* 1,050	*+83* 1,133
Donnelly P. (WP)	614	*+2* 616	*+2* 618	*+18* 636	*+38* 674			
Larkin A. (GA)	504	*+7* 511	*+7* 518	*+3* 521				
Donnelly N. (SF)	423	*+1* 424	*+2* 426					
Doolin G. (Ind)	95	*+5* 100						
Hyland B	33							

139

JIM TUNNEY (FF) First elected 1969. Appointed Leas Cheann Comhairle Mar 1987. Leas Cheann Comhairle, 1981-82. Minister of State at the Department of Education 1978-81. Parliamentary Secretary to the Minister for Education 1977-1978; 1972-1973. Opposition frontbench spokesman on the Gaeltacht 1973-77. Chairman FF parliamentary party since 1982. Lord Mayor of Dublin 1985-86.
Home address: Rosebank, Navan Road, Dublin 7.
Tel: 01 304267.
Born: Finglas, Co Dublin, Dec 1923.
Married: Cathleen Byrne. 2 sons, 2 daughters.
Education: St. Brigid's Convent, Finglas; St Vincent's CBS Glasnevin; UCD.
Occupation: Public representative. Former civil servant, teacher and headmaster. Governor National Institute for Higher Education, Dublin. Member of the New Ireland Forum; Comhdhail Náisiúnta na Gaeilge; Vocational Teachers' Association. Former Gaelic footballer with Dublin County teams; holder of a Junior All-Ireland Medal. Son of the late James Tunney, Dáil Deputy for Dublin County 1943-44 and a former Senator.

MICHAEL BARRETT (FF) First elected 1981. Member Dublin City Council since 1979. Re-elected to Dublin Corporation in 1985 as Alderman.
Home address: 102 Glasnevin Avenue, Dublin 11.
Tel: 01 422480.
Born: Loughglynn, Co Roscommon, Jan 1927.
Married: Theresa Kelly. 1 daughter.
Education: Loughglynn NS.
Occupation: Public representative. Member Pro-Life; Society for the Protection of the Unborn Child; Pioneer Association. Director of Dublin and Eastern Tourism.

PROINSIAS DE ROSSA (WP) First elected Feb 1982. Member Dublin Corporation since 1985; Eastern Health Board.
Home address: 39 Pinewood Crescent, Dublin 11.
Tel: Home 01 425644; Office 01 766554.
Born: May 1940.
Married: Monica Kelly. 1 daughter, 2 sons.
Occupation: Public representative. Vice-Chairman of The Workers Party; Chairman of the Party's Political Committee. Member ITGWU; Irish Anti-Apartheid Movement.

MARY D. FLAHERTY (FG) First elected 1981. Minister of State at the Department of Health and Social Welfare 1981-82.
Home address: 2 Richmond Place, Rathmines, Dublin 6.
Tel: 01 976620.
Born: Dublin, May 1953.
Married: Alexis Fitzgerald, Senator. Two children.
Education: Holy Faith Convent, Glasnevin; UCD.
Occupation: Public representative. Former secondary school teacher.
Member Oireachtas Joint Committees on Women's Rights and Legislation 1982-87. Member Dublin City Council 1979; City of Dublin VEC; Eastern Health Board Local Health Committee. Member Women's Political Association; An Taisce.

DUBLIN SOUTH (5)

Elected: Anne Colley (PD), *Seamus Brennan (FF) 1st Count; Tom Kitt (FF) 10th Count; *John Kelly (FG), *Alan Shatter (FG) 13th Count.

All through the eighties this was a FG stronghold with the party taking three of the five seats until this election and the advent of the PDs. The FG vote dropped by more than 20 per cent in this middle class heartland stretching from Ailesbury Road to Kilternan and Glencullen. The PDs' Anne Colley, daughter of the late George Colley, picked up almost all the votes lost by FG, topping the poll with nearly 12,000 votes. Fine Gael's John Kelly was the poll-topper here in successive elections but this time he had to settle for fourth place, running behind FF's Seamus Brennan and Tom Kitt. Labour's share of the vote was down 3.5 per cent, despite Eithne FitzGerald's efforts in the constituency since 1981 to build up a base here. On the FG side, the loser to the PDs was Nuala Fennell, the first Minister for Womens' Affairs in the history of the State. In all the pre-election speculation it was assumed that the PDs would take a seat in Dublin South — it was only a question of which of the two FG candidates, Fennell or Shatter, would suffer. It was all made clear on the 13th count when John Kelly was elected and Alan Shatter took the last seat by a margin of 760 votes from his party colleague. On the FF side, there was never any doubt about their two seats despite Niall Andrews opting for Europe.

FEB 87		NOV 82		Electorate:	77,519	
% Poll		% Poll				
FF	35.8	FF	36.6	Total poll:	57,667	(74.4%)
FG	30.9	FG	52.5	Spoiled votes:	336	
PD	20.9	—	—	Total valid poll:	57,331	
LAB	4.7	LAB	8.2	Quota:	9,556	
WP	2.3	WP	—			
OTH	5.6	OTH	2.7	15 Candidates.		

COUNTS	1st	2nd Colley Surplus (2,401)	3rd Brennan Surplus (384)	4th MacFeorais Votes (110)	5th Hyland Votes (127)	6th O'Neill Votes (170)	7th Sharkey Votes (240)	8th O Liathain Votes (1,400)	9th Duchon Votes (1,566)	10th Garland Votes (2,155)	11th Kitt Surplus (238)	12th Ormonde Votes (2,691)	13th FitzGerald Votes (4,772)
				(NT) (4)	(NT) (6)	(NT) (7)	(NT) (21)	(NT) (113)	(NT) (119)	(NT) (379)	(NT) (26)	(NT) (1607)	(NT) (1450)
Colley A. (PD)	**11,957**												
Brennan S. (FF)	**9,940**												
Kitt T. (FF)	8,423	+217 8,640	+289 8,929	+25 8,954	+5 8,959	+24 8,983	+40 9,023	+217 9,240	+296 9,536	+258 **9,794**			
Kelly J. (FG)	7,247	+728 7,975	+11 7,986	+13 7,999	+16 8,015	+20 8,035	+10 8,045	+48 8,093	+224 8,317	+282 8,599	+21 8,620	+257 8,877	+952 **9,829**
Shatter A. (FG)	5,720	+483 6,203	+7 6,210	+2 6,212	+11 6,223	+11 6,234	+16 6,250	+53 6,303	+124 6,427	+239 6,666	+17 6,683	+168 6,851	+1,080 **7,931**
Fennell N. (FG)	4,737	+532 5,269	+8 5,277	+1 5,278	+9 5,287	+8 5,295	+15 5,310	+55 5,365	+143 5,508	+212 5,720	+11 5,731	+150 5,881	+1,290 7,171
FitzGerald E. (Lab)	2,684	+149 2,833	+8 2,841	+6 2,847	+10 2,857	+7 2,864	+19 2,883	+457 3,340	+263 3,603	+639 4,242	+21 4,263	+509 4,772	
Ormonde A. (FF)	2,133	+50 2,183	+51 2,234	+7 2,241	+11 2,252	+5 2,257	+16 2,273	+64 2,337	+66 2,403	+146 2,549	+142 2,691		
Garland R. (GA)	1,377	+78 1,455	+2 1,457	+9 1,466	+17 1,483	+23 1,506	+54 1,560	+264 1,824	+331 2,155				

O Liathain E.E. (WP)	1,308	+39 / 1,347	+3 / 1,350	+2 / 1,352	+5 / 1,357	+16 / 1,373	+27 / 1,400	
Duchon M. (TRL)	1,253	+85 / 1,338	+4 / 1,342	+21 / 1,363	+21 / 1,384	+31 / 1,415	+22 / 1,437	+129 / 1,566
Sharkey T. (Ind)	189	+14 / 203	+1 / 204	+9 / 213	+9 / 222	+18 / 240		
O'Neill P. (Ind)	142	+12 / 154	+0 / 154	+9 / 163	+7 / 170			
Hyland B.	114	+11 / 125	+0 / 125	+2 / 127				
MacFeorais M. (Ind)	107	+3 / 110	+0 / 110					

ANNE COLLEY (PD) First elected 1987.
Address: Liscannor, Beaumont Avenue, Churchtown, Dublin 14.
Tel: 01 986276.
Born: 1952.
Married: Dr Gerry Ormond, 3 children.
Education: Notre Dame Convent, Churchtown; Sacred Heart Convent, Mount Anville, Dublin; Incorporated Law Society, Blackhall Place, Dublin.
Occupation: Public representative. Former solicitor. Member of organising committee for the First National Conference of the Progressive Democrats, May 1986.

TOM KITT (FF) First elected 1987. Member Dublin County Council since 1979. Member of the County Dublin Education Committee; Cultural and Environmental Committee; Roads and Transport Committee; Local Health Committee.
Home address: 3 Pine Valley Drive, Rathfarnham, Dublin 16; business address: Our Lady's Boys NS, Ballinteer, Dublin 16.
Tel: Home 01 946507; Business 01 945616.
Born: Galway, Jul 1952.
Married: Jacinta Burke-Walshe. 2 sons, 1 daughter.
Education: St Jarlath's College, Tuam, Co Galway; St Patrick's Teacher Training College, Drumcondra, Dublin.
Occupation: Public representative and primary school teacher. County Councillor. Member Amnesty International; Irish Anti-Apartheid Movement; Irish CND; St John's GAA Club, Ballinteer.

SEAMUS BRENNAN (FF) First elected 1981. Appointed Junior Minister for Trade and Marketing Mar 1987. Senator 1977-81. Member Oireachtas Committee on Procedure and Privileges 1977-81. Vice-Chairman Oireachtas Committee on State Sponsored Bodies; Oireachtas Committee on EEC Legislation 1982. Government Deputy Whip Seanad 1977-81. General Secretary Fianna Fáil 1973-80. Founded Fianna Fáil youth movement 1974.
Home address: 17 Hollywood Drive, Goatstown, Dublin 14; constituency office: 9 Braemor Road, Churchtown, Dublin 14.
Tel: Home 01 987518; Business 01 951717.
Born: Galway, Feb 1948.
Married: Ann O'Shaughnessy. 1 son, 4 daughters.
Education: St Joseph's Secondary School, Galway; UCG.
Occupation: Public representative, accountant and management consultant.

ALAN SHATTER (FG) First elected June 1981. Member Joint Oireachtas Committee on Marital Breakdown 1982-87. Member Dublin County Council since June 1979. Chairman Dublin County Health Committee (1982-83).
Home address: 14 Crannagh Park, Rathfarnham, Dublin 14; business
    address: 4, Ely Place, Dublin.
Tel: Home 0l 900033; Business 01 681874
Born: Dublin, Feb 1951.
Married: Carol Danker. 1 son, 1 daughter.
Education: High School, Dublin; TCD; University of Amsterdam; Law
    School of the Incorporated Law Society of Ireland.
Occupation: Public representative, solicitor, author and lecturer.
    Former Director Free Legal Advice Centres. Member CARE
    (Chairman 1977); Mental Health Association of Ireland; Anti-
    Apartheid Movement; Irish Council of the European Movement.
    Consultant on family law to the Incorporated Law Society and author
    of *Family Law in the Republic of Ireland.*

JOHN KELLY (FG) First elected 1973. Senator 1969-73. Minister for Industry, Commerce and Tourism 1981-82; Acting Minister for Foreign Affairs 1981. Parliamentary Secretary to the Taoiseach 1973-77; to the Minister for Foreign Affairs 1975-77. Government Chief Whip 1973-77. Opposition spokesman on Industry and Commerce 1977-79; Economic Planning and Development and Energy 1979-81.
Home address: 17 Ailesbury Road, Dublin 4.
Tel: 01 694138.
Born: Dublin, Aug 1931
Married: Delphine Dudley. 3 sons, 2 daughters.
Education: Glenstal Abbey, Co Limerick; UCD; Heidelberg
    University; Oxford University; Kings Inns, Dublin.
Occupation: Public representative, university professor and senior
    counsel. Member New Ireland Forum; Joint Oireachtas Committee
    on Public Expenditure 1982-87. Professor of Jurisprudence and
    Roman Law at UCD since 1965; Fellow and lecturer in law at
    Trinity College, Oxford 1961-65. Practised at the Irish Bar 1957-62.
    Author of *Fundamental Rights in the Irish Law and Constitution,*
    Roman Litigation, Studies in the Civil Judicature of the Roman
    Republic and *The Irish Constitution.*

DUBLIN SOUTH CENTRAL (5)

Elected: *Ben Briscoe (FF) 1st Count; *Gay Mitchell (FG) 8th Count; *Fergus O'Brien (FG) 9th Count; *Frank Cluskey (LAB), Mary Mooney (FF) 11th Count.

Despite predictions that both Fergus O'Brien and Frank Cluskey were likely to lose their seats, it was the legendary vote-getter, John O'Connell of FF, who was the unexpected casualty, with his personal vote down significantly on 1981 (he was Ceann Comhairle for both elections in 1982 and was returned automatically). His seat was taken by Mary Mooney, a 28-year-old Alderman contesting her first general election. Although she had fewer first-preference votes than John O'Connell, she improved her position as the count continued and finally overtook him after the elimination of Eric Byrne of the WP and the distribution of his votes. Fine Gael saw its share of first-preference votes drop by 12 per cent, though Fergus O'Brien managed to poll well enough to stay in the race until he exceeded the quota with the distribution of Ronnie McBrien's (PD) vote. O'Brien took 3,211 of McBrien's 5,842 votes. For Lab Frank Cluskey defied those preparing to write his political obituary. It was transfers from Eric Byrne (WP) and, ironically, Ronnie McBrien (PD), together with Fergus O'Brien's surplus which secured a seat in the 25th Dáil for the former Lab leader.

FEB 87 % Poll		NOV 82 % Poll		Electorate:	78,116	
FF	40.9	FF	37.1	Total poll:	52,317	(67%)
FG	27.6	FG	39.6	Spoiled votes:	625	
PD	10.1	—	—	Total valid poll:	51,692	
LAB	9.1	LAB	14.0	Quota:	8,616	
WP	7.6	WP	8.2			
SF	2.4	—	—			
OTH	2.2	OTH	1.1	13 Candidates		

COUNTS	1st	2nd Briscoe Surplus (966) (NT) (6)	3rd Wall Votes (102) (NT) (1)	4th Hyland Votes (155) (NT) (9)	5th Buggle Votes (265) (NT) (20)	6th Cahill Votes (777) (NT) (49)	7th O'Muireagain Votes (1,343) (NT) (238)	8th Byrne Votes (4,638) (NT) (678)	9th McBrien Votes (5,842) (NT) (641)	10th Mitchell Surplus (152)	11th O'Brien Surplus (1,114)
Briscoe B. (FF)	**9,582**										
Mitchell G. (FG)	8,107	+38 8,145	+3 8,148	+15 8,163	+6 8,169	+90 8,259	+47 8,306	+462 **8,768**			
O'Brien F. (FG)	6,160	+23 6,183	+1 6,184	+8 6,192	+4 6,196	+71 6,267	+41 6,308	+211 6,519	+3,211 **9,730**		
O'Connell J. (FF)	5,911	+346 6,257	+2 6,259	+1 6,260	+11 6,271	+39 6,310	+178 6,488	+365 6,853	+358 7,211	+28 7,239	+141 7,380
Mooney M. (FF)	5,656	+445 6,101	+0 6,101	+12 6,113	+18 6,131	+61 6,192	+255 6,447	+606 7,053	+469 7,522	+37 7,559	+153 **7,712**
McBrien R. (PD)	5,212	+24 5,236	+3 5,239	+20 5,259	+7 5,266	+154 5,420	+36 5,456	+386 5,842			
Cluskey F. (Lab)	4,701	+37 4,738	+3 4,741	+15 4,756	+39 4,795	+181 4,976	+134 5,110	+1930 7,048	+1163 8,203	+87 8,290	+820 **9,110**
Byrne E. (WP)	3,946	+32 3,978	+19 3,997	+17 4,014	+95 4,109	+115 4,224	+414 4,638				
O'Muireagain M. (SF)	1,266	+5 1,271	+10 1,281	+1 1,282	+44 1,326	+17 1,343					
Cahill T. (TRL)	711	+4 715	+1 716	+40 756	+21 777						
Buggle D. (CPI)	186	+6 192	+56 248	+17 265							
Hyland B	152	+0 152	+3 155								
Wall M. (CPI)	102	+0 102									

BEN BRISCOE (FF) First elected 1965. Represented four different Dublin constituencies in successive Dáileanna: Dublin South-West 1965-69, Dublin South-Central 1969-77, Dublin Rathmines West 1977-81 and Dublin South Central since 1981. Member Committee of Public Accounts 1965-72; Committee of Selection since 1969; Committee on Procedure and Privileges since 1977. Assistant Chief Whip 1977-83. Member Dublin Corporation since 1967.
Home address: Shenandoah, Newtown, Celbridge, Co Kildare.
Tel: 01 288426.
Born: Ballybrack, Co Dublin, Mar 1934.
Married: Carol Ann Ward. 2 sons, 2 daughters.
Education: St Andrew's College, Dublin.
Occupation: Public representative. Chairman of Dublin Corporation Cultural Committee. Member Eastern Health Board; Finance Committee of Cheeverstown House for Mentally Handicapped. Son of Robert Briscoe, Dail Deputy 1927-65 and Lord Mayor of Dublin 1956-57 and 1961-62.

GAY MITCHELL (FG) First elected 1981. Party Spokesman on Health Boards 1982. Member Dublin City Council since 1979. Member Local Government Reform Committee; Public Accounts Committee. Chairman Motor Insurance Committee. Vice-Chairman Dáil Committee on Crime Lawlessness and Vandalism.
Home address: 192 Upper Rathmines Road, Dublin 6.
Tel: 01 972475.
Born: Inchicore, Dublin 1951.
Married: Norma O'Connor. 3 children.
Education: St Michael's CBS Inchicore; Emmet Road Vocational School, Dublin; College of Commerce, Rathmines; UCD.
Occupation: Public representative. Former accountant. Member City of Dublin VEC since 1979. Chairman Rathmines College of Commerce Committee since 1979. Member Dublin Institute of Technology and Bolton Street College Councils. Member Anti-Apartheid Movement.

FERGUS O'BRIEN (FG) First elected 1973. Government Chief Whip and Minister of State Departments of the Taoiseach, Environment and Defence, 1986-87. Minister of State Department of the Environment 1983-87; 1981-82; Department of Social Welfare 1982-83. Member Committee on Procedure and Privileges 1973-77; All-Party Committee on State Sponsored Bodies 1976-77.
Home address: 60 Ranelagh Road, Dublin 6.
Tel: 01 979546.
Born: Dublin, Mar 1930.
Married: Margaret Moylan. 1 son, 5 daughters.
Education: College of Technology, Kevin Street, Dublin; College of Industrial Relations, Sandford Road, Dublin.
Occupation: Public representative. Former ESB official. Dublin City Commissioner 1973-74. Member Dublin City Council 1974-81. Lord Mayor of Dublin 1980-81.

FRANK CLUSKEY (LAB) First elected 1965. Junior Minister for Health and Social Welfare 1973-77. Leader of the Labour Party 1977-81. Elected to the European Parliament in 1979. Became Minister for Industry Commerce and Energy in Nov 1982 and resigned from the Ministry over the Dublin Gas issue a year later.
Home address: 1 Glasnevin Park, Ballymun, Dublin 11.
Tel: 01 422818.
Born: Dublin 1930.
Married: Eileen Gillespie (dec.). 1 son, 2 daughters.
Occupation: Public representative. Former trade union official.

MARY MOONEY (FF) First elected 1987.
Home address: Glenora, Strawberry Beds, Lucan; business address: 67/68 Meath St, Dublin 2.
Tel: Home 01 213457; Business 01 757296.
Born: Liberties, Dublin 1958.
Marital status: Single.
Education: St Theresa's Presentation College, Dublin.
Occupation: Public representative and shopkeeper. Joined FF Dublin South-Central 1983. Alderman South Inner City 1985. Member Houses & General Purposes Committee.

DUBLIN SOUTH EAST (4)

Elected: *Garret FitzGerald (FG) 1st Count; *Gerry Brady (FF) 12th Count; Michael McDowell (PD) 14th Count; *Ruairi Quinn (LAB) 15th Count.

FF were hoping to return to the Jun 1981 situation when they held two seats here. It was also widely predicted that this would prove a good battleground for the PDs. In the event the PD challenge succeeded with Michael McDowell, Dr FitzGerald's former director of elections in this constituency, easily taking a seat from FG's Joe Doyle while benefiting from 61 per cent of Doyle's transfers. In the Taoiseach's base, the FG vote was down 15.4 per cent — almost exactly the share achieved by the PDs on their first outing, 15.6 per cent. Fianna Fáil increased their vote by 1.6 per cent but were still nearly six points off their 1981 performance and, with too many candidates in the field, failed to improve on Nov '82. Former Lab Minister Ruairi Quinn saw his vote drop by 5.7 per cent, but with 31 per cent of Green Alliance transfers and 30 per cent from the WP, he stayed ahead of the row of FF candidates and Joe Doyle to pass the quota on the 15th count with a massive 80 per cent of McDowell's transfers. These votes came down from Joe Doyle — and showed that in South East the FG/Lab Coalition was not forgotten that quickly, to Ruairi Quinn's benefit. Dublin South East had the lowest turnout in the country at 56.5 per cent — reflecting the high flat-dwelling population in Rathmines, Rathgar and Ranelagh — and the Green Alliance vote of 3 per cent could be an interesting base for the future.

FF % Poll		FG % Poll		Electorate:	68,286	
FF	32.7	FF	31.1	Total poll:	38,614	(56.5%)
FG	32.0	FG	47.4	Spoiled votes:	344	
PD	15.6	—	—	Total valid poll:	38,270	
LAB	9.1	LAB	14.8	Quota:	7,655	
WP	5.0	WP	4.6			
SF	2.1	—	—			
OTH	3.5	OTH	2.1	16 Candidates		

COUNTS	1st	2nd Fitz-Gerald Surplus (413)	3rd Clarke Votes (29)	4th Hyland Votes (68)	5th Brennan Votes (173)	6th Crilly Votes (694)	7th O'Snod-aigh Votes (845)	8th Egan Votes (989)	9th Mull-amey Votes (1,340)	10th Ryan Votes (1,972)	11th Smith Votes (2,315)	12th McAleese Votes (3,712)	13th Brady Surplus (355)	14th Doyle Votes (4,663)	15th McDowell Surplus (2,117)
FitzGerald G. (FG)	**8,068**														
(NT)			(NT) (1)	(NT) (1)	(NT) (9)	(NT) (10)	(NT) (117)	(NT) (14)	(NT) (111)	(NT) (1)	(NT) (632)	(NT) (192)	(763)	(NT) (261)	(NT)
McDowell M. (PD)	5,961	+74 6,035	+0 6,035	+5 6,040	+9 6,049	+27 6,076	+23 6,099	+184 6,283	+206 6,489	+86 6,575	+170 6,745	+178 6,923	+12 6,935	+2,837 **9,772**	
Brady G. (FF)	5,560	+5 5,565	+2 5,567	+1 5,568	+7 5,575	+19 5,594	+87 5,681	+12 5,693	+28 5,721	+713 6,434	+228 6,662	+1348 **8,010**			
Quinn R. (Lab)	3,480	+26 3,506	+1 3,507	+9 3,516	+19 3,535	+64 3,599	+72 3,671	+42 3,713	+418 4,131	+104 4,235	+839 5,074	+170 5,244	+16 5,260	+876 6,136	+1,704 **7,840**
Doyle J. (FG)	3,323	+175 3,498	+1 3,499	+3 3,502	+10 3,512	+29 3,541	+14 3,575	+699 4,254	+129 4,383	+55 4,438	+151 4,589	+67 4,656	+7 4,663		
Donnelly M. (FF)	2,838	+2 2,840	+3 2,843	+2 2,845	+8 2,853	+22 2,875	+61 2,936	+9 2,945	+28 2,973	+421 3,394	+143 3,537	+1,157 4,694	+320 5,014	+187 5,201	+152 5,353
McAleese M. (FF)	2,243	+4 2,247	+0 2,247	+4 2,251	+7 2,258	+9 2,267	+90 2,357	+13 2,370	+87 2,457	+503 2,960	+152 3,112				
Ryan E. (FF)	1,881	+2 1,883	+0 1,883	+2 1,885	+2 1,887	+13 1,900	+33 1,933	+4 1,937	+35 1,972						
Smith A. (WP)	1,250	+2 1,252	+1 1,253	+1 1,254	+19 1,273	+455 1,728	+196 1,924	+4 1,928	+298 2,226	+89 2,315					
Mullarney M. (GA)	1,094	+4 1,098	+1 1,099	+21 1,120	+46 1,166	+18 1,184	+148 1,332	+8 1,340							

Egan W. (FG)	860	+116 976	+0 976	+2 978	+1 979	+6 985	+4 989
O'Snodaigh A. (SF)	811	+0 811	+2 813	+0 813	+10 823	+22 845	
Crilly J. (WP)	660	+1 661	+6 667	+1 668	+26 694		
Brennan G. (Ind)	147	+1 148	+9 157	+16 173			
Hyland B. (Ind)	65	+1 66	+2 68				
Clarke P. (Ind)	29	+0 29					

MICHAEL MC DOWELL (PD) First elected 1987. Founding member, joint trustee and Chairman of the national executive of the Progressive Democrats. He is a grandson of Eoin McNeill, founder of the Irish Volunteers and Minister of Finance in Dáil Éireann. Former FG Chairman of Dublin South East Constituency. Member and Honorary Secretary of the Council at Kings Inns, and the Incorporated Council of Law Reporting for Ireland.
Home address: 15 Mount Pleasant Square, Dublin 6.
Tel: Home 01 974955; Business 01 720622.
Born: Dublin, May 1951.
Married: Niamh Brennan.
Education: Pembroke School; Gonzaga College; UCD. Kings Inns.
Occupation: Public representative and barrister.

RUAIRI QUINN (LAB) First elected 1977. Minister for Labour and the Public Service 1986-87. Minister for Labour 1983-86. Senator 1981-82. Junior Minister Department of the Environment 1982-83.
Home address: 7 Railway Cottages, Dublin 4.
Tel: Home 01 602367; Business 01 742961
Born: Dublin, Apr 1946.
Married: Nicola Underwood. 1 daughter, 1 son.
Education: Blackrock College, Dublin; UCD; Athens Centre of Ekistics.
Occupation: Public representative, architect and lecturer. Partner in Burke-Kennedy, Doyle and Partners.

GARRET FITZGERALD (FG) First elected 1969. Taoiseach 1982-87; 1981-82. Minister for Foreign Affairs 1973-77. Leader of Fine Gael 1977-87. Opposition spokesman on Education 1969-72; Finance 1972-73. Senator 1965-69. Co-signatory Anglo-Irish Agreement Nov 1985; President European Council Jun-Dec 1984.
Home address: 30 Palmerston Road, Dublin 6.
Tel: 01 767803.
Born: Dublin 1926.
Married: Joan O'Farrell. 1 daughter, 2 sons.
Education: St Brigid's School, Bray; Colaiste na Rinne, Waterford; Belvedere College, Dublin; UCD; Kings Inns, Dublin.
Occupation: Public representative. Former economist, lecturer, financial journalist and Aer Lingus Research & Schedules Manager. Founder New Ireland Forum. Member Executive Committee and Council of Institute of Public Administration since 1961. Member Governing Body of UCD since 1964; Senate of the National University of Ireland since 1973. Author of *State-Sponsored Bodies* (1959); *Planning in Ireland* (1968); *Towards a New Ireland* (1972); and *Unequal Partners* (UNCTAD 1979). Governor Atlantic Institute on International Relations, Paris. Son of Desmond FitzGerald, substitute Director of Propaganda in first Dáil, Minister for External Affairs in the Provisional Government, Minister for External Affairs and later Minister for Defence in the Executive Councils up to 1932.

GERRY BRADY (FF) First elected 1977. Minister for Education Oct-Dec 1982. Minister of State at the Department of the Environment Mar-Oct 1982. Member Dublin City Council since 1974.
Home address: 9 Greenfield Park, Donnybrook, Dublin 4.
Tel: Home 01 694172; Business 01 758484.
Born: Dublin 1936.
Married: Antoinette Freeman. 3 sons, 1 daughter.
Education: St Mary's College, Rathmines; College of Science and Technology; College of Pharmacy.
Occupation: Public representative and opthalmic optician. Son of Philip A. Brady, TD for Dublin South-Central 1951-54, 1957-77, and Lord Mayor of Dublin 1959-60.

DUBLIN SOUTH WEST (4)

Elected: *Mary Harney (PD) 8th Count; Chris Flood (FF) 10th Count; *Sean Walsh (FF) 12th Count; *Mervyn Taylor (LAB) 13th Count.

The result here gave FF back the two seats it held before Mary Harney was expelled from the party, and her subsequent involvement in setting up the PDs. Going through that political firestorm did Harney no harm electorally — her first-preference vote went up 77 per cent — at the expense of FG, whose vote collapsed by more than 20 per cent. Senator Larry McMahon's words to the FG selection convention proved prophetic. He said the party which had credibly aimed just a few years ago at two seats in the constituency would be hard pressed to retain one seat. McMahon was chosen to fly the flag once again with two others, after being ousted from his seat in Nov '82 by FG's new recruit, the former Labour Party leader, Michael O'Leary. On the eve of the convention O'Leary announced his resignation from politics — there were strong doubts anyway about his re-selection by the convention.

Fianna Fáil's strategy of running just two candidates worked well with their men evenly balanced on the 1st count. One of the most notable features was the strong poll by the WP's Pat Rabbitte who ran nearly 500 votes ahead of Lab's former poll-topper, Mervyn Taylor, making inroads into the working class-vote in Tallaght and Greenhills. This constituency must be a target for the WP in the next election. Mervyn Taylor had to wait on a 53 per cent transfer from the eliminated Larry McMahon to hold his seat on the 13th count.

FEB 87		NOV 82		Electorate:	59,955	
% Poll		% Poll				
FF	38.6	FF	36.5	Total poll:	41,902	(69.9%)
FG	12.7	FG	33.5	Spoiled votes:	448	
PD	19.7	—	—	Total valid poll:	41,454	
LAB	12.2	LAB	20.7	Quota:	8,291	
WP	12.3	WP	6.3			
SF	3.3	—	—			
OTH	1.2	OTH	3.0	15 Candidates		

COUNTS	1st	2nd O'Flangan Votes (64)	3rd Hyland Votes (73)	4th Jago Votes (177)	5th Maloney Votes (239)	6th Dunne Votes (400)	7th Walsh Votes (484)	8th Ridge Votes (666)	9th Harney Surplus (137)	10th Noonan Votes (1,320)	11th Cass Votes (1,449)	12th Flood Surplus (199)	13th McMahon Votes (4,819)
		(NT) (4)		(NT) (16)	(NT) (13)	(NT) (7)	(NT) (5)	(NT) (7)		(NT) (357)	(NT) (92)	(NT) (18)	(NT) (1,645)
Harney M. (PD)	8,169	+3 8,172	+6 8,178	+21 8,199	+37 8,236	+16 8,252	+20 8,272	+156 **8,428**					
Flood C. (FF)	8,082	+6 8,088	+4 8,092	+35 8,127	+18 8,145	+34 8,179	+62 8,241	+14 8,255	+8 8,263	+227 **8,490**			
Walsh S. (FF)	7,922	+6 7,928	+3 7,931	+5 7,936	+7 7,943	+12 7,955	+49 8,004	+11 8,015	+10 8,025	+167 8,192	+28 8,220	+138 **8,358**	
Rabbitte P. (WP)	5,086	+9 5,095	+5 5,100	+40 5,140	+67 5,207	+23 5,230	+41 5,271	+25 5,296	+15 5,311	+384 5,695	+86 5,781	+19 5,800	+608 6,408
Taylor M. (Lab)	4,607	+8 4,615	+6 4,621	+22 4,643	+43 4,686	+11 4,697	+291 4,988	+48 5,036	+28 5,064	+152 5,216	+141 5,357	+19 5,376	+2566 **7,942**
McMahon L. (FG)	3,407	+4 3,411	+1 3,412	+7 3,419	+8 3,427	+4 3,431	+11 3,442	+219 3,661	+31 3,692	+20 3,712	+1102 4,814	+5 4,819	
Cass B. (FG)	1,187	+1 1,188	+4 1,192	+4 1,196	+11 1,207	+3 1,210	+1 1,211	+181 1,392	+44 1,436	+13 1,449			
Noonan J. (SF)	1,001	+1 1,002	+2 1,004	+4 1,008	+17 1,025	+287 1,312	+2 1,314	+5 1,319	+1 1,320				
Ridge T. (FG)	656	+0 656	+2 658	+2 660	+4 664	+0 664	+2 666						
Walsh E. (Lab)	458	+4 462	+3 465	+5 470	+11 481	+3 484							
Dunne C. (SF)	378	+2 380	+11 391	+6 397	+3 400								
Maloney E. (DSP)	223	+2 225	+4 229	+10 239									
Jago G. (Ind)	143	+12 155	+22 177										
Hyland B	71	+2 73											
O'Flanagan D. (Ind)	64												

SEAN WALSH (FF) First elected in 1973 for Dublin North County. Elected 1977 for Dublin Mid County. Senator from 1969-73. Chairman Belgard Council 1985-87. Member Dublin County Council since 1967 (Vice-Chairman 1972); Dublin County VEC since 1974.
Home address: 62 St Columba's Road, Greenhills Estate, Dublin 12. Tel: 01 509767.
Born: Birchfield, Co Kilkenny, Apr 1927.
Marital status: Single.
Education: De La Salle Secondary School, Kilkenny.
Occupation: Public representative. Former farmer and market gardener.
    Member GAA.

155

CHRIS FLOOD (FF) First elected 1987. Member Dublin County Council since 1979. Member of the Get Tallaght Working Co-Operative; West Tallaght Enterprise Committee. Chairman Deansrath Community College Board of Management; Enterprise and Employment Committee of Dublin County Council.
Home address: 22 Birchview Lawn, Kilnamanagh, Tallaght, Dublin 24; business address: Apex House, Greenmount Industrial Estate, Harolds Cross, Dublin 12.
Tel: Home 01 518574; Business 01 533177.
Born: Westmeath, May 1947.
Married: Carmel O'Dwyer. 1 son, 3 daughters.
Education: St Norbert's College, Ballyjamesduff, Co Cavan.
Occupation: Public representative and businessman.

MERVYN TAYLOR (LAB) First elected 1981. Member Dublin County Council since 1974. Vice-Chairman of the Labour Party and Parliamentary Whip. Former Chairman of the Joint Oireachtas Committee on Legislation.
Home address: 4 Springfield Road, Dublin 14.
Tel: Home 01 758221; Business 01 904569.
Born: Dublin 1931.
Married: Marilyn Fisher. 2 sons, 1 daughter.
Education: Zion NS; Wesley College, Dublin; TCD.
Occupation: Public representative and solicitor.

MARY HARNEY (PD) First elected for FF 1981. Senator 1977-81. Founder members PDs, Dec 1985. Member Dublin County Council since 1979. First female Auditor Trinity College Historical Society.
Home address: Upperlands, Newcastle, Co Dublin.
Tel: 01 589651.
Born: Ballinasloe, Co Galway 1953.
Education: Newcastle NS; Convent of Mercy, Inchicore; Presentation Convent, Clondalkin; TCD.
Occupation: Public representative. Former researcher and teacher.

DUBLIN WEST (5)

Elected: *Brian Lenihan (FF) 12th Count; *Tomas McGiolla (WP) 13th Count; *Jim Mitchell (FG) 16th Count; Pat O'Malley (PD), Liam Lawlor (FF) 17th Count.

The FG vote here took one of its biggest tumbles in the country, down 21 per cent. The party, which had held two seats here in Nov '82 and three in Jun '81 and Feb '82, was reduced to a meagre one seat. The background to this disaster is well known. Liam Skelly, the high-profile dissident who threatened repeatedly to bring down the government over his plan for a major development scheme in Dublin city centre (see chapter one), was refused a nomination for FG and stood as an Independent. When he was eliminated on the 13th count his votes scattered everywhere, with the biggest share, 27 per cent, going to elect the WP's Tomas McGiolla. When the PDs' second candidate, James Fay, a former member of FG, was eliminated, 63.5 per cent of his votes transferred to Des O'Malley's cousin Pat O'Malley, the leading PD candidate, putting him in a strategic position to benefit from transfers from FG's Brian Fleming, and then Jim Mitchell's surplus, to bring him home on the 17th count. Fianna Fáil expressed some hopes of getting three seats, but though their vote was up 3.9 per cent it was not enough. The last hours of the campaign were marred by allegations of dirty tricks, with Liam Lawlor accusing unnamed supporters of his party running mate, Brian Lenihan, of spreading misleading literature about his views on a constituency road scheme. Lawlor slipped comfortably into the FF seat vacated by Eileen Lemass when she opted for Europe.

For FG, there was heavy irony in their result here. Liam Skelly, then a political unknown, won a seat for them in the famous by-election of May 1982. Charles Haughey had appointed the sitting FG TD, Dick Burke, as Ireland's European Commissioner, precipitating the by-election. It had been intended as a master stroke; a FF victory would strengthen Mr Haughey's minority government. In the event Liam Skelly took the seat for FG. His win helped to restore FG's morale after their defeat in the Feb by-election and it paved the way for the party's success in Nov '82 when it won the biggest number of seats in its history.

FEB 87 % Poll		NOV 82 % Poll		Electorate:	75,366	
FF	40.5	FF	36.6	Total poll:	52,246	(69.3%)
FG	22.2	FG	43.2	Spoiled votes:	534	
PD	11.6	—	—	Total valid poll:	51,712	
LAB	2.3	LAB	3.9	Quota:	8,619	
WP	12.9	WP	14.7			
SF	2.0	—	—			
OTH	8.6	OTH	1.6	20 Candidates		

COUNTS	1st	2nd Hyland Vote (43)	3rd Roche Votes (72)	4th Montgomery Votes (225)	5th McMenamy Votes (244)	6th Gallagher Votes (319)	7th O'Connor Votes (620)	8th Conaghan Votes (690)	9th Lyons Votes (815)	10th Loftus Votes (943)	11th Delaney Votes (1,196)	12th Tuffy Votes (1,448)	13th Skelly Votes (2,326)	14th Fay Votes (3,213)	15th Mac Giolla Surplus (235)	16th Fleming Votes (5,508)	17th Mitchell Surplus (3,224)
		(NT) (2)	(NT) (3)	(NT) (13)	(NT) (6)	(NT) (8)	(NT) (12)	(NT) (26)	(NT) (61)	(NT) (10)	(NT) (216)	(NT) (86)	(NT) (214)	(NT) (192)		(NT) (381)	(NT) (173)
Lenihan B. (FF)	8,278	+6 8,284	+1 8,285	+4 8,289	+7 8,296	+47 8,343	+15 8,358	+26 8,384	+71 8,455	+19 8,474	+123 8,597	+53 **8,650**					
Lawlor L. (FF)	7,020	+4 7,024	+0 7,024	+11 7,035	+12 7,047	+32 7,079	+12 7,091	+19 7,110	+54 7,164	+5 7,169	+98 7,267	+48 7,315	+268 7,583	+153 7,736	+43 7,779	+192 7,977	+141 **8,112**
MacGiolla T. (WP)	6,651	+2 6,653	+5 6,658	+66 6,724	+41 6,765	+34 6,799	+119 6,918	+214 7,132	+100 7,232	+15 7,247	+392 7,639	+581 8,220	+634 **8,854**				
Mitchell J. (FG)	6,585	+1 6,586	+1 6,587	+11 6,598	+41 6,639	+19 6,658	+29 6,687	+93 6,780	+68 6,848	+284 7,132	+50 7,182	+136 7,318	+329 7,647	+275 7,922	+42 7,964	+3879 **11,843**	
Bennett O. (FF)	5,622	+1 5,623	+3 5,626	+9 5,635	+34 5,669	+28 5,697	+26 5,723	+47 5,770	+58 5,828	+14 5,842	+116 5,958	+50 6,008	+195 6,203	+129 6,332	+38 6,370	+105 6,475	+90 6,565
Fleming B. (FG)	4,011	+1 4,012	+0 4,012	+2 4,014	+7 4,021	+17 4,038	+39 4,077	+18 4,095	+67 4,162	+455 4,617	+18 4,635	+164 4,799	+245 5,044	+423 5,467	+41 5,508		
O'Malley P. (PD)	3,308	+2 3,310	+1 3,311	+4 3,315	+12 3,327	+7 3,334	+41 3,375	+33 3,408	+44 3,452	+49 3,501	+11 3,512	+93 3,605	+256 3,861	+2041 5,902	+71 5,973	+951 6,924	+2820 **9,744**
Fay J. (PD)	2,706	+2 2,708	+0 2,708	+1 2,709	+2 2,711	+20 2,731	+23 2,754	+51 2,805	+91 2,896	+62 2,958	+26 2,984	+44 3,028	+185 3,213				
Skelly L. (Ind)	1,734	+5 1,739	+2 1,741	+8 1,749	+12 1,761	+21 1,782	+63 1,845	+45 1,890	+110 2,000	+21 2,021	+112 2,133	+193 2,326					
Tuffy E. (Lab)	1,185	+2 1,187	+3 1,190	+18 1,208	+9 1,217	+4 1,221	+85 1,306	+61 1,367	+39 1,406	+8 1,414	+34 1,448						

Candidate	1st Count	Count 2	Count 3	Count 4	Count 5	Count 6	Count 7	Count 8	Count 9	Count 10
Delaney J. (SF)	1,041	+0 1,041	+4 1,045	+52 1,097	+7 1,104	+11 1,115	+25 1,140	+36 1,176	+19 1,195	+1 1,196
Loftus E. (FG)	860	+1 861	+1 862	+0 862	+2 864	+6 870	+36 906	+4 910	+33 943	
Lyons S. (Ind)	675	+3 678	+0 678	+2 680	+20 700	+52 752	+46 798	+17 815		
Conaghan M. (DSP)	600	+2 602	+0 602	+10 612	+25 637	+4 641	+49 690			
O'Connor B. (GA)	587	+6 593	+6 599	+10 609	+2 611	+9 620				
Gallagher G. (Ind)	312	+1 313	+0 313	+1 314	+5 319					
McMenamy B. (Ind)	239	+2 241	+0 241	+3 244						
Montgomery J. (CPI)	183	+42 225								
Roche J. (CPI)	72	+0 72								
Hyland B. (Ind)	43									

BRIAN LENIHAN (FF) First elected in 1961 for Roscommon/Leitrim. Appointed Tanaiste and Minister for Foreign Affairs Mar 1987. Minister for Agriculture Mar-Dec 1982; Minister for Foreign Affairs 1979-81; Jan-Mar 1973; Minister for Forestry and Fisheries 1977-1979; Minister for Transport and Power 1969-73; Minister for Education 1968-69; Minister for Justice 1964-68. Parliamentary Secretary to the Minister for Lands and Fisheries 1961-64; to the Minister for Justice Oct-Nov 1964. Leader of the FF party in the Seanad 1973-77. Dáil deputy for Roscommon/Leitrim 1961-73. Member European Parliament and leader of the FF delegation 1973-77. Senator 1957-61. Deputy leader FF since 1983.
Home address: 24 Park View, Castleknock, Co Dublin.
Tel: 01 213453.
Born: Dundalk, Co Louth, Nov 1930.
Married: Ann Devine. 4 sons, 1 daughter.
Education: Marist Brothers Secondary School, Athlone; UCD; Kings Inns, Dublin.
Occupation: Public representative and barrister-at-law. Member Dublin County Council 1974-77; Roscommon County Council 1955-61. Son of Patrick Lenihan, Dáil deputy for Longford/Westmeath 1965-70.

PAT O'MALLEY (PD) First elected 1987.
Home address: Leys Lodge, Lucan, Co Dublin.
Tel: 01 280812.
Born: Limerick 1943.
Married: Anne Heaveney. 3 sons, 1 daughter.
Education: UCD.
Occupation: Public representative and Company Director. Chairman of Lucan Constituency Council.

LIAM LAWLOR (FF) First elected in 1977. Lost his seat in 1982. Member Dublin County Council since 1979; Eastern Regional Development Organisation since 1979.
Home address: Somerton, Lucan, Co Dublin.
Tel: Home 01 241842; Business 01 280507.
Born: Dublin, Oct 1944.
Married: Hazel Barber. 3 sons, 1 daughter.
Education: Synge Street CBS; College of Technology, Bolton Street, Dublin.
Occupation: Public representative. Member Trilateral Commission. Member Board of Management Coolmine, Lucan and Collinstown Colleges.

TOMAS MAC GIOLLA (WP) First elected in Nov 1982. Member Dublin Corporation since 1979. Leader of the Workers Party.
Home address: 49 St Laurence's Road, Chapelizod, Dublin 20.
Tel: 01 267429.
Born: Nenagh, Co Tipperary, Jan 1924.
Married: May McLoughlin.
Education: Nenagh Boys NS; CBS Nenagh; St Flanan's College, Ennis; UCD.
Occupation: Public representative. Former ESB employee.

JIM MITCHELL (FG) First elected 1977. Minister for Transport; Minister for Posts and Telegraphs 1982-83; Minister for Communications Dec 1983-87; Minister for Justice Jun 1981-Feb 1982. Opposition spokesman on Labour and the Public Service 1977-81; on Justice Mar-Dec 1982.
Home address: 10 Dargle Valley, Marley Grange, Dublin 16.
Tel: 01 947580.
Born: Inchicore, Dublin 1946.
Married: Patricia Kenny. 2 sons, 2 daughters.
Education: James' CBS, Dublin; Vocational School, Inchicore; Emmet Road Vocational School; College of Commerce Rathmines; TCD.
Occupation: Public representative. Member Dublin City Council 1974-81. Lord Mayor 1976-77. President EEC Council of Transport.

DUN LAOGHAIRE (5)

Elected: *David Andrews (FF) 7th Count; *Sean Barrett (FG) 10th Count; Geraldine Kennedy (PD), *Barry Desmond (LAB) 12th Count; *Monica Barnes (FG) 13th Count.

Known in FG electoral folklore as the "premier constituency" because of the party's long dominance — in the past due to the polling power of the former Taoiseach Liam Cosgrave. His son took over his seat in 1981 but with Liam Junior falling victim to the PD surge on the 9th count, the unbroken tradition of a Cosgrave presence in the Dail since 1918 came to an end. Once again it was a FG-dominated constituency where most observers agreed that the PDs were likely to gain a seat, though the imposition of former political journalist Geraldine Kennedy along with the two local candidates caused some resentment. Helen Keogh, the local candidate with the best chance of taking a seat, told the selection convention that she would work to ensure nobody else was added to the ticket. On the day she polled well and was just 1,000 votes behind Geraldine Kennedy on the 1st count, justifying the local organisation's belief that they could win the seat without a "name" candidate. The FF performance was deeply disappointing to them, because Dun Laoghaire was one constituency where the party expected to take a second seat. They needed a swing of just 1.3 per cent - but in fact their vote was down 3.9 per cent on Nov '82. At the highest level in the party there is an admission that the campaign was badly split and suffered because of in-fighting between the two new candidates. Barry Desmond once again defied the prophets of doom who predicted that his high profile as a Minister for Health in the Coalition, with tough reforms introduced during his stewardship, would lead to his downfall. He looked comfortable on the 1st count, his vote slipping just 0.6 per cent — far less than the Lab national average. On the 9th count he benefited from the big WP vote, up nearly 5 per cent, and he took the fourth seat with over 500 transfers from Helen Keogh on the 12th count. The real struggle of the count was between Monica Barnes and Liam Cosgrave. With Cosgrave trailing his party colleague by 23 votes on the 9th, he called for a total recount — but it was in vain. The margin was adjusted by just two votes, and Cosgrave was eliminated. Monica Barnes took the last seat on the 13th count.

FEB 87 % Poll		NOV 82 % Poll		Electorate:	77,325	
				Total poll:	56,096	(72.5%)
FF	26.2	FF	30.0	Spoiled votes:	394	
FG	30.7	FG	52.5	Total valid poll:	55,702	
PD	19.8	—	—	Quota:	9,284	
LAB	11.6	LAB	12.2			
WP	7.3	WP	2.7			
SF	2.2	—	—			
OTH	2.3	OTH	2.5	15 Candidates		

COUNTS	1st	2nd Hyland	3rd Abel-O'Reilly	4th McGolddrick	5th Fitzpatrick	6th Lohan	7th Conroy	8th Andrews	9th Gilmore	10th Cosgrave	11th Barrett	12th Keogh	13th Kennedy
		Votes (124)	Votes (236)	Votes (982)	Votes (1,253)	Votes (1,656)	Votes (3,033)	Surplus (1,103)	Votes (4,872)	Votes (5,290)	Surplus (1,705)	Votes (5,824)	Surplus (1,707)
		(NT) (2)	(NT) (13)	(NT) (49)	(NT) (125)	(NT) (10)	(NT) (38)		(NT) (957)	(NT) (180)		(NT) (303)	
Andrews D. (FF)	8,414	+4 8,418	+38 8,456	+54 8,510	+234 8,744	+33 8,777	+1610 **10,387**						
Barrett S. (FG)	7,284	+10 7,294	+22 7,316	+52 7,368	+41 7,409	+99 7,508	+56 7,564	+18 7,582	+433 8,015	+2974 **10,989**			
Desmond B. (Lab)	6,484	+16 6,500	+25 6,525	+217 6,742	+86 6,828	+69 6,897	+82 6,979	+33 7,012	+1543 8,555	+380 8,935	+108 9,043	+532 **9,575**	
Kennedy G. (PD)	5,228	+13 5,241	+13 5,254	+68 5,322	+29 5,351	+446 5,797	+57 5,854	+24 5,878	+415 6,293	+314 6,607	+165 6,772	+4219 **10,991**	
Barnes M. (FG)	4,923	+4 4,927	+13 4,940	+112 5,052	+18 5,070	+26 5,096	+15 5,111	+7 5,118	+193 5,311	+1085 6,396	+1294 7,690	+629 8,319	+1491 **9,810**
Cosgrave L.T. (FG)	4,870	+9 4,879	+14 4,893	+37 4,930	+29 4,959	+39 4,998	+42 5,040	+8 5,048	+242 5,290				
Keogh H. (PD)	4,203	+8 4,211	+12 4,223	+69 4,292	+15 4,307	+866 5,173	+41 5,214	+16 5,230	+245 5,475	+229 5,704	+120 5,824		
Gilmore E. (WP)	4,054	+16 4,070	+17 4,087	+173 4,260	+480 4,740	+39 4,779	+68 4,847	+25 4,872					
McDonald E. (FF)	3,265	+5 3,270	+9 3,279	+38 3,317	+114 3,431	+14 3,445	+1024 4,469	+972 5,441	+844 6,285	+128 6,413	+18 6,431	+141 6,572	+216 6,788
Conroy R. (FF)	2,897	+6 2,903	+16 2,919	+28 2,947	+71 3,018	+15 3,033							
Lohan L. (PD)	1,592	+2 1,594	+7 1,601	+44 1,645	+11 1,656								
Fitzpatrick K. (SF)	1,202	+1 1,203	+9 1,212	+41 1,253									
McGoldrick A. (GA)	929	+25 954	+28 982										
Abel-O'Reilly P. (Ind)	233	+3 236											
Hyland B. (Ind)	124												

163

DAVID ANDREWS (FF) First elected 1965. Parliamentary Secretary to the Taoiseach and to the Minister for Defence 1970-73. Chief Whip of the Government 1970-73. Minister of State at the Department of Foreign Affairs from 1977-79; at the Department of Justice 1979. Opposition frontbench spokesman on Justice and Social Welfare 1973-77.
Home address: 8 Glenart Avenue, Blackrock, Co Dublin.
Tel: Home 01 887655; Business 01 789911.
Born: Dublin, Mar 1935.
Married: Annette Cusack. 2 sons, 3 daughters.
Education: Colaiste Mhuire, Dublin; Mount St Joseph's, Roscrea, Co
    Tipperary; UCD; Kings Inns, Dublin.
Occupation: Public representative and barrister-at-law. Member
    Committee on the Constitution 1967; New Ireland Forum. President
    UCD Association Football Club. Played rugby for Galwegians RFC
    and Palmerston RFC; represented Connaught at an inter-provincial
    level, and played soccer for UCD. Brother of Niall Andrews, MEP
    and former TD for Dublin South.

BARRY DESMOND (LAB) First elected 1969. Minister for Health and Social Welfare 1982-86; for Health 1986-87. Junior Minister for Finance 1981-82. Member of Dublin County Council 1974-1985. Deputy leader of the Labour Party.
Home address: 2 Taney Avenue, Goatstown, Dublin 14.
Tel: 01 985719.
Born: Cork 1935.
Married: Stella Murphy. 4 sons.
Occupation: Public representative. Former trade union official.
    Education Officer and Industrial Officer ICTU 1960-69; Member
    ITGWU since 1956. Member Maritime Institute. President Irish
    Council against Blood Sports.

GERALDINE KENNEDY (PD) First elected 1987.
Home address: 27 Fortwilliam, Mount Merrion Ave, Blackrock, Co Dublin.
Tel: 01 882148
Born: Glenbower, Carrick-on-Suir 1952.
Marital status: Single.
Occupation: Public representative. Former Journalist.

SEAN BARRET (FG) First elected 1981. Minister for Sport 1986-87. Leader of the House 1986-87. Minister of State at the Department of the Taoiseach and Department of Defence 1982-87. Government Chief Whip 1982-87; Assistant Government Whip 1981-82; FG Chief Whip 1982.
Home address: 56 Arnold Park, Glenageary, Co Dublin.
Tel: Home 01 852077; Business 01 767591.
Born: Dublin 1944.
Married: Sheila Hyde. 5 children.
Education: CBC Monkstown; Presentation College, Glasthule.
Occupation: Public representative. Former insurance broker. Member Dublin County Council since 1974; County Dublin VEC since 1974; County Dublin Health Committee since 1974; Joint Committee of the three local authorities in Dublin.

MONICA BARNES (FG) First elected Nov 1982. Senator 1982. Fine Gael spokesperson on Law Reform and Assistant Whip Senate 1982.
Home address: 5 Arnold Park, Glenageary, Co Dublin.
Tel: 01 853751.
Born: Carrickmacross 1936.
Married: Bob Barnes. 1 son, 2 daughters.
Education: St Louis Convent, Carrickmacross; Oranges' Academy, Belfast.
Occupation: Public representative and lecturer. Founder Member Council for the Status of Women 1973; Vice-Chairperson Women's Political Association 1973-74; Secretary-General Women's Federation, European People's Party since 1978. First Woman Vice-President FG 1980-81. Member Executive Committee Irish Council of European Movement; Irish Anti-Apartheid Movement.

GALWAY EAST (3)

Elected: *Michael Kitt (FF) 2nd Count; *Paul Connaughton (FG) 3rd Count; *Noel Treacy (FF) 5th Count.

Despite getting over 2,400 more votes than when he ran for FG in Nov 1982, PD candidate Joe Burke broke no moulds in Galway East. The result was widely predicted and the same three sitting TDs were returned to the Dáil. At the end of the 4th count the PDs called for a recount. At that stage Joe Burke was 127 votes behind FF's Noel Treacy. After the recount the gap was narrowed to 116 — but Treacy was waiting to pick up 815 from Kitt's surplus and the final outcome was never in any doubt, with Treacy elected on the 5th count, 883 votes clear of Joe Burke.

FEB 87 % Poll		NOV 82 % Poll			
				Electorate:	42,587
				Total poll:	33,169 (77.9%)
FF	51.8	FF	51.5	Spoiled votes:	231
FG	31.6	FG	45.2	Total valid poll:	32,938
PD	16.6	—	—	Quota:	8,235
LAB	—	LAB	2.8		
OTH	—	OTH	0.5	6 Candidates	

COUNTS	1st	2nd Hussey Votes (3,463)	3rd Burke Votes (3,762) (NT) (46)	4th Connaughton Surplus (1,323) (NT) (95)	5th Kitt Surplus (863)
Kitt M. (FF)	6,831	+2,267 **9,098**			
Treacy N. (FF)	6,762	+585 7,347	+309 7,656	+134 7,790	+815 **8,605**
Connaughton P. (FG)	6,719	+232 6,951	+2607 **9,558**		
Burke J. (PD)	5,463	+271 5,734	+751 6,485	+1189 7,674	+48 7,722
Burke U. (FG)	3,700	+62 3,762			
Hussey T. (FF)	3,463				

MICHAEL KITT (FF) First elected 1975 for the old constituency of Galway North-East, winning his seat at a by-election caused by the death of his father, Michael Kitt. Re-elected 1981 after an absence of four years. Senator 1977-81. Member Galway County Council; Galway County VEC; Galway County Committee of Agriculture since 1975. Chairman Galway County Council 1985-86. Vice-Chairman Galway/Mayo Regional Development Organisation 1985-86.
Home address: Castleblakeney, Ballinasloe, Galway.
Tel: 0905 78147.
Born: Tuam, Co Galway, May 1950.
Married: Catherine Mannion. 2 sons, 1 daughter.
Education: St Jarlath's College, Tuam; UCD; St Patrick's Teachers Training College, Dublin; University College Galway.
Occupation: Public representative. Former national school teacher. Member INTO; Caltra GAA; Comhaltas Ceoltoiri Eireann. Son of Michael F. Kitt, Dáil deputy for Galway constituencies 1948-51 and 1957-75 and Parliamentary Secretary to the Minister for the Gaeltacht 1970-73.

NOEL TREACY (FF) First elected 1982 when he won a by-election in Galway East caused by the death of John Callanan (FF). Appointed Minister of State Department of Finance (Office of Public Works) Mar 1987. Frontbench spokesman on Defence 1983-87. Member Dáil All Party Committee on Public Expenditure. Member Galway County Council since Jun 1985; Chairman Galway County Council since 1986. Chairman Galway/Mayo Regional Development Organisation. Member County Galway VEC; Local Health Committee.

Home address: Gurteen, Ballinasloe, Co Galway; constituency office: Main St, Loughrea, Co Galway.

Tel: Home 0905 77094; Office 091 41311.

Born: Galway, Dec 1952.

Married: Mary Clonan. 3 daughters.

Education: Gurteen NS; St Joseph's College, Ballinasloe, Co Galway.

Occupation: Public representative. Former auctioneer and farmer. Member Macra na Feirme since 1968; former Chairman County Executive Macra na Feirme. Member Irish Auctioneers and Valuers Institute; Irish Livestock Auctioneers Association.

PAUL CONNAUGHTON (FG) First elected 1981. Senator 1977-81. Minister of State Department of Agriculture 1982-87. Member Galway County Council 1979-85.

Home address: Mount Bellew, Co Galway.

Tel: Home 0905 79249; Business 01 789911.

Born: Mount Bellew, Jun 1944.

Married: Bernadette Keating. 2 sons, 3 daughters.

Education: St Mary's Secondary School, Ballygar; Vocational School, Mount Bellew; Athenry Agricultural Colleges; IMI Management Course.

Occupation: Public representative and farmer. Member Macra na Feirme; IFA; Mount Bellew Town Development Association; Tuam Chamber of Commerce; GAA.

GALWAY WEST (5)

Elected : *Bobby Molloy (PD) 1st Count; *Frank Fahey (FF) 10th Count; *John Donnellan (FG) 12th Count; Michael D. Higgins (LAB), *Maire Geoghegan-Quinn (FF) 13th Count.

This marginal five-seater provided some of the richest territory for speculation in the run-up to the election. There was Bobby Molloy's defection to the PDs, FF battling to regain its three seats, hampered in the latter stages by internal divisions leading to an independent campaign by Michael "The Stroke" Fahey. Labour Party Chairman Michael D. Higgins once again attempted to regain the seat he first won in Jun 1981, only to lose again in Feb 1982. Then, after a "Today Tonight" poll, there were fears in the FG camp that one of their TDs might be in danger. Those fears were justified because the FG vote slumped, and Fintan Coogan's seat fell to Lab. FG accepted in the constituency that there was a strong anti-government reaction on the doorsteps, that their election machine was working below par, and that they lost massively to the PDs. Bobby Molloy headed the poll, but it was felt locally that he should have polled better than his 9,216 first preferences. However the crowded field may well account for that.

Michael D. Higgins survived a nail-biting two-day count to be elected to the second last seat on the 13th count. His election was assured when sitting FG TD Fintan Coogan from Galway city was eliminated; he picked up a steady stream of transfers from all candidates, particularly those who were city based. Fianna Fáil had been hoping that Coogan would stay ahead of his running mate, Junior Minister Donnellan, and at one stage only a few votes separated them. They believed they would have taken the third seat if Coogan had been elected, and Donnellan eliminated, because the Lab Party Chairman would not have got enough transfers to stay ahead of their third contender, Mark Killilea. It was not the way it went. Michael "The Stroke" Fahey polled a creditable 3,100 votes under the Ind FF banner. Neil Blaney turned up for the launching of his campaign. The travellers' rights candidate Margaret Sweeney got over 500 votes.

FEB 87 % Poll		NOV 82 % Poll				
				Electorate:	77,542	
				Total poll:	53,214	(68.6%)
FF	37.9	FF	53.3	Spoiled votes:	452	
FG	18.2	FG	34.1	Total valid poll:	52,762	
PD	21.5	—	—	Quota:	8,794	
LAB	7.3	LAB	9.0			
WP	3.0	WP	3.6			
OTH	12.1	OTH	—	17 Candidates		

COUNT	1st	2nd Molloy	3rd Shanley Mannion Sweeney	4th Duffy	5th O'Malley	6th Brick	7th O Tuathail	8th O'Neill	9th M. Fahy	10th O Cuiv	11th F.Fahey	12th Coogan	13th Donnellan
		Surplus (422)	Votes (655)	Votes (925)	Votes (940)	Votes (1,741)	Votes (1,926)	Votes (2,885)	Votes (3,440)	Votes (4,808)	Surplus (158)	Votes (5,989)	Votes (1,582)
			(NT) (20)	(NT) (36)	(NT) (24)	(NT) (132)	(NT) (430)	(NT) (554)	(NT) (434)	(NT) (430)		(NT) (585)	
Molloy B. (PD)	**9,216**												
Fahey F. (FF)	6,488	+13 6,501	+14 6,515	+51 6,566	+9 6,575	+108 6,683	+32 6,715	+160 6,875	+1,049 7,924	+1028 **8,952**			
Killilea M. (FF)	5,053	+12 5,065	+6 5,071	+35 5,106	+10 5,116	+56 5,172	+28 5,200	+131 5,331	+569 5,900	+1076 6,976	+68 7,044	+135 7,179	+103 7,282
Geoghegan-Quinn M. (FF)	4,607	+15 4,622	+28 4,650	+55 4,705	+17 4,722	+76 4,798	+270 5,068	+88 5,156	+263 5,419	+1715 7,134	+78 7,212	+153 7,365	+149 **7,514**
Donnellan J. (FG)	4,476	+19 4,495	+56 4,551	+51 4,602	+314 4,916	+57 4,973	+62 5,035	+467 5,572	+475 5,977	+136 6,113	+3 6,116	+4260 **10,376**	
Coogan F. (FG)	4,206	+33 4,239	+47 4,286	+109 4,395	+351 4,746	+226 4,976	+112 5,084	+578 5,662	+210 5,872	+114 5,986	+3 5,989		
Higgins M.D. (Lab)	3,878	+34 3,912	+225 4,137	+238 4,375	+20 4,395	+877 5,272	+360 5,632	+546 6,178	+260 6,438	+309 6,747	+6 6,753	+856 7,609	+1,330 **8,939**
O Cuiv E. (FF)	3,831	+17 3,848	+30 3,878	+42 3,920	+23 3,943	+28 3,971	+434 4,405	+223 4,628	+180 4,808				
Fahey M. (Ind FF)	3,139	+9 3,148	+10 3,158	+31 3,189	+8 3,197	+60 3,257	+45 3,302	+138 3,440					
O'Neill M. (PD)	2,144	+243 2,387	+40 2,427	+140 2,567	+71 2,638	+94 2,732	+153 2,885						
O Tuathail P. (Ind)	1,724	+6 1,730	+53 1,783	+33 1,816	+83 1,899	+27 1,926							
Brick J. (WP)	1,567	+10 1,577	+58 1,635	+96 1,731	+10 1,741								
O'Malley J. (FG)	918	+6 924	+8 932	+8 940									
Duffy M. (PAYE)	862	+3 865	+60 925										
Sweeney M. (Ind)	511	+1 512											
Mannion B. (Ind)	101	+1 102											
Shanley D. (Ind)	41												

FRANK FAHEY (FF) First elected in Feb 1982. Appointed Minister of State at the Department of Education Mar 1987. Member Galway County Council; Western Health Board; Fianna Fáil National Executive.
Home address: Kilbeacanty, Gort, Co Galway.
Tel: 091 31254.
Born: Dublin, Jun 1951.
Married: Ethelle Griffin. 2 sons, 1 daughter.
Education: St Mary's College, Galway; Our Lady's College, Gort; UCG.
Occupation: Public representative. Former secondary school teacher.

MARIE GEOGHEGAN-QUINN (FF) First elected Mar 1975 when she won a seat in a by-election in the old three-seat constituency of Galway West caused by the death of her father, Johnny Geoghegan, Dáil Deputy for Galway West from 1954 until his death in 1975. Appointed Minister of State at the Department of the Taoiseach Mar 1987. Minister of State at the Department of Education 1982. Minister for the Gaeltacht 1979-81. Parliamentary Secretary to the Minister for Industry, Commerce and Energy 1977-78; Minister of State at that Department 1978-79 with special responsibility for Consumer Affairs. First woman Cabinet Minister since the foundation of the state. The only woman to previously hold the position of Minister was Countess Markievicz in the Second Ministry 1919-21.
Home address: 6 Beach Close, Glenoran, Renmore, Galway.
Tel: 091 66369.
Born: Carna, Connemara, Sept 1950.
Married: John Quinn. 2 sons.
Education: Coláiste Muire, Túr Mhic Eadaigh, Co Mhaigheo; Carysfort Training College, Co Dublin.
Occupation: Public representative. Former national school teacher. Elected to Galway Borough Council 1985; Member Galway City VEC.

MICHAEL D. HIGGINS (LAB) First elected Jun 1981. Member of Seanad Éireann. Member Galway Corporation; Galway County Council since 1984. Chairman Labour Party since 1978. Member of the International Affairs Committee.
Home address: 6 Sylvan Avenue, Fairlands Park, Newcastle, Galway.
Tel: 091 24513.
Born: 1941.
Married: Sabina Coyne. 1 daughter, 3 sons.
Occupation: Public representative, lecturer in Politics and Sociology at UCG.

BOBBY MOLLOY (PD) First elected for FF 1965. Minister for Local Government 1970-73; Minister for Defence 1977-79. Parliamentary Secretary to the Minister for Education 1969-70. Opposition spokesman on Local Government 1973-75; on Posts and Telegraphs 1975; on Environment 1984-86. Member Progressive Democrats since 1986.
Home address: 1 D'Alton Drive, Salthill, Co Galway.
Tel: 091 21765.
Born: Galway 1936.
Married: Phyllis Barry. 2 sons, 2 daughters.
Education: St Ignatius College, Galway; UCG.
Occupation: Public representative. Member Committee on the Constitution 1967. Member Galway County Council 1967-70 and 1974-77; Galway Borough Council 1967-70. Mayor of Galway 1968-69. Member Western Region Tourism Organisation.

JOHN DONNELLAN (FG) First elected 1964. Minister of State at the Department of Transport and Department of Posts and Telegraphs 1982-87. Opposition spokesman on Office of Public Works 1977-81; on Sport 1982.
Home address: Cloonmore, Dunmore, Co Galway.
Tel: 093 38111.
Born: Cloonmore 1937.
Married: Fidelma Mannion. 3 sons, 2 daughters.
Education: St Jarlath's College, Tuam, Co Galway.
Occupation: Public representative and farmer. Member Galway County Council since 1967. Member GAA. All-Ireland medal winner with Galway, 1964 (capt), '65, '66. Son of Michael Donnellan, founder of Clann na Talmhan 1938, TD 1943-64, and Parliamentary Secretary to the Minister for Finance in Inter-Party Governments of 1948-51 and 1954-57.

KERRY NORTH (3)

Elected: Jimmy Deenihan (FG) 1st Count; *Denis Foley (FF) 5th Count; *Dick Spring (LAB) 6th Count.

While FG were successfully mounting a big push to get Jimmy Deenihan in here, no one anticipated the drama that would unfold. The former Tanaiste and Lab leader Dick Spring's first-preference vote slumped by over 3,000 and at the end of a tense count he was left hanging onto his seat by a bare five votes over FF's Tom McEllistrim. Immediately FF called for a recount and for seven hours every packet of votes was re-checked. For the last couple of hours dozens of votes challenged by both sides were scrutinised one by one. Through all this Dick Spring sat on a ledge at one end of the hall, swinging his legs and looking pale. An equally tense Tom McEllistrim, accompanied by Donal Spring, Dick's brother, and a group of tallymen, pored over the votes as the Returning Officer gave her verdict, vote by vote. Shortly after 5 am on Thursday morning, the recount finished with Spring hanging onto victory — by just four votes. North Kerry is noted for narrow margins on the last count. In 1977 Dick's father Dan Spring held onto his seat by just 44 votes from FG after more than three decades in the Dáil. In 1981 Dick himself took his father's seat by 144 votes over FG, and last time out Jimmy Deenihan was pipped at the post by FF's Denis Foley, again by 144 votes. This time FF were just 670 votes short of two quotas on the first count — and they could reasonably have expected to get two seats through SF's 1,200 transfers. However, 269 of those went to Spring which, together with 816 of Deenihan's surplus and a leakage of 72 from Denis Foley's surplus, gave him victory.

FEB 87		NOV 82		Electorate:	45,602	
% Poll		% Poll				
				Total poll:	35,061	(76.9%)
FF	48.1	FF	51.2	Spoiled votes:	296	
FG	29.0	FG	19.9	Total valid poll:	34,765	
LAB	19.4	LAB	28.9	Quota:	8,692	
SF	3.5	—	—	7 Candidates		

COUNTS	1st	2nd Deenihan Surplus (1,395)	3rd Leen's Votes (576)	4th Finucane Votes (1,061)	5th Kiely's Votes (3,370)	6th Foley's Surplus (927)	Recount
			(NT) 18	(NT) 294	(NT) 308		
Deenihan J. (FG)	**10,087**						
Foley D. (FF)	7,612	+166 7,778	+110 7,888	+230 8,118	+1501 **9,619**		
Spring D. (Lab)	6,739	+816 7,555	+80 7,635	+189 7,824	+487 8,311	+72 8,383	−4 **8,379**
McEllistrim T. (FF)	6,161	+132 6,293	+51 6,344	+105 6,449	+1074 7,523	+855 8,378	−3 8,375
Kiely D. (FF)	2,939	+180 3,119	+8 3,127	+243 3,370			
Finucane D. (SF)	668	+84 752	+309 1,061				
Leen D. (SF)	559	+17 576					

DENIS FOLEY (FF) First elected in 1981. Member All-Party Public Accounts Committee since 1981 and Chairman since 1982. Member Kerry County Council since 1979; Regional Development Organisation since 1979 (Chairman 1985-86 and 1986-87); Tralee Vocational Eduation Committee from 1979-85; Kerry County Library Committee since 1979 (Chairman 1984); Member Kerry Health Committee since 1979 (Chairman 1983-84 and 1986-87).

Home address: St Joseph's Guest House, Staughtons Row, Tralee, Co Kerry.

Telephone: 066 21174.

Born: Tralee, May 1934.

Married: Hanna O'Halloran. 1 son, 3 daughters.

Education: CBS; St Mary's Secondary School; Central Technical School, Tralee.

Occupation: Public representative. Director Cork and Kerry Tourism since 1980; Tralee Development Association 1970-79; Tralee Tourism 1970-81. Member Irish Local Government Officials' Union since 1958. National Executive Member Catholic Young Men's Society of Ireland 1968-72.

DICK SPRING (LAB): First elected in 1981, succeeding his father Dan Spring. Tanaiste 1982-87; Minister for the Environment 1982-83; Minister for Energy 1983-87. Junior Minister for Justice 1981-82. Became leader of the Labour Party following the resignation of Michael O'Leary in autumn 1982. First elected to Kerry County Council in 1979.
Home Address: 17 Cloonanorig, Tralee, Co. Kerry.
Tel: 066 25337.
Born: Tralee 1950.
Married: Kristi Hutcheson. 1 son, 1 daughter.
Education: CBS, Tralee; Mount St Joseph's College, Roscrea; TCD; Kings Inns.
Occupation: Public representative, barrister.

JIMMY DEENIHAN (FG) First elected 1987. Senator (Taoiseach's nominee) 1983-87. Government spokesperson on Youth and Sport in the Seanad. Member Kerry County Council since 1985; Kerry VEC.
Home address: Finuge, Co Kerry.
Tel: 068 40235; 40154.
Born: Finuge, Co Kerry, Sept 1953.
Married: Mary Dowling.
Education: Dromclough NS; St Michael's College, Listowel, Co Kerry; National College of Physical Education, Limerick; Strawberry Hill, Twickenham, London.
Occupation: Public representative. Former teacher. Winner of 5 All-Ireland football medals; Captain of Kerry All Ireland team 1981.

KERRY SOUTH (3)

Elected: *John O'Leary (FF) 6th Count; John O'Donoghue (FF) 7th Count; *Michael Begley (FG) 8th Count.

The Fianna Fáil strategy in this constituency worked well: three candidates recaptured two of the three seats with a swing to the party of 8.2 per cent. The 70-year-old former Lab Minister of State Michael Moynihan was the victim, and FG's Michael Begley held his seat despite a drop of nearly 2,600 first preferences and a very poor showing by the second FG candidate. Overall, the FG vote was down 7.6 per cent. The PDs' Michael Ahern polled a creditable 3,215 first preferences, just under 10 per cent. The transfers to FG were notably lower from PD to FG here than in other constituencies, with 31.8 per cent going to Michael

Begley and 26.8 per cent to Michael Moynihan, reflecting the "Killarney factor" which favoured the latter. Ahern is a solicitor from Glenbeigh with a practice in Killarney and Moynihan is also based in Killarney.

FEB 87 % Poll		NOV 82 % Poll				
				Electorate:	42,701	
				Total poll:	33,498	(78.4%)
FF	54.0	FF	45.8	Spoiled votes:	287	
FG	17.9	FG	25.5	Total valid poll:	33,211	
PD	9.7	—	—	Quota:	8,303	
LAB	13.7	LAB	23.1			
WP	2.2	WP	2.1			
OTH	2.5	OTH	3.5	10 Candidates		

COUNTS	1st	2nd Falvey Votes (122) (NT) (5)	3rd Counihan Votes (721) (NT) (35)	4th O'Grady Votes (898) (NT) (71)	5th Sheahan Votes (975) (NT) (21)	6th Ahern Votes (3,654) (NT) (285)	7th MacGearailt Votes (4,947) (NT) (484)	8th O'Donoghue Surplus (909) (NT) (194)
O'Leary J. (FF)	7,839	+18 7,857	+72 7,929	+210 8,139	+36 8,175	+494 **8,669**		
O'Donoghue J. (FF)	5,606	+7 5,613	+33 5,646	+41 5,687	+46 5,733	+438 6,171	+3041 **9,212**	
Begley M. (FG)	5,036	+21 5,057	+55 5,112	+45 5,157	+634 5,791	+1161 6,952	+897 7,849	+350 **8,199**
Moynihan M. (Lab)	4,559	+22 4,581	+124 4,705	+266 4,971	+103 5,074	+981 6,055	+525 6,580	+365 6,945
MacGearailt B. (FF)	4,481	+8 4,489	+82 4,571	+66 4,637	+15 4,652	+295 4,947		
Ahern M. (PD)	3,215	+18 3,233	+138 3,371	+163 3,534	+120 3,654			
Sheahan D. (FG)	910	+4 914	+25 939	+36 975				
O'Grady S. (WP)	735	+6 741	+157 898					
Counihan M. (GA)	708	+13 721						
Falvey J. (Ind)	122							

JOHN O'LEARY (FF) First elected in the Dec 1966 by-election. Minister of State at the Department of the Environment 1977-79. Member Consultative Assembly of the Council of Europe 1973-75. Opposition spokesman on Physical Planning and the Environment 1975-77. Member Dáil Public Accounts Committee 1983-87; Committee on Procedure and Privileges 1969-77. Delegate to New Ireland Forum. Member of Governing Body of UCC.

Home address: Beechcroft, Killarney, Co Kerry; business address: 89 New St Killarney.
Tel: Home 064 31565; Business 064 31762.
Born: Kilcummin, Killarney, May 1933.
Married: Judy O'Brien. 7 sons.
Education: St Brendan's College, Killarney.
Occupation: Public representative, auctioneer and building society manager. Member Irish Local Government Officials' Union 1952-74; Institute of Public Administration since 1962.

JOHN O'DONOGHUE (FF) First elected in 1987. Member Kerry County Council since June 1985.

Home address: Garranearagh, Cahirciveen, Co Kerry.
Tel: 0667 2413.
Born: Cahirciveen, May 1956.
Married: Kate Ann Murphy. 2 sons.
Education: CBS, Cahirciveen; UCC; Blackhall Place, Dublin.
Occupation: Public representative and solicitor. Member Southern Health Board; Psychiatric Services Committee. Kerry County Committee of Agriculture.

MICHAEL BEGLEY (FG) First elected in 1969. Minister of State at the Department of Trade, Commerce and Tourism 1981-82. Parliamentary Secretary to Minister for Finance and Minister for Defence 1975-77. Opposition spokesman on the Gaeltacht 1970-73 and 1977-81; Fisheries 1972-73; Defence 1982.

Home address: Dyke Gate Street, Dingle, Co Kerry.
Tel: 066 51117
Born: Dingle 1932.
Married: Eleanor Crowley. 1 daughter, 2 sons.
Education: CBS, Dingle.
Occupation: Public representative. Former contractor. Member Kerry County Council since 1960; Kerry County Library Committee since 1963; Kerry County VEC.

KILDARE (5)

Elected: *Paddy Power (FF), Emmet Stagg (LAB) 5th Count; *Alan Dukes (FG) 6th Count; *Bernard Durkan (FG) 7th Count; *Charlie McCreevy (FF) 8th Count.

Fianna Fáil had hopes of taking three seats to return them to their Feb 1982 position. But the strong performance of Lab's Emmet Stagg put paid to that. Pundits had suggested he would not be able to hold the seat of former Minister of State Joe Bermingham, who had resigned from the Party in a row over the choice of his successor. Bermingham had wanted Senator Timmy Conway to be the Lab candidate. When Stagg was chosen, Conway defected to the PDs and was denied selection by that party as well. The only question after the 1st count was whether Gerry Brady would oust party colleague Charlie McCreevy, whom he led by five votes. In the event McCreevy, as the sitting TD, picked up enough transfers on succeeding counts to lead by 401 votes on the 8th when he was elected to the last seat. This constituency was also a disappointment for the PDs. Despite the fact that they had two strong candidates — Frank Masterson, who had IFA connections, and Owen McBennett, a financial controller who gave up his job with an American company to fight the election — they were still 2,600 short of a quota on the 1st count. With a 70 per cent transfer rate between them perhaps they would have been better to run just one candidate.

FEB 87 % Poll		NOV 82 % Poll			
				Electorate:	74,340
				Total poll:	54,126 (72.8%)
FF	42.7	FF	47.8	Spoiled votes:	421
FG	26.3	FG	36.5	Total valid poll:	53,705
PD	11.8	—	—	Quota:	8,951
LAB	14.1	LAB	15.2		
WP	2.3	—	—		
SF	2.6	—	—		
OTH	0.2	OTH	0.4	12 Candidates	

COUNTS	1st	2nd Leavy Purcell Votes (1,361) (NT) (85)	3rd Wright Votes (1,528) (NT) (192)	4th O'Fearghall Votes (2,798) (NT) (49)	5th Masterson Votes (3,112) (NT) (70)	6th McBenett Votes (5,713) (NT) (999)	7th Dukes Surplus (1,186)	8th Durkan Surplus (714) (NT) (288)
Power P. (FF)	7,649	+45 7,694	+263 7,957	+942 8,899	+88 **8,987**			
Stagg E. (Lab)	7,567	+728 8,295	+473 8,768	+120 8,888	+116 **9,004**			
Dukes A. (FG)	7,453	+37 7,490	+94 7,584	+85 7,669	+385 8,054	+2083 **10,137**		
Durkan B. (FG)	6,671	+92 6,763	+32 6,795	+21 6,816	+137 6,953	+1608 8,561	+1104 **9,665**	
Brady G. (FF)	6,297	+73 6,370	+99 6,469	+709 7,178	+33 7,211	+438 7,649	+39 7,688	+176 7,864
McCreevy C. (FF)	6,292	+65 6,357	+147 6,504	+776 7,280	+107 7,387	+585 7,972	+43 8,015	+250 **8,265**
Bennett E. (PD)	3,407	+61 3,468	+35 3,505	+34 3,537	+2176 5,713			
Masterson F. (PD)	2,913	+46 2,959	+91 3,050	+62 3,112				
O'Fearghail S. (FF)	2,675	+21 2,696	+102 2,798					
Wright P. (SF)	1,420	+108 1,528						
Purcell C. (WP)	1,238							
Leavy F. (Ind)	123							

CHARLIE McCREEVY (FF) First elected in 1977. Member Kildare County Council from 1979-85.
Home address: Celbridge, Co Kildare; business address: 57 Amiens St, Dublin 1; 56 South Main Street, Naas, Co Kildare; Ballyhaunis Co Mayo.
Tel: 045 76816.
Born: Sallins, Co Kildare, Sept 1949.
Married: Kitty O'Connor. 1 son, 3 daughters.
Education: Naas CBS; Franciscan College, Gormanston; UCD.
Occupation: Public representative and chartered accountant.

PADDY POWER (FF) First elected in 1969. Minister for Defence 1982; Minister for Fisheries and Forestry 1979-81. Member European Parliament 1977-79. Member of Council of Europe since 1984.
Home address: Caragh, Naas, Co Kildare.
Tel: 045 97820
Born: The Curragh, Co Kildare, Nov 1928.
Married: Kitty Martin. 7 sons, 3 daughters.
Education: Presentation Convent and De La Salle NS; St Joseph's Academy, Kildare; St Patrick's Teachers' Training College, Dublin.
Occupation: Public representative. Former national school teacher. Member Kildare County Council 1967-79, re-elected 1985; Kildare Vocational Committee 1967-79 (Chairman 1985); Kildare Health Committee 1972-79. Member Droichead Nua branch of the Irish National Teachers' Organisation since 1950; Kildare Archaeological Society; GAA.

EMMET STAGG (LAB) First elected in 1987. First elected to Kildare County Council in 1979.
Home address: Lodge Park, Straffan, Co Kildare.
Tel: 01 272149
Born: Oct 1944.
Married: Mary Morris. 2 children.
Education: Robeen NS, Hollymount; CBS Ballinrobe, Co Mayo; College of Technology, Kevin St, Dublin.
Occupation: Public representative and medical technologist (on leave of absence from TCD). Member Administrative Council of the Labour Party since 1982 and has served on the Organisation Sub-Committee. Member Kildare VEC; Eastern Health Board. Secretary of Kildare Constituency Council of the Labour Party.

ALAN DUKES (FG) First elected in 1981. Minister for Justice 1986-87; Minister for Finance 1982-86; Minister for Agriculture 1981-82. Opposition spokesman on Agriculture 1982. Elected leader of Fine Gael Mar 1987. Like Dr Noel Browne, Kevin Boland and Dr Martin O'Donoghue, he was appointed a Cabinet minister on his first day in the Dáil.
Home address: Tranquilla, Tully West, Co Kildare.
Tel: Home 045 21912 ; Business 01 789681
Born: Dublin, Apr 1945.
Married: Fionnula Corcoran. 2 daughters.
Education: Scoil Columcille, Marlborough Street, Dublin; Coláiste Mhuire, Parnell Square, Dublin; UCD.
Occupation: Public representative. Former economist. Chief Economist IFA 1967-72; Director IFA Brussels 1973-76; Personal Adviser EEC Commissioner Richard Burke 1977-80; Governor European Investment Bank and IMF 1982-86.

BERNARD DURKAN (FG) First elected in 1981; re-elected Nov 1982. Senator 1982. Member Kildare County Council since 1976.
Home address: Timard, Maynooth, Co Kildare.
Tel: 01 286063.
Born: Killaser, Co Mayo 1945.
Married: Hilary Spence. 2 sons.
Education: St John's School, Corramore.
Occupation: Public representative. Member Eastern Health Board; Kildare Local Health Committee; Vice-Chairman Eastern Regional Development Organisation. Member of All-Party Committee dealing with Irish prisoners overseas.

LAOIS OFFALY (5)

Elected: *Brian Cowen (FF), *Liam Hyland (FF) 4th Count; *Ger Connolly (FF) 8th Count; Charles Flanagan (FG), *Tom Enright (FG) 9th Count.

In all three elections in the early eighties FF averaged 50 per cent of the first-preference vote in this stronghold and no one expected any upsets this time. In fact, FF increased their first-preference vote by 3.5 per cent, returning their three sitting TDs. The nationally unknown PD candidate, Cathy Honan, came close to upsetting the apple-cart for FG by polling extremely well, beating all three of their candidates on first preferences and coming within 493 votes of FG's Tom Enright on the 9th count for the last seat. The FG vote was down 14.5 per cent. The local PD branch said it had wanted to run two candidates. They might have taken the seat if they had had a ''sweeper''. Certainly, the constituency will be a target for a PD seat next time out. Brian Cowen consolidated his hold on the FF seat that he won after his father's death in 1984 and Charles Flanagan replaced his father, Oliver J. Flanagan, for FG.

FEB 87 % Poll		NOV 82 % Poll		Electorate:	75,021	
				Total poll:	56,683	(75.6%)
FF	53.8	FF	50.3	Spoiled votes:	561	
FG	31.1	FG	45.6	Total valid poll:	56,122	
PD	9.5	—	—	Quota:	9,354	
LAB	1.5	LAB	3.7			
SF	2.5	—	—			
OTH	1.5	OTH	0.3	13 Candidates.		

COUNTS	1st	2nd McCormack Votes (354) (NT) (49)	3rd Phelan Keeley Votes (1,372) (NT) (109)	4th Carroll Votes (1,529) (NT) (225)	5th Fox Votes (3,295) (NT) (90)	6th Cowen Surplus (282)	7th McDonald Votes (4,511) (NT) (146)	8th Larch Votes (4,849) (NT) (537)	9th Connolly Surplus (2,498) (NT) (1,808)
Hyland L. (FF)	9,208	+35 9,243	+88 9,331	+87 **9,418**					
Cowen B. (FF)	9,168	+4 9,172	+124 9,296	+340 **9,636**					
Connolly G. (FF)	7,472	+8 7,480	+140 7,620	+296 7,916	+251 8,167	+179 8,346	+76 8,422	+3430 **11,852**	
Honan C. (PD)	5,353	+36 5,389	+229 5,618	+153 5,771	+479 6,250	+11 6,261	+536 6,797	+408 7,205	+324 7,529
Flanagan C. (FG)	5,317	+28 5,345	+139 5,484	+87 5,571	+1164 6,735	+21 6,756	+2216 8,972	+295 9,267	+214 **9,481**
Enright T. (FG)	5,136	+26 5,162	+95 5,257	+172 5,429	+876 6,305	+30 6,335	+1356 7,691	+179 7,870	+152 **8,022**
Lodge J. (FF)	4,356	+59 4,415	+86 4,501	+93 4,594	+34 4,628	+40 4,668	+181 4,849		
McDonald C. (FG)	3,921	+38 3,959	+130 4,089	+20 4,109	+401 4,510	+1 4,511			
Fox M. (FG)	3,105	+6 3,111	+128 3,239	+56 3,295					
Carroll J. (SF)	1,405	+20 1,425	+104 1,529						
Phelan T. (Lab)	818	+35 853							
Keeley T. (Ind)	509	+10 519							
McCormack J. (Ind)	354								

LIAM HYLAND (FF) First elected in 1981. Former spokesman on Justice. Senator 1977-81. Member Laois County Council since 1967; Laois County Committee of Agriculture since 1974; Midland Health Board 1971-82; General Council of County Committees of Agriculture 1974-85. First ever FF Chairman of Laois County Council.
Home address: Fearagh, Ballacolla, Portlaoise, Co Laois.
Tel: 0502 34051.
Born: Ballacolla, Co Laois, Apr 1935.
Married: Agnes Rafter. 5 sons, 1 daughter.
Education: Ballacolla NS; UCD.
Occupation: Public representative.

BRIAN COWEN (FF) First elected in the Jun 1984 by-election caused by the death of his father Ber Cowen, who had held a seat in the Dáil from 1969-73; 1977-84. Member of Offaly County Council.
Home address: River Street, Clara, Co Offaly.
Tel: 0506 31160.
Born: Tullamore, Jan 1960.
Education: Clara NS; Ard Scoil Naoimh Chiarain, Clara; Cistercian College Roscrea, UCD; Incorporated Law Society of Ireland.
Occupation: Public representative and solicitor. Member Select Committee on Crime Lawlessness and Vandalism. Member Offaly VEC; Offaly Committee of Agriculture; GAA.

GER CONNOLLY (FF) First elected in 1969. Appointed Minister of State at the Department of the Environment Mar 1987. Minister of State at Department of the Environment 1979-81 and 1982. Former deputy spokesman on Trade, Commerce and Tourism.
Home address: Bracknagh, Co Offaly.
Tel: 0502 29025
Born: Bracknagh, Co Offaly, Apr 1937.
Married: Mary Dunne. 3 sons, 1 daughter.
Education: CBS, Portarlington, Co Offaly.
Occupation: Public representative, farmer and businessman. Member Offaly County Council since 1967; Offaly County Committee of Agriculture since 1967; Vice-Chairman Offaly Health Board since 1972. Member Council of Europe 1977-79; and from 1984. President Bracknagh GAA Club since 1975.

CHARLES FLANAGAN (FG) First elected 1987. Son of Oliver J. Flanagan, TD for Laois Offaly 1943-87.
Home address: Oaklawn, Ballyfin Road, Portlaoise, Co Laois.
Tel: Home 0502 22100; Business 0502 20232.
Born: 1957.
Married: Mary McCormack.
Education: Mountmellick NS; Colaiste na Rinne, Waterford; Knockbeg College Carlow; UCD; Incorporated Law Society.
Occupation: Public representative and solicitor. Founder member Young Fine Gael; Secretary Portlaoise Fine Gael; policy officer Laois/Offaly constituency committee.

TOM ENRIGHT (FG) First elected in 1969. Former Dáil spokesman on Tourism and Consumer Affairs. Member Fine Gael Parliamentary Party Agricultural Committee; Industry and Energy Committee.
Home address: Hillside, Birr, Co Offaly.
Tel: 0509 20293
Born: Shinroone, Co Offaly 1940.
Married: Rita Mary Hanniffy. 1 son, 4 daughters.
Education: Cistercian College, Roscrea; UCD; Law School of the Incorporated Law Society of Ireland.
Occupation: Public representative. Member Offaly County Council since 1967. Member Offaly Health Committee. Chairman Midland Regional Development Committee 1977-85.

LIMERICK EAST (5)

Elected: Des O'Malley (PD), Willie O'Dea (FF) 1st Count; Peadar Clohessy (PD) 2nd Count; Jim Kemmy (DSP) 12th Count; Michael Noonan (FG) 13th Count.

As the cheering and stamping of feet erupted around the count centre Des O'Malley roared into the RTE microphone: "We have smashed them! We have smashed them here tonight in Limerick East." He was referring to FF and FG who both suffered badly, losing a seat each to the PDs. For O'Malley there was the personal victory of topping the poll with a record 12,358 votes; the election of his running mate, former FF TD Peadar Clohessy, on the 2nd count was the icing on the cake. Fianna Fáil's hopes of regaining a second seat were dashed, and FG also took a crushing blow with the loss of their veteran TD and MEP Tom O'Donnell. His vote collapsed, down from 9,058 in 1982 to just 2,968, and his running mate, outgoing Industry Minister Michael Noonan had to wait until the final count to be elected. O'Donnell blamed his loss on what he called the "Tom will be alright: let's worry about Michael Noonan" policy of the constituency party. Fianna Fáil's campaign was divided and personalised and the party appears to have paid the price. Their sitting TD, Willie O'Dea, was elected on the 1st count — but the other two candidates had only 3,365 first preferences between them.

Labour's sitting TD Frank Prendergast lost his seat to Jim Kemmy, leader of the Democratic Socialist Party, who had previously lost his seat to Lab in Nov '82. Kemmy felt considerable pleasure in retaking his seat, having lost it in a particularly bitter contest last time when he was castigated as a pro-abortionist by the *Limerick Leader* newspaper. Frank Prendergast's first-preference vote was halved.

FEB 87 % Poll		NOV 82 % Poll				
				Electorate:	67,301	
				Total poll:	49,910	(74.2%)
FF	25.5	FF	46.5	Spoiled votes:	297	
FG	17.9	FG	33.9	Total valid poll:	49,613	
PD	37.1	—	—	Quota:	8,269	
LAB	4.4	LAB	10.1			
WP	0.5	WP	—			
SF	1.1	—	—			
OTH	13.4	OTH	9.4	15 Candidates.		

COUNTS	1st	2nd O'Malley Surplus (4,089)	3rd O'Dea Surplus (999)	4th Clohessy Surplus (832)	5th O'Donovan Votes (63) (NT) (4)	6th O'Riordan Votes (92) (NT) (13)	7th O'Lehane Votes (264) (NT) (18)	8th Grant Votes (295) (NT) (27)	9th Neugent Votes (463) (NT) (66)	10th Malone Votes (664) (NT) (137)	11th Parkes Votes (1,657) (NT) (140)	12th Prendergast Votes (2,707) (NT) (443)	13th O'Donnell Votes (3,820) (NT) (737)
O'Malley D. (PD)	12,358												
O'Dea W. (FF)	9,268												
Clohessy P. (PD)	6,069	+3,032 9,101											
Kemmy J. (DSP)	5,920	+308 6,228	+81 6,309	+220 6,529	+15 6,544	+12 6,556	+98 6,654	+153 6,807	+159 6,966	+274 7,240	+147 7,387	+1,025 8,412	
Noonan M. (FG)	5,913	+304 6,217	+39 6,256	+254 6,510	+3 6,513	+23 6,536	+37 6,573	+23 6,596	+37 6,633	+15 6,648	+79 6,727	+576 7,303	+2,819 10,122
O'Donnell T. (FG)	2,968	+158 3,126	+53 3,179	+126 3,305	+7 3,312	+14 3,326	+9 3,335	+5 3,340	+44 3,384	+17 3,401	+62 3,463	+357 3,820	
Prendergast F. (Lab)	2,201	+110 2,311	+38 2,349	+113 2,462	+8 2,470	+5 2,475	+32 2,507	+24 2,531	+50 2,581	+52 2,633	+74 2,707		
O'Flaherty R. (FF)	2,111	+74 2,185	+537 2,722	+41 2,763	+1 2,764	+7 2,771	+13 2,784	+8 2,792	+43 2,835	+127 2,962	+1,155 4,117	+306 4,423	+264 4,687
Parkes M. (FF)	1,254	+63 1,317	+228 1,545	+35 1,580	+2 1,582	+4 1,586	+5 1,591	+5 1,596	+19 1,615	+42 1,657			
Malone P. (SF)	565	+7 572	+7 579	+3 582	+5 587	+0 587	+8 595	+24 619	+45 664				
Nugent M. (Ind)	353	+18 371	+10 381	+21 402	+3 405	+7 412	+25 437	+26 463					
Grant E. (WP)	246	+7 253	+2 255	+7 262	+11 273	+3 276	+19 295						
O'Lehane D. (GA)	241	+6 247	+3 250	+7 257	+3 260	+4 264							
Riordan D. (Ind)	87	+2 89	+0 89	+2 91	+1 92								
Donovan J. (Ind)	59	+0 59	+1 60	+3 63									

DESMOND O'MALLEY (PD) First elected in 1968 in a by-election following the death of his uncle Donogh O'Malley, then Minister for Education. Des O'Malley is the leader of the Progressive Democrats which he founded in Dec 1985. While a member of FF he was Minister for Trade, Commerce and Tourism 1982; Minister for Industry Commerce and Tourism 1980-81; Minister for Industry, Commerce and Energy 1977-80; Minister for Justice 1970-73. Parliamentary Secretary to the Taoiseach, Minister for Defence and Government Chief Whip 1969-70. Opposition spokesman on Health 1973-75; Industry and Commerce 1975-77.

Address: 37 Abbey Avenue, Corbally, Limerick.

Born: Limerick, Feb 1939.

Married: Patricia McAleer. 2 sons, 4 daughters.

Education: Crescent College, Limerick; UCD; Incorporated Law Society of Ireland.

Occupation: Public representative.

WILLIAM O'DEA (FF) First elected in Feb 1982.
Home address: Miltown, Kilteely, Co Limerick; 2 Glenview Gardens,
    Farranshore, Limerick.
Tel: Home 061 54488; Business 061 54522.
Born: Limerick, Nov 1952.
Education: Patrician Brothers' Ballyfin, Co Laois; UCD; Kings Inns;
    Institute of Certified Accountants.
Occupation: Public representative and accountant. Partner in O'Dea,
    Ryan, Kinirons & Co Auditors and Accountants.

PEADAR CLOHESSY (PD) First elected in Jun 1981.
Home address: Fanningstown, Crecora, Co Limerick.
Tel: 061 351190.
Born: Fedamore, Co Limerick 1933.
Married: Jean McMahon. 3 sons, 3 daughters.
Education: CBS, Limerick.
Occupation: Public representative. Former company representative.
    Member County Limerick Health Committee; Roads Committee
    and Tourist Committee; General Council of County Councils.
    Markets' Trustee.

MICHAEL NOONAN (FG) First elected in 1981, taking a second
seat for FG in this marginal constituency. Minister for Justice 1982-86;
Minister for Industry and Commerce 1986-87. Opposition spokesman
on Education 1982. Member of ASTI.
Address: 18 Gouldavoher Estate, Fr Russell Road, Limerick.
Born: Limerick, May 1943.
Married: Florence Knightly.
Education: St. Patrick's Teacher Training College, Drumcondra,
    Dublin; UCD.
Occupation: Public representative. Former teacher.

JIM KEMMY (DSP) First elected in 1981, taking a seat from Lab's Mick Lipper. Brought down the first FitGerald government in Feb '82 with his vote against the budget. He retained his seat in the election which followed and then lost his seat in Nov '82. He is the leader of the Democratic Socialist Party, of which he is a founder. Member Limerick Corporation since 1974. Editor of the *Old Limerick Journal*. Address: 33 Greenhill Road, Garryowen, Limerick.
Tel: 061 42966.
Marital status: Single.
Education: CBS, Limerick; Municipal Technical College, Limerick.
Occupation: Public representative. Former stonemason.

LIMERICK WEST (3)

Elected: *Gerry Collins (FF) 1st Count; *Michael J. Noonan (FF) 2nd Count; John McCoy (PD) 5th Count.

They never saw a night like it in Rathkeale. Against all the odds and the political predictions the PDs upset the status quo in one of the most traditional constituencies in the country. Some weeks before the election, Martin Byrnes, a journalist with the *Limerick Leader,* predicted that the PD candidate, John McCoy, would take the third seat in the constituency from FG. At the time few believed him. Events proved him right. Fine Gael's tactic of running three candidates, one of them imposed by the National Executive, proved disastrous. The PDs' first-preference total of 6,580 was 3,228 votes clear of the nearest FG candidate, Jimmy Houlihan. The order of elimination was against FG and their transfers put McCoy above the quota on the 5th count. The two FF candidates elected were, as usual, Gerry Collins and Michael Noonan.

FEB 87 % Poll		NOV 82 % Poll		Electorate:	43,418	
				Total poll:	34,294	(79%)
FF	51.3	FF	62.2	Spoiled votes:	288	
FG	27.8	FG	37.7	Total valid poll:	34,006	
PD	19.3	—	—	Quota:	8,502	
LAB	1.5	—	—	7 Candidates		

COUNTS	1st	2nd Collins Surplus (2,310)	3rd Brennan Votes (539) (NT) (121)	4th Neville Votes (3,012) (NT) (206)	5th Houlihan Votes (4,357) (NT) (489)
Collins G. (FF)	**10,812**				
Noonan M. (FF)	6,631	+1873 **8,504**			
McCoy J. (PD)	6,580	+209 6,789	+182 6,971	+777 7,748	+1334 **9,082**
Houlihan J. (FG)	3,352	+56 3,408	+49 3,457	+900 4,357	
Finucane M. (FG)	3,218	+96 3,314	+125 3,439	+1129 4,568	+2534 7,102
Neville D. (FG)	2,894	+56 2,950	+62 3,012		
Brennan P. (Lab)	519	+20 539			

MICHAEL J. NOONAN (FF) First elected in 1969. Appointed Minister for Defence Mar 1987. Opposition spokesman on Agriculture 1983-87. Member RTE Authority 1965-69. National President Macra na Feirme 1963-65.
Home address: Crean, Kilmallock, Limerick.
Tel: 061 89718.
Born: Bruff, Co Limerick, Sept 1935.
Education: Salesian College, Pallaskenry, Co Limerick; UCC.
Married: Helen Sheahan. 2 sons, 4 daughters.
Occupation: Farmer and public representative. Member Limerick County Council; Limerick VEC since 1967; Limerick County Committee of Agriculture since 1967; Limerick Health Advisory Committee since 1971. Member Muintir na Tire; GAA.

GERARD COLLINS (FF) First elected in 1967 when he was returned in a by-election in Limerick West caused by the death of his father, James Collins TD 1948-67. Appointed Minister for Justice Mar 1987. Minister for Foreign Affairs 1982; Minister for Justice 1977-81; Minister for Posts and Telegraphs 1970-73. Parliamentary Secretary to the Minister for Industry and Commerce and to the Minister for the Gaeltacht 1969-70. Member Consultative Assembly and Council of Europe since 1973. Frontbench spokesman on Agriculture 1973-75; Justice 1975-77; Foreign Affairs 1982-86.
Home address: The Hill, Abbeyfeale, Co Limerick.
Tel: 068 31126.
Born: Abbeyfeale, Co Limerick, Oct 1938.
Education: St Ita's College, Abbeyfeale; Patrician College, Ballyfin; UCD.
Married: Hillary Tattan.
Occupation: Public representative. Former vocational school teacher. Member Limerick County Council 1974-77; Assistant General Secretary of FF 1965-67.

JOHN McCOY (PD) First elected in 1987. Former FF councillor on Limerick County Council.
Home address: The Square, Newcastlewest, Co Limerick.
Tel: Home 069 62ll7; Business 069 62096.
Born: Newcastlewest, Jul 1940.
Married: Ann Burke. 3 sons, 1 daughter.
Education: Mount Sion Waterford; UCC.
Occupation: Public representative and senior manager, Kentoher Co-Op, Limerick. Member Newcastlewest Action Group on Unemployment.

LONGFORD WESTMEATH (4)

Eected: *Albert Reynolds (FF) 1st Count; Henry Abbott (FF) 6th Count; *Mary O'Rourke (FF), *Pat Cooney (FG) 7th Count.

Albert Reynolds' arrival in this constituency in 1977 changed the pattern of support, from an even balance between FF and FG to one of FF dominance. With a near-perfect division of the constituency among their candidates this time, FF reached their optimistic target of three out of four seats. The retirement of FG stalwart, Gerry L'Estrange, made it that bit easier for FF. A FG candidate, who lived across the constituency border in Meath, tried to hold the L'Estrange vote in the Mullingar area. The FF strategy, led by Albert Reynolds, was to leave Mullingar to Henry Abbott, a barrister. Mary O'Rourke had free rein around Athlone, in the south west of the constituency, where she was marking FG's Pat Cooney. Albert Reynolds concentrated on Longford. Fianna Fáil increased their share of the vote by 4.6 per cent — a total increase of 10 per cent on their performance in Jun 1981. The only surprise was that Henry Abbott came ahead of Mary O'Rourke in first preferences. Fine Gael did badly, their vote dropping by almost 16 per cent. The PDs, who may have been mistaken in running two candidates, got many votes at FG's expense. Outgoing Minister Paddy Cooney had a bad showing on the 1st count with just 5,680 votes. But the transfers of his two running mates saw him home safely by the 7th count.

FEB 87 % Poll		NOV 82 % Poll		Electorate:	61,253	
				Total poll:	45,489	(74.3%)
FF	57.6	FF	53.0	Spoiled votes:	337	
FG	27.5	FG	43.2	Total valid poll:	45,152	
PD	12.0	—	—	Quota:	9,031	
LAB	2.3	LAB	3.8			
OTH	0.6	OTH	—	10 Candidates		

COUNTS	1st	2nd Reynolds Surplus (1,511)	3rd Murphy Votes (314) (NT) (33)	4th McNamee Votes (1,078) (NT) (152)	5th O'Sullivan Votes (2,062) (NT) (74)	6th Smyth Votes (3,312) (NT) (50)	7th Finnan Votes (4954) (NT) (383)
Reynolds A. (FF)	**10,542**						
Abbott H. (FF)	8,035	+463 8,498	+36 8,534	+271 8,805	+74 8,879	+154 **9,033**	
O'Rourke M. (FF)	7,440	+779 8,219	+64 8,283	+101 8,384	+314 8,698	+55 8,753	+198 **8,951**
Cooney P. (FG)	5,680	+51 5,731	+19 5,750	+102 5,852	+430 6,282	+1701 7,983	+3760 **11,743**
Finnan S. (FG)	3,642	+109 3,751	+76 3,827	+75 3,902	+90 3,992	+962 4,954	
McAuliffe-Ennis H. (PD)	3,463	+31 3,494	+24 3,518	+182 3,700	+999 4,699	+390 5,089	+613 5,702
Smyth C. (FG)	3,094	+7 3,101	+4 3,105	+126 3,231	+81 3,312		
O'Sullivan D. (PD)	1,938	+29 1,967	+26 1,993	+69 2,062			
McNamee S. (Lab)	1,038	+8 1,046	+32 1,078				
Murphy P. (Ind)	280	+34 314					

ALBERT REYNOLDS (FF) First elected in 1977. Appointed Minister for Industry and Commerce Mar 1987. Minister for Industry and Energy 1982; Minister for Posts and Telegraphs and Minister for Transport 1979-81. Frontbench spokesman on Industry and Employment 1983-85; Energy 1985-87.
Home address: Mount Carmel House, Dublin Road, Longford.
Tel: 043 41333.
Born: Rooskey, Co Roscommon, Nov 1935.
Married: Kathleen Coen. 2 sons, 5 daughters.
Education: Summerhill College, Sligo.
Occupation: Public representative and company director. Member Longford County Committee of Agriculture 1974-79; Chairman Longford Recreational Development Committee. President Longford Chamber of Commerce 1974-78.

MARY O'ROURKE (FF) First elected in 1982. Appointed Minister for Education Mar 1987. Senator 1981-82. Fianna Fáil spokesperson on Education 1982-87. Sister of Brian Lenihan, FF TD for Dublin West; daughter of the late P.J. Lenihan, TD for Longford Westmeath 1965-70.
Home address: "Aisling", Arcadia, Athlone.
Tel: 0902 75065
Born: Athlone 1937.
Married: Enda O'Rourke. 2 sons.
Education: St Peter's Convent, Athlone; Loreto Convent, Bray; UCD; Maynooth College, Co Kildare.
Occupation: Public representative. Former secondary school teacher. Member Athlone Urban District Council since 1974; Westmeath County Council since 1979; Board of Management Athlone Regional Technical College 1974-79; Westmeath VEC since 1979; Athlone and District Soroptimist Society.

HENRY ABBOTT (FF) First elected in 1987. Chairman of Westmeath County Council.
Home address: Monilea, Mullingar, Co Westmeath.
Tel: 044 72110.
Born: Mullingar, Dec 1947
Married: Pauline Heffernan. 3 girls, 1 boy.
Education: Taughmon NS; St Mary's, Mullingar; UCD; TCD; Kings Inns.
Occupation: Public representative, farmer and barrister. Member Westmeath VEC; Midlands Regional Development Organisation; Westmeath Health Committee; GAA.

PATRICK COONEY (FG) First elected in 1970. Minister for Education 1986-7; Minister for Defence 1982-86; Minister for Transport and for Posts and Telegraphs 1981-82; Minister for Justice 1973-77. Fine Gael leader in the Seanad 1977-81. Frontbench spokesman on Justice 1972-73. Vice-Chairman Joint Oireachtas Committee on State-Sponsored Bodies 1977-81.
Home address: Garnafailagh, Athlone, Co Westmeath.
Tel: 0902 75531.
Born: Dublin 1931.
Married: Brigid McMenamin. 3 sons, 1 daughter.
Education: Castleknock, Co Dublin; UCD.
Occupation: Public representative. Former solicitor. Member Westmeath County Council 1967-73. Member Incorporated Law Society of Ireland since 1956. Served in Forsa Cosanta Áitiúl 1948-53.

LOUTH (4)

Elected: *Brendan McGahon (FG) 6th Count; *Seamus Kirk (FF) 7th Count; Dermot Ahern (FF), *Michael Bell (LAB) 9th Count.

Fianna Fáil were hoping to get three seats here, repeating their 1977 performance. But the strong showing of PD Frank Aiken, son of one of the founding fathers of FF and a FF TD from 1927-73, helped to end their hopes. The FF vote dropped by 3.6 per cent. They held their two seats, with Dermot Ahern, a solicitor based in Dundalk, winning the seat of outgoing TD Padraig Faulkner, who had retired. Surprising some senior FF people, Ahern went comfortably ahead of former county footballer, Jimmy Mulroy, on the elimination of Tom Bellew, a former FF TD who was standing as an Ind. Bellew is based in Dundalk and 25 per cent of his transfers went to FG's Brendan McGahon, 21 per cent to Ahern. All of the major parties were surprised at the 5,219 first preferences polled by Aiken, and the PDs will target this constituency in the next election. Sinn Féinn, with a new candidate, dropped nearly 3 per cent on their Feb 1982 performance.

FEB 87 % Poll		NOV 82 % Poll				
				Electorate:	61,991	
				Total poll:	47,301	(76.3%)
FF	39.5	FF	43.1	Spoiled votes:	492	
FG	23.1	FG	33.8	Total valid poll:	46,809	
PD	11.1	—	—	Quota:	9,362	
LAB	13.3	LAB	14.7			
WP	1.2	WP	1.5			
SF	5.6	—	—			
OTH	6.3	OTH	6.9	14 Candidates		

COUNT	1st	2nd Hyland MacRaghnaill Ross Smith	3rd O'Dowd	4th Morgan	5th Bellew	6th Lennon	7th Mulroy	8th McGahon	9th Kirk
		Votes (787)	Votes (1,964)	Votes (2,693)	Votes (3,082)	Votes (4,282)	Votes (5,970)	Surplus (675)	Surplus (1704)
		(NT) (57)	(NT) (24)	(NT) (523)	(NT) (306)	(NT) (126)	(NT) (208)		
Kirk S. (FF)	7,156	+41 7,197	+12 7,209	+515 7,724	+391 8,115	+234 8,349	+2717 **11,066**		
Bell M. (Lab)	6,205	+260 6,465	+377 6,842	+312 7,154	+286 7,440	+188 7,628	+1295 8,923	+125 9,048	+143 **9,191**
Ahern D. (FF)	5,822	+54 5,876	+8 5,884	+430 6,314	+638 6,952	+79 7,031	+1549 8,580	+42 8,622	+1506 **10,128**
Mulroy J. (FF)	5,492	+46 5,538	+88 5,626	+192 5,818	+102 5,920	+50 5,970			
McGahon B. (FG)	5,319	+59 5,378	+657 6,035	+220 6,255	+764 7,019	+3018 **10,037**			
Aiken F. (PD)	5,219	+67 5,286	+248 5,534	+138 5,672	+499 6,171	+587 6,758	+201 6,959	+508 7,467	+55 7,522
Lennon J. (FG)	3,560	+19 3,579	+526 4,105	+81 4,186	+96 4,282				
Bellew T. (Ind)	2,709	+78 2,787	+13 2,800	+282 3,082					
Morgan A. (SF)	2,599	+83 2,682	+11 2,693						
O'Dowd F. (FG)	1,941	+23 1,964							
MacRaghnaill D. (WP)	570								
Smyth R. (Ind)	86								
Ross C. (Ind)	66								
Hyland B. (Ind)	65								

SEAMUS KIRK (FF) First elected in Nov 1982. Appointed Junior Minister for Horticulture Mar 87. Member of Louth County Council since 1974. Seamus Kirk is a former Louth footballer. Opposition spokesman on Horticulture 1983-87.
Home address: Rathiddy, Knockbridge, Dundalk.
Tel: 046 31032.
Born: Dunkeith, Apr 1945.
Married: Mary McGeough. 3 sons, 1 daughter.
Education: Drumsinnott NS; CBS, Dundalk.
Occupation: Public representative and farmer.

DERMOT AHERN (FF) First elected 1987. Member Louth County Council since 1979; Louth VEC.
Home address: Hill Cottage, The Crescent, Blackrock, Co Louth.
Tel: Home 042 21473; Business 042 34250.
Born: 1956.
Married: Maeve Coleman.
Education: Marist College, Dundalk; UCD.
Occupation: Public representative, solicitor and Commissioner for
    Oaths.

MICHAEL BELL (LAB) First elected Nov 1982. Chairman Parliamentary Lab Party on the retirement of Joe Bermingham in 1986.
Home address: 110 Brookville, Drogheda, Co Louth; business address:
    Connolly Hall, Drogheda.
Tel: 041 38573.
Married: Betty Plunkett. 3 daughters, 2 sons.
Occupation: Public representative and trade union official (on
    secondment to Dáil). Member Drogheda Corporation; Louth County
    Council 1974. Director Institute for Industrial Research and Standards
    since 1974.

BRENDAN MCGAHON (FG) First elected Nov 1982. Member Louth County Council.
Home address: 4 Faughart Terrace, St Mary's Road, Dundalk, Co Louth.
Tel: 042 32620
Born: Dundalk 1936.
Married: Celine Lundy. 3 sons, 2 daughters.
Education: St Mary's College, Dundalk.
Occupation: Public representative and newspaper distributor. Member Louth VEC; Dundalk Urban District Council; Dundalk Harbour Commissioners. Former soccer player for Dundalk FC in the League of Ireland.

MAYO-EAST (3)

Elected: *Sean Calleary (FF), *P.J. Morley (FF), Jim Higgins (FG) 3rd Count.

The major surprise here was the defeat of Paddy O'Toole, the outgoing Minister for Defence and the Gaeltacht. He lost his seat to his party colleague, Senator Jim Higgins, who was making his fourth attempt to win a seat. Higgins, who is from Ballyhaunis, topped the poll with 7,263 votes, just 468 short of a quota. He had a high profile through an imaginative plan for Knock Airport: he was going to fly in pilgrims from the "Blue Army", an American organisation of Marian devotees with a membership of three million. Stories in the local press refuting his claims seem to have had no adverse affect on their popularity. Paddy O'Toole attributed his failure to government policy on the airport and the time-consuming commitment to government business which kept him out of the constituency. As expected, Sean Calleary, a former Minister for State, and P.J.Morley retained their seats with Padraig Gavin's Swinford-based transfers.

FEB 87 % Poll		NOV 82 % Poll			
				Electorate:	41,247
				Total poll:	31,179 (75.6%)
FF	55.7	FF	53.2	Spoiled votes:	259
FG	42.1	FG	45.4	Total valid poll:	30,920
SF	2.2	—	—	Quota:	7,731
LAB	—	LAB	1.4	6 Candidates	

COUNT	1st	2nd McHale Votes (668)	3rd Gavin Votes (4,203)
		(NT) (104)	(NT) (74)
Higgins J. (FG)	7,263	+65 7,328	+501 **7,829**
Calleary S. (FF)	6,779	+176 6,955	+1605 **8,560**
Morley P.J. (FF)	6,382	+115 6,497	+1798 **8,295**
O'Toole P. (FG)	5,765	+68 5,833	+225 6,058
Gavin P. (FF)	4,063	+140 4,203	
McHale J. (SF)	668		

SEAN CALLEARY (FF) First elected in 1973. Appointed Minister of State at the Department of Foreign Affairs Mar 1987. Minister of State at the Department of Labour and Department of the Public Service 1979-81; Department of Trade, Commerce and Tourism 1982. Member Mayo County Council since 1967; Mayo VEC.
Home address: Quay Road, Ballina, Co Mayo; business address: Pearse St, Ballina, Co Mayo.
Tel: Home 096 22475; Business 096 21154.
Born: Killala, Co Mayo, Oct 1931.
Married: Doris Brogan. 3 sons, 1 daughter.
Education: St Joseph's College, Ballinasloe, Co Galway; UCG.
Occupation: Public representative. Former civil engineer. Member Ballina UDC since 1981; Mayo/Galway Regional Development Organisation. Played rugby for Galwegians, UCG and Connaught 1952-60. Former Member Mayo GAA County Board. Son of the late Phelim A. Calleary, Dáil Deputy for Mayo North 1952-69.

P.J.MORLEY (FF) First elected in 1977. Member Mayo County Council since 1967; Western Health Board since 1971, currently Chairman. Member Irish National Teachers' Organisation since 1952. Member Council of Europe since 1983.
Home address: Bekan, Claremorris, Co Mayo.
Tel: 094 80217
Born: Bekan, Claremorris, Co Mayo, Mar 1931.
Married: Mary O'Boyle. 3 sons, 1 daughter.
Education: St Colman's College, Claremorris; St Patrick's Teachers' Training College, Dublin; UCG.
Occupation: Public representative. Former national school teacher.

JIM HIGGINS (FG) First elected in 1987. Senator 1981-87. Member Mayo County Council since 1979.
Home address: Devlis, Ballyhaunis, Co Mayo.
Tel: 0907 30052
Born: Ballyhaunis, May 1945.
Married: Marian Hannan. 4 daughters.
Education: St Jarlath's College, Tuam; UCG.
Occupation: Public representative. Former teacher. Member Western Care Association; Junior Chamber Ireland; Save the West Campaign.

MAYO-WEST (3)

Elected: *Denis Gallagher (FF), *Padraig Flynn (FF), *Enda Kenny (FG) 2nd Count.

While few people would have predicted any change in this constituency, FG had hoped to make some inroads into FF's vote. They planned their strategy back in 1982 when Westport-based solicitor, Patrick Durcan, was nominated by the Taoiseach to the Seanad. However, their hopes did not materialise and FF, in fact, increased their original 10 per cent lead by over 3 per cent. After the election Durcan criticised his running-mate, Enda Kenny, a Junior Minister, for breaking a pre-election agreement to divide the constituency between them. According to Durcan, Kenny sent 800 letters into Westport town, Durcan's base. However, it is extremely unlikely that the agreement — if it had been kept — would have made any difference to the final outcome. Labour and the PDs did not put up any candidates. Fianna Fáil, once again, had a strong team: Denis Gallagher and Padraig Flynn — two former Cabinet Ministers — were joined by Padraig Cosgrove, a county councillor and vocational school teacher from Belmullet.

FEB 87 % Poll		NOV 82 % Poll		Electorate:	40,739	
				Total poll:	30,514	(74.9%)
FF	56.8	FF	52.9	Spoiled votes:	224	
FG	43.2	FG	42.8	Total valid poll:	30,290	
LAB	—	LAB	4.2	Quota:	7,573	
				5 Candidates		

COUNTS	1st	2nd Cosgrove Votes (3091) (NT) (50)
		+164
Kenny E. (FG)	7,410	**7,574**
		+1052
Flynn P. (FF)	7,198	**8,250**
		+1553
Gallagher D. (FF)	6,908	**8,461**
		+272
Durcan P. (FG)	5,683	5,955
Cosgrove P. (FF)	3,091	

PADRAIG FLYNN (FF) First elected in 1977. Appointed Minister for the Environment Mar 1987. Minister for Trade, Commerce and Tourism Oct-Dec 1982; Minister for the Gaeltacht 1982. Minister of State at the Department of Transport and Power 1980-81. Frontbench spokesman on Trade, Commerce and Tourism 1982-87.
Home address: Newtown Street, Castlebar, Co Mayo.
Tel: 094 22686.
Born: Castlebar, May 1939.
Married: Dorothy Tynan. 3 daughters, 1 son.
Education: St Gerald's Secondary School, Castlebar; St Patrick's Teachers' Training College, Dublin.
Occupation: Public representative and publican. Former national school teacher. Member Mayo County Council 1967-86. Member Irish National Teachers' Organisation.

DENIS GALLAGHER (FF) First elected Dáil 1973. Appointed Minister of State at the Department of the Gaeltacht Mar 1987. Minister for the Gaeltacht Oct-Dec 1982; 1977-79. Minister of State at the Department of Social Welfare 1982; Department of Industry, Commerce and Tourism 1980-81. Opposition spokesman on Fisheries 1974-77; the Gaeltacht 1982-86.
Home address: Currane, Achill Sound, Co Mayo.
Tel: 094 45126
Born: Currane, Achill Sound, Nov 1923.
Married: Hannah McHugh. 5 sons, 7 daughters.
Education: St Enda's College, Galway; St Patrick's Teachers Training College, Dublin.
Occupation: Public representative. Former national school teacher. Member Mayo County Council 1967-77; Board Iascaigh Mhara 1969-77. Secretary and founder member Achill Fishermen's Co-Operative.

ENDA KENNY (FG) First elected in 1975, in a by-election following the death of his father, Henry Kenny, Dáil Deputy 1969-75 and Parliamentary Secretary to the Minister for Finance 1973-75. Minister of State Departments of Education and Labour 1986-87. Spokesman on Gaeltacht 1982; Youth Affairs and Sport 1977-80. Member Dáil Committee on Procedure and Privileges. Member New Ireland Forum. Founder member Young Fine Gael. Member Mayo County Council since 1975.
Home address: Derrycoosh, Castlebar, Co Mayo.
Tel: Home 094 22720; Business 094 22299.
Born: Castlebar, Co Mayo 1951.
Marital status: Single.
Education: Coornanool NS; St Gerard's College, Castlebar; St Patrick's Teacher Training College, Dublin; UCG.
Occupation: Public representative.

MEATH (5)

Elected: *John Bruton (FG), Michael Lynch (FF) 10th Count; *John Farrelly (FG), *Colm Hilliard (FF), Noel Dempsey (FF) 13th Count.

This was a five seater where it was generally agreed that FF were likely to take three seats — but on the day they were even in the hunt for a fourth. This was because of an impressive first-time performance from a 25-year-old hospital administrator, Mary Wallace. With 5,681 first preferences, she out-polled sitting TDs John Farrelly and Frank McLoughlin. Labour's McLoughlin was the one who fell victim to the FF thrust and there were anxious moments for FG's John Farrelly as he waited for PD transfers (41 per cent) to take him finally above Mary Wallace for election on the 13th count. Fianna Fáil had a well-managed vote-splitting exercise which brought Michael Lynch, an Oldcastle publican, back to the Dáil along with Noel Dempsey. It was Dempsey's first time contesting a general election. The chairman of Trim Urban Council, he did fatal damage to Frank McLoughlin's vote in the area. Michael Lynch topped the poll, which reflected the fact that he was the only FF candidate in the north of the county. Colm Hilliard from Kilmessan moved into the Navan area to take over the FF vote of Jim Fitzsimons who had opted for Europe. Overall, the FF vote was up 2.7 per cent but that was on an electorate that had increased by 7,000. Fine Gael's vote was down by 10.6 per cent and Lab's down 9.6 per cent.

FEB 87 % Poll		NOV 82 % Poll		Electorate:	73,904	
				Total poll:	55,597	(75.2%)
FF	50.2	FF	47.5	Spoiled votes:	402	
FG	25.7	FG	36.3	Total valid poll:	55,195	
PD	8.8	—	—	Quota:	9,200	
LAB	6.6	LAB	16.2			
WP	1.4	—	—			
SF	1.8	—	—			
OTH	5.6	OTH	—	16 Candidates		

COUNTS	1st	2nd Gormley Votes (36) (NT) (3)	3rd Archer Votes (395) (NT) (8)	4th Cummins Votes (654) (NT) (35)	5th McMahon Votes (767) (NT) (10)	6th McDonagh Votes (938) (NT) (98)	7th Reilly Votes (1,198) (NT) (213)	8th Maher Votes (1,734) (NT) (38)	9th Marry Votes (2,681) (NT) (356)	10th McLoughlin Votes (4,223) (NT) (973)	11th Bruton Surplus (646) (NT) (85)	12th Lynch Surplus (149) (NT) (7)	13th Andrews Votes (5,659) (NT) (1,608)
Lynch M. (FF)	8,712	+4 8,716	+2 8,718	+25 8,743	+3 8,746	+30 8,776	+205 8,981	+20 9,001	+129 9,130	+219 **9,349**			
Bruton J. (FG)	8,084	+2 8,086	+40 8,126	+50 8,176	+235 8,411	+38 8,449	+41 8,490	+201 8,691	+433 9,124	+722 **9,846**			
Hilliard C. (FF)	6,763	+2 6,765	+10 6,775	+42 6,817	+15 6,832	+79 6,911	+187 7,098	+35 7,133	+364 7,497	+425 7,922	+44 7,966	+53 8,019	+616 **8,635**
Dempsey N. (FF)	6,538	+4 6,542	+14 6,556	+38 6,594	+7 6,601	+35 6,636	+113 6,749	+36 6,785	+232 7,017	+496 7,513	+45 7,558	+37 7,595	+661 **8,256**
Wallace M. (FF)	5,681	+3 5,684	+23 5,707	+35 5,742	+17 5,759	+72 5,831	+122 5,953	+57 6,010	+532 6,542	+289 6,831	+24 6,855	+13 6,868	+437 7,305
Farrelly J. (FG)	5,345	+2 5,347	+18 5,365	+30 5,395	+345 5,740	+32 5,772	+23 5,795	+71 5,866	+143 6,009	+463 6,472	+333 6,805	+23 6,828	+2337 **9,165**
McLoughlin F. (Lab)	3,237	+2 3,239	+206 3,445	+87 3,532	+28 3,560	+244 3,804	+123 3,927	+68 3,995	+228 4,223				
Andrews P. (PD)	3,227	+0 3,227	+19 3,246	+76 3,322	+30 3,352	+50 3,402	+54 3,456	+1172 4,628	+264 4,892	+636 5,528	+115 5,643	+16 5,659	
Marry G. (Ind)	2,393	+0 2,393	+10 2,403	+47 2,450	+16 2,466	+79 2,545	+100 2,645	+36 2,681					
Maher B. (PD)	1,604	+2 1,606	+10 1,616	+41 1,657	+33 1,690	+27 1,717	+17 1,734						
Reilly J. (SF)	1,012	+0 1,012	+2 1,014	+19 1,033	+11 1,044	+154 1,198							
McDonagh S. (WP)	790	+4 794	+18 812	+109 921	+17 938								
McMahon B. (FG)	743	+0 743	+4 747	+20 767									
Cummins C. (Ind)	636	+7 643	+11 654										
Archer P. (Lab)	394	+1 395											
Gormley S. (Ind)	36												

COLM HILLIARD (FF) First elected in Feb 1982. Member Meath County Council and Meath County Committee of Agriculture. Member Oireachtas All Party Committee on Public Expenditure. Member Fianna Fáil Policy Committees for Agriculture, Finance and Taxation.
Home address: Ringlestown, Kilmessan, Co Meath.
Tel: 046 25236
Born: Navan, May 1936.
Married: Margaret Quinn. 3 sons, 1 daughter.
Education: Carmelite College, Castlemartyr, Co Cork.
Occupation: Public representative and farmer. Former livestock marketing manager, auctioneer and accountant. Former Member Meath GAA Finance and Grounds Committee and delegate to the Leinster GAA Convention and Congress. Son of Michael Hilliard, former Minister of Posts and Telegraphs, Minister for Defence and MEP.

MICHAEL LYNCH (FF) First elected 1982, losing his seat in the Nov election that year. Re-elected 1987. Senator 1982-87. Member Meath County Council since 1967; North Eastern Health Board since 1979. Vice-Chairman of the Joint Oireachtas Committee on Small Businesses. Member Joint Oireachtas Committee on Irish Language.
Home address: Cogan St, Oldcastle, Co Meath.
Tel: 049 41307.
Born: Summerbank, Oldcastle, Aug 1934.
Married: Maureen Cahill. 2 sons, 2 daughters.
Education: Gibson National and Secondary Schools, Oldcastle, Co Meath.
Occupation: Public representative and publican. Member Comhaltas Ceoltóirí Éireann.

NOEL DEMPSEY (FF) First elected 1987. Chairman Meath County Council 1986-1987.
Home address: 58 Castle Abbey, Trim, Co Meath.
Tel: 046 31146.
Born: Trim, Jan 1953.
Married: Bernadette Rattigan. 2 sons, 2 daughters.
Education: St Brid's NS, Trim; St Michael's CBS, Trim; UCD; St Patrick's College, Maynooth.
Occupation: Public representative and career guidance counsellor. Member Meath Library Committee; Meath VEC; Meath County Health Committee; Meath County Council Sub Committees on Employment, Tourism and Housing; Eastern Regional Development Organisation Dublin. Director Eastern Regional Tourism Organisation.

JOHN BRUTON (FG) First elected 1969. Minister for Finance 1986-87; Minister for Industry and Commerce 1984-86; Minister for Industry and Energy 1982-84; Minister for Finance 1981-82. Parliamentary Secretary to Minister for Education 1973-77; to Minister for Industry and Commerce 1975-77. Opposition frontbench spokesman on Agriculture 1972-73 and 1977-81.

Home address: Cornelstown, Dunboyne, Co Meath.

Born: Dublin 1947.

Married: Fiona Gill. 1 son.

Education: St Dominic's College, Cabra; Clongowes Wood, Dublin; UCD; Kings Inns, Dublin.

Occupation: Public representative and farmer. Member Council of the European Movement since 1972. Member An Taisce since 1972; Irish Cattle Traders and Stockowners Association; IFA. Member FCA 1963-66.

JOHN FARRELLY (FG) First elected 1981. Member Dáil Public Expenditure Committee. Member Meath County Council since 1974.

Home address: Eden, Kilmainhamwood, Kells, Co Meath.

Tel: Home 046 21153; Business 046 2276.

Born: Kilmainhamwood 1954.

Married: Gwen Murphy. 1 daughter.

Education: St Finian's College, Mullingar; Warrenstown Agricultural College.

Occupation: Public representative, farmer and auctioneer. Member Meath County Committee of Agriculture; General Council of County Councils since 1979. Member North Eastern Health Board. Member Meath ACOT; IFA. Member GAA.

ROSCOMMON (3)

Elected: *Sean Doherty (FF) 1st Count; *Terry Leyden (FF) 2nd Count; *Liam Naughton (FG) 4th Count.

Roscommon is normally one of the most predictable constituencies in the country, returning two FF and one FG deputies. No change was expected this time. But the candidacy of Eithne Quinn, Ind, campaigning for the retention of services at Roscommon County Hospital, raised the possibility of a change in the FG representation. However, nobody anticipated that two marathon recounts would be required to decide the FG winner. As expected, the controversial former Justice Minister, Sean Doherty, topped the poll on the 1st count. His 853 surplus votes ensured that party colleague Terry Leyden made it on the 2nd count. Then followed the distribution of Eithne Quinn's impressive 4,067 first preferences. On the 4th count outgoing FG deputy Liam Naughten had a margin of just one vote over party colleague and long-time rival John Connor. A first recount put Connor ahead of Naughten by two votes. The issue was finally resolved after a second recount which saw Naughten regaining his seat by 18 votes. Ironically, Roscommon announced the first TD of the 25th Dáil, Sean Doherty, and — because of the lengthy recounts — also announced the last.

FEB 87 % Poll		NOV 82 % Poll		Electorate:	41,515	
				Total poll:	32,681	(78.7%)
FF	50.1	FF	53.3	Spoiled votes:	320	
FG	37.4	FG	46.7	Total valid poll:	32,361	
OTH	12.6	OTH	—	Quota:	8,091	
				5 Candidates		

COUNTS	1st	2nd Quinn Votes (4,067) (NT) (409)	3rd Doherty Surplus (853)	4th Leydon Surplus (715)
Doherty S. (FF)	**8,944**			
Leyden T. (FF)	7,257	+1549 **8,806**		
Connor J. (FG)	6,144	+1010 7,154	+462 7,616	+260 7,876
Naughten L. (FG)	5,949	+1099 7,048	+391 7,439	+455 **7,894**
Quinn E. (Ind)	4,067			

TERRY LEYDEN (FF) First elected in 1977. Appointed Minister of State at the Department of Health Mar 1987. Minister of State at the Department of Transport; Department of Posts and Telegraphs 1982. Opposition spokesman on Communications in the last Dáil.
Home address: Castlecoote, Roscommon.
Tel: 0903 7380
Born: Roscommon, Oct 1945.
Married: Mary Margaret O'Connor. 1 son, 3 daughters.
Education: CBS Roscommon; Roscommon Vocational School.
Occupation: Public representative and architect. Member Dáil Committee on Small Businesses. Member Roscommon County Council since 1974; Roscommon VEC since 1985. Chairman Roscommon Local Health Committee since 1985. Member Roscommon Agricultural and Industrial Society; CCE and GAA. Board member Athlone Regional College. Fellow of the Irish Architects' Society.

SEAN DOHERTY (FF) First elected in 1977. Minister for Justice 1982. Minister of State Department of Justice 1979-81. Member Roscommon County Council since 1973.
Home address: Cootehall, Boyle, Co Roscommon.
Tel: 079 67005
Born: Roscommon, Jun 1944.
Married: Maura Nangle. 4 daughters.
Education: Presentation Brothers, Carrick-on-Shannon; UCD; Kings Inns.
Occupation: Public representative and company director. Vice-Chairman Western Health Board. Member Midland Regional Development Organisation. Chairman Regional Tourism Organisation.

LIAM NAUGHTEN (FG) First elected Feb 1982. Senator 1981-82. Member Dáil Committee on Public Accounts.
Home address: Drum, Athlone, Co Roscommon.
Tel: 0902 37100.
Born: Drum, Athlone 1944.
Married: Mary Murray. 6 sons.
Education: Athlone Vocational School; St Isidore's College, Multyfarnham.
Occupation: Public representative and farmer. Member Roscommon County Council; Roscommon VEC; Roscommon Health Committee since 1974; Western Health Board since 1979. Member IFA; GAA.

SLIGO LEITRIM (4)

Elected: *Ray McSharry (FF) 1st Count; *Ted Nealon (FG), *Matthew Brennan (FF), John Ellis (FF) 7th Count.

Sligo Leitrim became a four-seat constituency in 1981, and the distribution of seats has changed at every election since then. In 1981, FF and FG got two seats each; in Feb 1982, FF won three seats, FG one; the Nov 1982 election resulted in two seats for each of the main parties and this time round, FF won three seats again. Fine Gael lost out because their share of the vote dropped by 10 per cent or some 5,000 first preferences below their Nov 1982 performance. Nealon's vote held up but Joe McCartin suffered and lost his seat. The vote of the third FG candidate, Tommy Lavin, was also badly down, which meant McCartin was unable to benefit from his transfers. The PDs, with 2,500 first preferences, took some FG votes but it is believed that many FG supporters simply did not vote. Fine Gael put a big effort into the constituency in an attempt to retain their two seats: there was a hospital extension for Sligo costing £44m; the "go-ahead" for a third bridge in Sligo and the promise of 938 jobs at an IDA-aided Korean video factory to replace the former Snia factory. Also, Joe McCartin was allowed to retain the dual mandate of MEP and TD in order to try to save the seat. Fianna Fáil spread their vote well to elect their three candidates.

Ray McSharry — who prematurely conceded defeat but eventually took the last seat in Nov 1982 — topped the poll. Declan Bree, an Independent Socialist, stayed in the race until the 6th count with nearly 3,500 votes. There was no challenge from Lab or the WP and Bree's first-preference vote was the highest given to a left-wing candidate since Lab's Dan Shaw stood in 1965. Bree received nearly the same number of votes in Sligo town as outgoing Minister of State, Ted Nealon. The SF vote was little different to Feb 1982 and their support came mainly from Leitrim.

FEB 87 % Poll		NOV 82 % Poll				
				Electorate:	59,740	
				Total poll:	46,079	(77.1%)
FF	51.6	FF	53.0	Spoiled votes:	373	
FG	31.0	FG	41.4	Total valid poll:	45,706	
PD	5.5	—	—	Quota:	9,142	
LAB	—	LAB	1.2			
SF	5.7	—	—			
OTH	6.2	OTH	4.3	10 Candidates		

COUNTS	1st	2nd McSharry Surplus (379)	3rd Gorman Votes (241)	4th Dobbs Votes (2570)	5th McGirl Votes (2722)	6th Lavin Votes (2906)	7th Bree Votes (3495)
			(NT) (19)	(NT) (116)	(NT) (408)	(NT) (70)	(NT) (904)
MacSharry R. (FF)	**9,521**						
Ellis J. (FF).	7,140	+58 7,198	+5 7,203	+161 7,364	+1097 8,461	+31 8,492	+348 **8,840**
Brennan M. (FF)	6,913	+241 7,154	+20 7,174	+230 7,404	+259 7,663	+472 8,135	+719 **8,854**
Nealon T. (FG)	6,483	+29 6,512	+22 6,534	+924 7,458	+103 7,561	+1414 8,975	+1233 **10,208**
McCartin J. (FG)	5,071	+7 5,078	+12 5,090	+491 5,581	+407 5,988	+866 6,854	+291 7145
McGirl J.J. (SF)	2,627	+7 2,634	+17 2,651	+71 2,722			
Lavin T. (FG)	2,606	+3 2,609	+6 2,615	+262 2,877	+29 2,906		
Bree D. (Ind.Soc.)	2,584	+24 2,608	+100 2,708	+315 3,023	+419 3,442	+53 3,495	
Dobbs F. (PD)	2,521	+9 2,530	+40 2,570				
Gorman N.F. (Ind.)	240	+1 241					

MATTHEW BRENNAN (FF) First elected Feb 1982. Member Sligo County Council since 1974.
Home address: Ragoora, Cloonacool, Tubbercurry, Co Sligo.
Tel: 071 85136.
Born: Cloonacool, Oct 1936.
Married: Mary Vesey. 1 son, 1 daughter.
Education: Cloonacool NS; Vocational School, Tubbercurry; Theodore Roosevelt High School, New York.
Occupation: Public representative. Member Local Health Advisory Committee; Sligo County Committee of Agriculture. Member GAA. Nephew of the late Dr Martin Brennan, FF TD Sligo Leitrim 1938-48.

JOHN ELLIS (FF) First elected in Jun 1981. Member Leitrim County Council since 1974. Senator 1977-81; 1982-87.
Home address: Fenagh, Co Leitrim.
Tel: Home 078 44252; Business 078 44399.
Born: Fenagh, Co Leitrim.
Married: Patricia Donnelly. 2 sons, 1 daughter.
Education: Fenagh NS; St Felim's College, Ballinamore, Co Leitrim. Member GAA.
Occupation: Public representative, farmer and businessman.

RAYMOND MCSHARRY (FF) First elected in 1969. Appointed Minister for Finance and the Public Service Mar 1987. Elected to European Parliament Jun 1984. Tánaiste and Minister for Finance 1982; Minister for Agriculture 1979-81. Minister of State at the Department of Finance and the Public Service 1978-79. Opposition spokesman on Agriculture 1981-82; Office of Public Works 1973-75. Member Committee of Public Accounts 1969-77.
Home Address: Alcantara, Pearse Road, Sligo.
Tel: 071 62525.
Born: Sligo, Apr 1938.
Married: Elaine Neilan. 3 sons, 3 daughters.
Education: St Vincent's NS; Ballincutranta NS, Beltra; Marist Brothers National School; Summerhill College, Sligo.
Occupation: Public representative. Governor European Investment Bank 1982. Member EEC Council of Ministers for over four years. President Budget Council dealing with European Parliament during Ireland's EEC Presidency 1979. Member New Ireland Forum.

TED NEALON (FG) First elected in 1981. Minister of State at the Department of the Taoiseach 1982-87; Department of Posts and Telegraphs 1982-87; Department of Agriculture, 1981-82. Government Information Officer 1975-77; Director Fine Gael Press and Information Service, 1977-81.
Home address: 31 Green Fort, Sligo.
Tel: 071 61428
Born: Aclare, Co Sligo, 1929.
Married: Jo Loughnane. 1 son, 1 daughter.
Education: St Nathy's College, Ballaghadreen.
Occupation: Public representative. Former journalist. Editor ''Nealon's Guides'' to Dáil. Former RTE current affairs reporter/presenter.

TIPPERARY NORTH (3)

Elected: Michael Smith (FF) 1st Count; *Michael O'Kennedy (FF) 2nd Count; Michael Lowry (FG) 6th Count.

The count in Nenagh was predictable from lunch-time on the day of the count. But it was not until 14 hours later that the three Michaels took the stage in the Scouts Hall, to promise a new era of co-operation. Labour's John Ryan said he would be watching their performance closely. The party faithful here celebrated the return of two FF TDs for the first time in a decade. It was a sweet moment for Michael Smith, who topped the poll exactly five years after he lost his seat to his running mate, Michael O'Kennedy. He was elected on the 1st count, with 8,978 votes, and his transfers elected O'Kennedy with a surplus on the 2nd count. Fianna Fáil's overall vote increased by 2 per cent from Nov 1982, and they took over half the overall vote. A close transfer agreement saw many ballots marked simply 1 and 2 FF. Their victory was at the expense of Leas Cheann Comhairle John Ryan, who had held a Lab seat for 14 years. His vote was down almost 40 per cent to 4,558 and he fared badly in the subsequent transfers. The end of the Coalition agreement with FG also cost him valuable votes, and the presence of a SF candidate and two Inds may also have reduced his share of first preferences. Fine Gael's vote was down 5 per cent, due to the national swing against the party and David Moloney's decision not to run for the 25th Dáil.

FEB 87 % Poll		NOV 82 % Poll		Electorate:	41,555	
				Total poll:	33,529	(80.7%)
FF	51.4	FF	49.0	Spoiled votes:	238	
FG	23.6	FG	28.7	Total valid poll:	33,291	
PD	7.3	—	—	Quota:	8,323	
LAB	13.7	LAB	22.3			
SF	2.6	—	—			
OTH	1.4	OTH	—	9 Candidates		

COUNTS	1st	2nd Smith Surplus (655)	3rd O'Kennedy Surplus (318)	4th Kealy Deegan Nolan Votes (1,413) (NT) (481)	5th D. Ryan Votes (2,191) (NT) (146)	6th Dwan Votes (2,987) (NT) (585)
Smith M. (FF)	**8,978**					
O'Kennedy M. (FF)	8,121	+520 **8,641**				
Lowry M. (FG)	5,821	+28 5,849	+35 5,884	+145 6,029	+1470 7,499	+1505 **9,004**
Ryan J. (Lab.)	4,558	+46 4,604	+109 4,713	+468 5,181	+351 5,532	+897 6,429
Dwan F. (PD)	2,444	+27 2,471	+57 2,528	+235 2,763	+224 2,987	
Ryan D. (FG)	2,038	+23 2,061	+46 2,107	+84 2,191		
Nolan J. (SF)	878	+7 885	+46 931			
Deegan S. (Ind.)	322	+3 325	+20 345			
Kealy D. ((Ind.)	131	+1 132	+5 137			

MICHAEL LOWRY (FG) First elected 1987. Member Tipperary (North Riding) County Council.
Home address: The Green, Holycross, Thurles, Co Tipperary.
Tel: 0504 43182.
Born: Holycross 1954.
Married: Catherine McGrath. 3 children.
Occupation: Public representative and company sales director. Member Tipperary (North Riding) County Development Team. Vice-Chairman Mid-Western Health Board. Chairman Tipperary County Board GAA.

MICHAEL O'KENNEDY (FF) First elected 1969. Appointed Minister for Agriculture Mar 1987. Minister for Finance 1979-80; Minister for Foreign Affairs 1977-79; Minister for Transport and Power 1973. EEC Commissioner 1981-82. Senator 1965-69. Parliamentary Secretary to Minister for Education 1970-72. Opposition frontbench spokesman on Foreign Affairs 1973-77; on Finance 1981-82 and 1982-87.
Home address: Gortlandroe, Nenagh, Co Tipperary.
Tel: 067 31484.
Born: Nenagh 1936.
Married: Breda Heavey. 2 daughters, 1 son.
Education: St Mary's NS, Nenagh; Nenagh CBS; St Flannan's College, Ennis, Co Clare; St Patrick's College, Maynooth; UCD; Kings Inns, Dublin.
Occupation: Public representative and barrister. Member All-Party Committee on Irish Relations 1973-77; Joint Oireachtas Committee on Secondary Legislation of the European Communities 1973-77; Committee on the Constitution 1967.

MICHAEL SMITH (FF) First elected 1969. Lost his seat in 1973, regaining it in 1977; lost it again in Feb 1982. Appointed Minister of State at the Department of Energy (Forestry) Mar 1987. Minister of State Department of Agriculture 1980-81. Senator 1982-87.
Home address: Lismackin, Roscrea.
Tel: 0505 43157.
Born: Roscrea, Nov 1940.
Married: Mary Therese Ryan. 1 son, 4 daughters.
Education: Templemore CBS, Co Tipperary.
Occupation: Public representative and farmer. Member Tipperary (North Riding) County Council since 1967. Member Mid-Western Health Board since 1970. Member IFA since 1969; ITGWU 1967-69. Member GAA.

TIPPERARY SOUTH (4)

Elected: *Brendan Griffin (FG), *Sean Treacy (IND) 7th Count; *Sean McCarthy (FF), Noel Davern (FF) 8th Count.

This constituency gave another example of an ironic transfer pattern. Sean Tracey had left the Lab Party over the issue of contraception and was fighting as an Ind. The key factor in bringing him above the quota was a transfer of 1,153 from Lab's Senator Michael Ferris. However, Treacy's first preferences dropped by a massive 3,000. With Michael Ferris standing at nearly 4,000 he must stand a fighting chance of taking a seat in the next election. Treacy's occupation of the Ceann Comhairle's chair means he is automatically re-elected next time, so the constituency will effectively be a three-seater in the next election. However, to get a seat, Michael Ferris will have to dislodge one of the other three sitting deputies, which will not be an easy task.

For FF, a long family tradition helped Noel Davern unseat the outgoing Sean Byrne, with the aid of 694 votes from the surplus of FG's Brendan Griffin. The FG vote dropped 13 per cent, the PDs took 10.6 per cent and probably would have been better off with just one candidate, and the effect of all this was a tussle between the sitting FG TD and the party's second candidate Jack Crowe with just 600 votes between them on the 1st count.

FEB 87 % Poll		NOV 82 % Poll		Electorate:	55,055	
				Total poll:	41,783	(75.9%)
FF	42.6	FF	46.4	Spoiled votes:	282	
FG	20.4	FG	33.6	Total valid poll:	41,501	
PD	10.6	—	—	Quota:	8,301	
LAB	9.2	LAB	20.0			
WP	1.0	—	—			
OTH	16.2	OTH	—	13 Candidates		

COUNTS	1st	2nd Hill Quigley Ryan	3rd Healy	4th Lonergan	5th Kehoe	6th Ferris	7th Crowe	8th Griffin
		Votes (555)	Votes (1,554)	Votes (1,928)	Votes (3,745)	Votes (4,539)	Votes (5,178)	Surplus (1,994)
		(NT) (32)	(NT) (105)	(NT) (13)	(NT) (261)	(NT) (469)	(NT) (280)	(NT) (472)
McCarthy S. (FF)	6,877	*+55* 6,932	*+98* 7,030	*+59* 7,089	*+242* 7,331	*+560* 7,891	*+330* 8,221	*+415* **8,636**
Davern N. (FF)	5,412	*+43* 5,455	*+196* 5,651	*+63* 5,714	*+408* 6,122	*+445* 6,567	*+330* 6,897	*+674* **7,571**
Byrne S. (FF)	5,372	*+25* 5,397	*+103* 5,500	*+151* 5,651	*+262* 5,913	*+468* 6,381	*+220* 6,601	*+433* 7,034
Treacy S. (Ind.)	5,126	*+118* 5,244	*+677* 5,921	*+160* 6,081	*+728* 6,809	*+1153* 7,962	*+365* **8,327**	
Griffin B. (FG)	4,542	*+21* 4,563	*+42* 4,605	*+178* 4,783	*+910* 5,693	*+949* 6,642	*+3653* **10,295**	
Crowe J. (FG)	3,938	*+27* 3,965	*+32* 3,997	*+135* 4,132	*+551* 4,683	*+495* 5,178		
Ferris M. (Lab.)	3,820	*+91* 3,911	*+177* 4,088	*+68* 4,156	*+383* 4,539			
Kehoe A. (PD)	2,524	*+32* 2,556	*+88* 2,644	*+1101* 3,745				
Lonergan T. (PD)	1,878	*+14* 1,892	*+36* 1,928					
Healy S. (Ind.)	1,457	*+97* 1,554						
Hill S. (WP)	407							
Quigley N. (Ind.)	76							
Ryan P. (Ind.)	72							

213

BRENDAN GRIFFIN (FG) First elected 1973. Vice-Chairman Fine
Gael parliamentary party. Member National Executive.
Home address: Cnoc Pio, St Michael St, Tipperary.
Tel: 062 51595.
Born: Tipperary 1935.
Married: Kay Armstrong. 3 daughters, 2 sons.
Education: CBS Primary School, Tipperary; Abbey CBS, Tipperary;
    St Patrick's Teacher Training College Dublin; UCD.
Occupation: Public representative. Former teacher. Member Joint
    Committee on Secondary Legislation of the European Communities.
    Member Council of Europe. Member Tipperary Urban District
    Council since 1967; Tipperary VEC.

SEAN TREACY (IND) First elected for Lab 1961. Appointed Ceann
Comhairle 25th Dáil Mar 1987; Ceann Comhairle 20th Dáil 1973-77.
Opposition spokesman on Education 1961-65; on Industry and
Commerce 1965-69; Local Government 1969-73. MEP 1981.
Independent TD since 1985.
Home address: Rossa, Haywood Rd, Clonmel, Co Tipperary.
Tel: 052 22747.
Born: Clonmel 1923.
Married: Catherine Connolly.
Education: St Mary's CBS, Clonmel; Clonmel Technical Institute;
    UCC.
Occupation: Public representative. Member Dáil Committee on Public
    Accounts; Joint Oireachtas Committee on the Secondary Legislation
    of the European Communities. Mayor of Clonmel 1957-58 and
    1961-62.

SEAN MCCARTHY (FF) First elected 1981. Appointed Minister of
State Department of Industry and Commerce (Science and Technology)
Mar 1987. Opposition spokesman on Social Welfare 1983-87. Member
Joint Oireachtas Committee on Legislation. Member Tipperary (South
Riding) County Council since 1979; Cashel Urban District Council
since 1979; South Tipperary Local Health Committee since 1977.
Home address: John Street, Cashel, Co Tipperary.
Tel: 062 61129.
Born: Cashel 1937.
Married: Mary O'Keefe. 3 sons, 2 daughters.
Education: Rockwell College, Tipperary; UCD.
Occupation: Public representative, doctor and physician.

NOEL DAVERN (FF) First elected 1969. Lost his Dáil seat in 1981. MEP 1979-84. Party spokesman on Agriculture European Parliament 1979-84.
Home address: Tannersrath, Clonmel, Co Tipperary.
Tel: 052 22991.
Born: Cashel, Dec 1945.
Married: Anne Marie Carroll. 2 sons, 1 daughter.
Education: Cashel Primary School; Franciscan College Gormanstown.
Occupation: Public representative. Member Tipperary (South Riding) County Council since 1985. Member ACOT; Tipperary VEC; Local Health Committee. Son of Michael Davern, Dáil deputy for Tipperary South 1948-65.

WATERFORD (4)

Elected: *Austin Deasy (FG) 4th Count; Martin Cullen (PD) 6th Count; *Jackie Fahey (FF), Brian Swift (FF) 7th Count.

The result here was reckoned to be solidly predictable: 2 FF and 2 FG seats, as it had been in recent years, with the exception of those few months in 1982 when the WP borrowed a FF seat and then gave it back. In the event Waterford produced three surprises: the PDs took a seat; former Minister for State Eddie Collins lost his seat for FG; and FF's Dr Donie Ormond lost his seat to fellow party man and Mayor of Waterford Brian Swift. A local newspaper poll had predicted that the PDs' Martin Cullen might have been "on for a seat", but few believed it. However the tallymen were able to say at 10.30 on the morning of the count that Eddie Collins would not survive his sacking as Minister for State. Even in the old Redmondite heartland of Ballybricken in the city, support had flagged. He took only 3,990 first preferences, 1,357 behind the little-known Martin Cullen for the PDs. Fine Gael officials said strategy was to blame. They should have run a third candidate, Senator Catherine Bulbulia, who had not run after she had clashed with Collins during the sacking controversy. She might have stemmed the PDs' advance and transferred a critical vote to save Collins, whose political passing means that for the first time since the foundation of the state there is no FG deputy in Waterford city. Then Minister for Agriculture Austin Deasy headed the poll and was first home, taking a seat on the 4th count. He gave the PDs 1,781 in transfers and that, added to 1,498 from the eliminated Lab candidate, elected Martin Cullen for the PDs on the 6th count. Jackie Fahey followed in on the 7th count for FF without reaching the quota. Sitting FF TD Dr Donie Ormonde had polled only 239 first preferences more than his party running mate Brian Swift. But Swift did slightly better at each stage of transfers and it was neck and neck until the 6th count with the transfers of the votes of Lab man Brian O'Shea. He lives in Tramore as does Swift. That mattered. Swift took 1,013 votes putting him ahead of Ormonde and giving him the seat on the 7th count without reaching the quota.

Waterford

FEB 87 % Poll		NOV 82 % Poll		Electorate:	59,904	
FF	42.6	FF	38.9	Total poll:	44,944	(75%)
				Spoiled votes	350	
FG	27.9	FG	39.6	Total valid poll	44,594	
PD	12.0	—	—	Quota:	8,919	
LAB	7.5	LAB	4.1			
WP	7.6	WP	10.7			
SF	1.7	—	—			
OTH	0.7	OTH	6.7	12 Candidates		

COUNTS	1st	2nd Lanigan Sweeney Wright Ryan Votes (1,614) (NT) (124)	3rd Gallagher Votes (3,408) (NT) (653)	4th Collins Votes (4,178) (NT) (132)	5th Deasy Surplus (2,789) (NT) (286)	6th O'Shea Votes (5069) NT) (1505)	7th Cullen Surplus (804) (NT) (152)
Deasy A. (FG)	8,430	+139 8,569	+225 8,794	+2914 **11,708**			
Fahey J. (FF)	7,321	+196 7,517	+330 7,847	+115 7,962	+87 8,049	+599 8,648	+207 **8,855**
Ormonde D. (FF)	5,959	+132 6,091	+249 6,340	+99 6,439	+91 6,530	+454 6,984	+135 7,119
Swift B. (FF)	5,720	+186 5,906	+449 6,355	+141 6,496	+111 6,607	+1013 7,624	+310 **7,930**
Cullen M. (PD)	5,347	+80 5,427	+434 5,861	+583 6,444	+1781 8,225	+1498 **9,723**	
Collins E. (FG)	3,990	+45 4,035	+143 4,178				
O'Shea B. (Lab.)	3,358	+159 3,517	+925 4,442	+194 4,636	+433 5,069		
Gallagher P. (WP)	2,855	+553 3,408					
Ryan N. (SF)	758						
Wright T. (WP)	552						
Sweeney P.	226						
Lanigan J.	78						

BRIAN SWIFT (FF) First elected in 1987. Mayor of Waterford City. Member of Waterford City Council; Waterford County Council; South Eastern Health Board; Board of Management of the County and City Infirmary.
Home address: 117 Roselawn, Tramore Heights, Tramore, Co Waterford.
Tel: 051 86278.
Born: May 1952.
Married: Sheila Gorman. 2 sons.
Education: Mount Sion CBS; UCC; Incorporated Law Society of Ireland.
Occupation: Public representative and solicitor. Member St Paul's Community College Board of Management; Waterford Regional Technical College Council; Waterford VEC. Member of Tramore GAA Club and Tramore Golf Club.

JACKIE FAHEY (FF) First elected 1965. Elected for Waterford 1977. Minister of State at the Department of the Environment 1979-81. Parliamentary Secretary to the Minister for Agriculture and Fisheries 1970-73. Member Dail and Seanad Joint Committee on Secondary Legislation of the European Communities 1973-77.
Home address: 95 Springfield, Dungarvan, Co Waterford.
Tel: Home 058 42514; Business 052 22536.
Born: Clonmel, Co Tipperary, Jan 1928.
Married: Maura Kenny. 4 sons, 4 daughters.
Education: Christian Brothers' Secondary School, Clonmel.
Occupation: Public representative.
Member Governing Body UCD 1965-69.

AUSTIN DEASY (FG) First elected 1977. Minister for Agriculture 1982-87. Senator 1973-77. Frontbench spokesman on Fisheries 1977-79; Transport 1979-81. Member Joint Oireachtas Committee on State-Sponsored Bodies 1979-81.
Home address: Durrow, Stradbally, Co Waterford.
Tel: 051 93151
Born: Dungarvan, Co Waterford 1936.
Married: Catherine Keating. 2 sons, 2 daughters.
Education: CBS Dungarvan, UCC.
Occupation: Public representative. Former schoolteacher. Member Waterford County Council since 1967; Dungarvan Urban District Council since 1967; South-Eastern Health Board; Waterford Harbour Commissioners. Member ASTI since 1963.

MARTIN CULLEN (PD) First elected 1987. Son of Tom Cullen, Ind. Mayor of Waterford 1967-68; grandson of Martin Cullen, Ind. Mayor 1952-53.
Home address: "St Helen's", Rockfield, Waterford.
Tel: 051 77820.
Born: Waterford 1954.
Married: Dorothea Larsen. 1 son.
Education: Waterpark College, Waterford; Waterford Regional Technical College.
Occupation: Public representative. Area sales manager, Edward Dillon and Co. Member Institute of Professional Auctioneers, Valuers and Livestock Salesmen. Member Marketing Institute of Ireland.

WEXFORD (5)

Elected: *John Browne (FF) lst Count; *Hugh Byrne (FF) 7th Count; *Ivan Yates (FG) 8th Count; *Avril Doyle (FG) 10th Count; Brendan Howlin (LAB) 11th Count.

Fianna Fáil were banking on an extra seat here, taking three of the five — but the strategy came unstuck. The party decided this time not to run a Wexford town candidate and instead manage the vote with just three candidates. But Lorcan Allen failed to regain the seat he had lost in Nov 1982, and the end result was that Lab's Brendan Howlin took a seat at FG's expense. After their traumatic experience in government, the result here was one of three — along with Galway West and Kildare — which gave the party fresh encouragement. Howlin succeeded, on his second attempt, in regaining the Lab seat held by the Corish family since 1921, latterly by Brendan Corish from 1945-82. Corish had failed to prepare adequately for a successor. His brother Des was beaten in Feb 1982, and Howlin failed by just 337 votes from Avril Doyle in Nov of that year. The FG vote was down by 9.7 per cent, less than the national average, and the FF share was down 2.3 per cent. The lack of a FF Wexford-town candidate probably helped Avril Doyle. She benefited from the transfers of former FF man Padge Reck (IND) from the town, the WP, and from the two PD candidates, more so than she did from the transfers of Michael D'Arcy. At the end of the day Howlin won his seat from Lorcan Allen by a margin of 350. Wexford, therefore, remains a key marginal for the next contest.

FEB 87		NOV 82			
% Poll		% Poll		Electorate:	69,658
				Total poll:	53,474 (76.8%)
FF	43.9	FF	46.2	Spoiled votes:	552
FG	31.7	FG	41.4	Total valid poll:	52,922
PD	8.9	—	—	Quota:	8,821
LAB	9.6	LAB	9.8		
WP	2.4	WP	1.8		
OTH	3.5	OTH	0.7	12 Candidates	

COUNTS	1st	2nd Tallon Votes (33)	3rd Browne Surplus (636)	4th Enright Votes (1,255)	5th Reck Votes (2,091)	6th G. Doyle Votes (2,206)	7th Minahan Votes (4,001)	8th Darcy Votes (6,062)	9th Byrne Surplus (216)	10th Yates Surplus (1,693)	11th A. Doyle Surplus (1,082)
(NT)		(3)		(58)	(175)	(56)	(399)	(390)			(461)
Browne J. (FF)	**9,457**										
Byrne H. (FF)	7,551	+0 7,551	+296 7,847	+111 7,958	+266 8,224	+111 8,335	+702 **9,037**				
Allen L. (FF)	6,225	+5 6,230	+216 6,446	+71 6,517	+179 6,696	+95 6,791	+147 6,938	+546 7,484	+110 7,594	+131 7,725	+148 7,873
Yates I. (FG)	6,018	+4 6,022	+48 6,070	+39 6,109	+74 6,183	+251 6,434	+1,020 7,454	+3,060 **10,514**			
Doyle A. (FG)	5,518	+1 5,519	+9 5,528	+110 5,638	+382 6,020	+118 6,138	+707 6,845	+1,635 8,480	+58 8,538	+1,365 **9,903**	
Darcy M. (FG)	5,247	+4 5,251	+11 5,262	+23 5,285	+44 5,329	+200 5,529	+533 6,062				
Howlin B. (Lab)	5,086	+6 5,092	+25 5,117	+500 5,617	+820 6,437	+144 6,581	+493 7,074	+431 7,505	+48 7,553	+197 7,750	+473 **8,223**
Minahan E. (PD)	2,630	+4 2,634	+6 2,640	+57 2,697	+73 2,770	+1,231 4,001					
Doyle G. (PD)	2,078	+1 2,079	+10 2,089	+39 2,128	+78 2,206						
Reck P. (Ind)	1,829	+4 1,833	+11 1,844	+247 2,091							
Enright M. (WP)	1,250	+1 1,251	+4 1,255								
Tallon J. (Ind)	33										

JOHN BROWNE (FF) First elected in Nov 1982. Assistant Chief Whip since 1982. Chairman of Ógra Fianna Fáil. Member of Wexford County Council since 1978; Enniscorthy Urban District Council since 1979.
Home Address: Kilcannon, Enniscorthy, Co Wexford.
Tel: 054 35046.
Born: Marshallstown, Co Wexford, Aug 1948.
Married: Judy Doyle. 1 son, 3 daughters.
Education: Marshallstown NS; St Mary's CBS, Enniscorthy.
Occupation: Public representative. Former salesman. Member Wexford VEC; Wexford Health Committee; Wexford Tourism Committee since 1979; Wexford County Council GP Committee; GAA. Nephew of Sean Browne, FF TD for Wexford 1957-61, 1969-81 and 1981-1982.

HUGH BYRNE (FF) First elected in 1981. Member Wexford County Council.
Home address: Air Hill, Fethard-on-Sea, Co Wexford.
Tel: 051 97125.
Born: Gusserane, Co Wexford, Sept 1943.
Married: Mary Murphy. 3 sons, 4 daughters.
Education: CBS, New Ross; St Peter's College, Wexford.
Occupation: Public representative and farmer. Member Wexford Committee on Agriculture. Vice Chairman Wexford VEC. Played inter-county football for Wexford and hurling for Kildare.

BRENDAN HOWLIN (LAB) First elected 1987. Senator 1982-87. Member Joint Oireachtas Committee on Legislation. Member Administrative Council of the Lab Party; Lab International Affairs Committee. Secretary of the Association of Labour Councillors. Member Wexford County Council since 1985. Alderman of Wexford Corporation. Mayor of Wexford.
Home address: 7 Upper William Street, Wexford.
Tel: Home 053 24036; Business 053 22848.
Born: Wexford, May 1957.
Marital Status: Single.
Education: CBS Wexford; St Patrick's Teacher Teacher Training College, Dublin.
Occupation: Public representative and former teacher.

AVRIL DOYLE (FG) First elected Nov 1982. Minister of State at the Departments of Finance and Environment 1986-1987. Member Wexford Corporation since 1974 (Mayor '75-76). Member Wexford County Council since 1974.
Home address: Rocklands, Wexford.
Tel: 053 22873.
Born: Dublin 1949.
Married: Fred Doyle. 3 daughters.
Education: Holy Child Convent, Killiney; UCD.
Occupation: Public representative and boutique director.

IVAN YATES (FG) First elected 1981. Chairman Oireachtas Committee on Small Businesses. Member New Ireland Forum. Member Wexford County Council; Enniscorthy Urban Council.
Home address: Blackstoops, Enniscorthy.
Tel: 054 33793.
Born: Enniscorthy 1959.
Married: Deirdre Boyd.
Education: St Mary's NS, Enniscorthy; Aravon School, Bray, County Wicklow; St. Columba's College, Rathfarnham; Gurteen Agricultural College, County Tipperary.
Occupation: Public representative. Member Wexford County Health Committee. Member County Committee on Agriculture; IFA.

WICKLOW (4)

Elected: Joe Jacob (FF) 5th Count; *Liam Kavanagh (LAB) 6th Count; *Gemma Hussey (FG) 7th Count; Dick Roche (FF) 8th Count.

The big surprise here was the defeat of sitting FG TD Godfrey Timmins. He lost to Dick Roche (FF) by 430 votes on the 8th count. Both of the new FF TDs were first-time runners. They benefited from divisions in the PD camp which led to two potential candidates withdrawing, one the former FF TD Ciaran Murphy, and then the selection by the PDs of three candidates to fight the constituency. There was also bitterness among Godfrey Timmins' supporters after the count, following what they felt was a hijacking of part of Timmins' vote by outgoing Social Welfare Minister Gemma Hussey, whose supporters they claimed had asked for first preferences on the basis that Timmins was safe and she was in trouble. However, it does seem that Gemma Hussey ran an effective campaign, and did well to retain her seat given the tough government brief she carried. The FF vote was down 3.1 per cent and FG down 10.2 per cent. The PDs took nearly 12 per cent, which must put them within striking distance next time with a better organised campaign and fewer candidates.

FEB 87 % Poll		NOV 82 % Poll			
				Electorate:	64,272
				Total poll:	46,391 (72.2%)
FF	32.6	FF	35.7	Spoiled votes:	388
FG	26.5	FG	36.7	Total valid poll:	46,003
PD	11.8	—	—	Quota:	9,202
LAB	16.9	LAB	18.3		
WP	7.6	WP	8.2		
OTH	4.6	OTH	1.1	12 Candidates	

COUNTS	1st	2nd DeSiun Hyland Votes (875) (NT) (38)	3rd Healy Votes (1,009) (NT) (12)	4th Wolahan Votes (1,365) (NT) (59)	5th Atkins Votes (2,452) (NT) (48)	6th McManus Votes (4,079) (NT) (512)	7th Murphy Votes (4,931) (NT) (1,268)	8th Kavanagh Surplus (1,045) (NT) (227)
Jacob J. (FF)	8,825	+51 8,876	+62 8,938	+258 9,196	+67 **9,263**			
Kavanagh L. (Lab)	7,754	+126 7,880	+93 7,973	+525 8,498	+160 8,658	+1589 **10,247**		
Hussey G. (FG)	6,474	+115 6,589	+103 6,692	+48 6,740	+302 7,042	+325 7,367	+1871 **9,238**	
Roche D. (FF)	6,163	+78 6,241	+10 6,251	+83 6,334	+56 6,390	+923 7,313	+542 7,855	+428 **8,283**
Timmins G. (FG)	5,710	+31 5,741	+72 5,813	+98 5,911	+113 6,024	+189 6,213	+1250 7,463	+390 7,853
McManus J. (WP)	3,509	+235 3,744	+21 3,765	+222 3,987	+92 4,079			
Murphy A. (PD)	2,461	+48 2,509	+236 2,745	+31 2,776	+1614 4,390	+541 4,931		
Atkins D. (PD)	2,014	+55 2,069	+342 2,411	+41 2,452				
Wolahan S. (Ind)	1,243	+64 1,307	+58 1,365					
Healy M. (PD)	975	+34 1,009						
DeSiun L. (GA)	658							
Hyland B. (Ind)	217							

JOE JACOB (FF) First elected 1987. Member of Wicklow County Council; County Committee of Agriculture; VEC; Dublin and Eastern Regional Tourism Organisation.
Home address: Jacob's Well, Rathdrum, Co Wicklow.
Tel: 0404 46282.
Born: Kilrush, Co Clare, Apr 1939.
Married: Patti Grant. 6 children.
Education: De La Salle, Wicklow; Terenure College, Dublin.
Occupation: Public representative and publican.

DICK ROCHE (FF) First elected in 1987. Private secretary to Minister of Economic Planning and Development 1977-78. Departmental Assistant Principal Officer 1978. Elected Greystones Town Commission 1984. Member Institute of Public Administration; Irish Council of European Movement. Chairman Episcopal Commission for Justice and Peace 1983-85.
Home address: 5 Rathdown Park, Greystones, Co Wicklow; business
    address: Faculty of Commerce, UCD.
Tel: Home 01 875471; Business 01 693244.
Born: Wexford, Mar 1946.
Married: Eleanor Griffin. 3 sons, 1 daughter.
Education: CBS Wexford; Institute of Public Administration; UCD.
Occupation: Public representative and lecturer.

LIAM KAVANAGH (LAB) First elected in 1969. Elected to the European Parliament in 1979. Resigned his seat on becoming Minister in Nov 1982. Minister for Labour 1982-83; Minister for the Environment 1983-86; Minister for Tourism, Forestry and Fisheries 1986-87. Minister for Labour and the Public Service 1981-82.
Home address: Mount Carmel, Convent Road, Wicklow.
Tel: 0404 67582.
Born: Wicklow, Feb 1935.
Married: Margaret Beatty. 1 daughter, 1 son.
Education: De La Salle, Wicklow; UCD.
Occupation: Public representative.

GEMMA HUSSEY (FG) First elected Feb 1982. Minister for Social Welfare 1986-87; Minister for Labour Jan-Mar 1987; Minister for Education 1982-86. Senator 1977-82. Spokesperson Womens Affairs 1980-81. Government leader of the Seanad 1981-82. Frontbench spokesperson on Arts, Culture and Broadcasting 1982. Member Seanad Committee on Procedure and Privilege 1977-81.
Home address: 29 Temple Road, Dublin 6.
Tel: 01 971169.
Born: Bray, Co Wicklow 1938.
Married: Derry Hussey. 1 son, 2 daughters.
Education: Loreto Convent, Bray; Convent of the Sacred Heart, Mount Anville, Dublin; UCD.
Occupation: Public representative. Member Joint Committee on EEC Legislation 1977-80. Chairperson Women's Political Association 1973-75. Member Council for the Status of Women 1973-75. Director The Abbey Theatre 1974-78. Member An Taisce, Bray Chamber of Commerce.